SPREAD
FORMATION

X F   OOXOO   Y Z

TAILGATING & HOME RECIPES FROM COLLEGE FOOTBALL GREATS!

LORAN SMITH

All the best
to my friend
Mato —
Great friend
of College football!

[signature]
10-3-'15

Spread Formation: Tailgating & Home Recipes From College Football Greats

ISBN: 0794842399
Printed and assembled in the United States of America.

To view other products by Whitman Publishing, please visit **www.Whitman.com**.

Table of Contents

THE HISTORY OF

I f you distinguish tailgating from picnicking, which accompanied football in the horse and buggy era, then you have to assume that tailgating officially began with the coming of the pickup truck. It makes sense that folding down the tailgate and spreading out food and drink brought about the term tailgating.

In 1921, the Graham Brothers started selling 1.5-ton trucks through Dodge dealers, the forerunners of the everyday pickup. Ford Motor Company came out with its modified rear body for its popular Model T in 1925. Soon after that, station wagons with rear tailgates began to make their way into the market place. Then there was always the boot of the car to accommodate picnicking and outdoor excursions.

Trying to determine the origin of tailgating is like trying to identify the first coach to run the spread formation (the spread is not a latent system when you consider that in the early 1950s, Southern Methodist coach Dutch Meyer wrote a book about the spread...no telling where he got the idea). There's nothing new under the sun, you know. Once the forward pass became standard, the spreading of the offense to flummox the defense became commonplace in football. While coaches were innovating to gain the advantage on the field, fans began making the picnic basket the centerpiece of pregame festivities.

TAILGATING

Author Loran Smith never met a tailgate party he didn't like. Photo courtesy of Sherry Thrift Bradshaw.

The advent of the pickup truck and the tradition of dinner on the grounds along with the popularity of college football, no doubt, coincided about the same time. The college game had taken root prior to the "roaring twenties," and would continue to grow and expand into what we have today: grills and cookers in place with tailgaters doing their thing in an all-day exercise to get everyone in the mood for the big game, accompanied by assorted snacks, chips and dip, libations galore and, of course, a wide-screen TV to keep everybody informed about what is taking place around the country. Fall Saturdays have become a happening. Tailgating today has energized momentum, which is a colossus with no backsliding in sight.

Before the pickup truck, there were other indications of pregame hoopla that might cause a historian to take a different stance. If you search the Internet, there is one notion that tailgating dates back to the Battle of Bull Run in 1861 when Union civilians brought picnic baskets and shouted, "Go Big Blue." That observation is duly noted by the American Tailgaters Association. That, to most of us, however, would be a big stretch, not so much that people gathered to watch death and destruction, but actually orchestrating in concert with the action, a modern-day football yell. I am *not* a believer.

It has been written that the first tailgating scene came about in 1869 when Rutgers and Princeton played that very first game of football. Rutgers fans wore scarlet colors to separate them from other fans, and that sausages were grilled at "the tail end of the horse." Rutgers gets credit for starting football. Tailgating? No horse's rear end could influence the tradition.

If you are not ready to accept the pickup-truck theory (something could be said about the invention of chuck wagon by a former Texas Ranger, Charles Goodnight, in 1866, confirming that, for work and play, food has been portable for a long, long time), then you have to say that tailgating began dating back to the time Eve offered the apple to Adam. We can't go back any further than that.

The Green Bay Packers take credit for coining the phrase "tailgating" during the team's first year of competition in 1919. According to the Internet, "fans backed their pickup trucks around the field, folded down the tailgates for seating. Naturally, food and beverages were brought along." Only one issue with that notion. If the pickup truck wasn't put into serious production until the mid-1920s, where did the Packer fans find those pickup trucks?

With the passing of time, the pickup truck would give way to the hatchback and more recently, the SUV. All across America today, you find SUVs accompanied by wide-screen televisions and spacious tents — with a generator for power. Under the tents are food spreads that would make any chef envious and the finest wines to make the pregame social as memorable as the game itself.

You are likely to get a lot of debate about the history of tailgating, where it originated and how it was established. In my own case, I have concluded that with the University of Georgia, my alma mater, the first game in 1893 was also the first tailgate party. Georgia defeated Mercer University 50-0, but a player on the team told longtime UGA historian John Stegeman that the score was wrong, noting that the scorekeeper missed two touchdowns when he went across the street to buy some booze.

What we do know about tailgating is that it has become almost as important as the games themselves. It has gone high tech. You may see someone during the long day, before a night kickoff, preparing chateaubriand for guests. Some of the most impressive cooking devices can be found at tailgate parties on today's college campuses. The menus are as varied and inviting as an upscale restaurant in big cities, although most tailgating menus are often dictated by local tastes: Maine lobster at Boston College; brisket seared by mesquite wood at Texas A&M; shucked oysters at an Auburn game, ferried upstate by a Mobile alumnus; Stromboli at Ohio State; Parmesan crisp potatoes at Idaho State; a Sonoran hot dog at Arizona; anything Mexican, beef or chili at Texas; bratwurst and cheese curds at Wisconsin; fried chicken at Notre Dame; boiled crawfish at LSU; and, as you might expect, Rocky Mountain oysters out West.

In the Southeast, you find a lot of beer and barbecue, boiled peanuts and corn on the cob. There's beer, wine and spirits unlimited. With some tailgaters, you have the same "call brand" option you have with the bartender at The Ritz. In the old days, according to old timers, moonshine was a staple of tailgate gatherings.

Tailgating tastes from the basic to the elite can be found at college football games every fall. There are pimento cheese sandwiches, fried chicken, hot dogs, burgers and deviled eggs. Food that could be brought to the campus for the day, without spoiling, has historically been a criteria for tailgaters, but that is not a big concern anymore since generators allow for refrigeration and power for the most sophisticated of grills.

One thing has become standard. Tailgating and technology has made it possible that college football fans can enjoy the tailgating experience without tickets to the game. All you have to do is park your SUV, sedan or van — pickups remain in style — and hook up your flat-screen TV. You can enjoy food and drink right up to kick-off, and then take in the game via one of the plethora of networks that cover college football on Saturday.

"Ole Miss," says Archie Manning, Hall of Fame quarterback for the Rebels, "has a stadium that seats only 62,000, but over 100,000 show up at The Grove to tailgate."

Ohio State estimates that 120,000 to 130,000 show up to tailgate, with 104,829 moving into the stadium for the game — meaning there are about 20,000 to 30,000 without tickets but come to campus for tailgating. "During the game," says Richard Mormon of the Ohio State police staff, "you can ride through the RV lots and find countless fans watching the game on wide-screen TVs. You know they are in the group of fans without tickets but, nonetheless, came to tailgate."

At Alabama, where Bryant-Denny Stadium seats 101,821, it has been estimated that 135,000 to 140,000 show up each home game to tailgate. "We have no way of knowing accurately," says Tide Athletic Director Bill Battle, "but we know that thousands of our fans come to tailgate with no ticket access to the game."

At Michigan, which has long had the biggest college football stadium in the country, there are 109,901 seats. While there is no official estimate with regard to how many fans tailgate at The Big House, the "guess" from athletic officials is "that it is in the thousands."

We hear that there is a hint of college football losing fans, especially with students sometimes taking a day off, depending on the strength of the schedule, but you wouldn't be able to tell it by visiting most college campuses in the fall.

The spectacle of college football and its rich traditions have been in place for over a century. We all know how important the performance of the band has been and continues to be. Mascots are beloved and adored. Beautiful coeds with the school logo painted on their cheeks. A stroll through the campus, remembering your first day at school. Your first football game and the place, with many, where you met your spouse.

Homecoming was once the biggest Saturday on campus in the fall. It still has its place, but the escalating interest in college football has made every Saturday a homecoming in recent years.

Let's not forget the bands that thrill us pregame and at halftime, and, of course, the cheerleaders. Every school likes to showcase its cheerleaders, which brings front and center a priceless story by the late Erskine Russell, a funny and charming raconteur. The head coach of the Georgia Southern Eagles, Erk said the origin of cheerleading began with Lady Godiva who, as history tells it, rode nude down the streets of Coventry, England, in the 13th century to protest taxation on the poor. Erk said he researched her famous ride and discovered that historians failed to note that she rode side-saddle.

"The folks on the side of the street she faced as she rode by," Erk said with a grin, "began to yell, 'Hooray for our side.'"

AN ALABAMA TAILGATING VETERAN

"**A** weekend of Alabama football, at home in Tuscaloosa, is one of those events that is one of life's rich experiences," says Frank Skinner Jr., who has been tailgating and partying with alumni and friends dating back to the Joe Namath era.

"Normally on a home game day," he says, "we travel Friday morning to Tuscaloosa to attend the 'Nick at Noon' fundraiser for Nick's Kids, and also the opportunity to listen to the coach provide an update on players and some insight to the team we are going to be playing. This carries us to about 1:30 Friday afternoon. Many times we use this downtime in the afternoon to obtain supplies and other items for the weekend.

"Normally, Tuesday or Wednesday our group of girls talk and decide on meals that we will be tailgating with, based on the time of the game," Frank continued. "Friday evening at 6 p.m., we move the motor home from its temporary location at University Mall to Coleman Coliseum, to our designated place and set up for the weekend. Usually on Friday evening, we go out to dinner with the Prines and the Yarbroughs, the other RVers of our little group. Many times we meet Bob and Phyllis, George and Jane, who live in the area. I'm sure sometimes the restaurant is glad when we leave.

"The next day begins with cooking outside and watching ESPN's 'GameDay' on the outside TVs. Breakfast consists of sausage and eggs — cooked on the grill — pancakes, biscuits, grits, lots of choices of fresh fruit, homemade jams and jellies, fruit juices and coffee. By this time, other friends have come and joined. Normally there are 10 or 12 people, at a minimum, and up to 25 and 30. We continue to hang out together, watching other games, if we are playing an afternoon or evening game. Certainly, the first game of the season for the last few years has been in Dallas or Atlanta. For those, we travel on Wednesday or Thursday morning to get to the location with our group and we set up and start our thing Friday afternoon.

"At least one time per year, if not more, our special friends from Mobile create a seafood feast for the mid-day meal, consisting of West Indies salad, crab claws, shrimp, fish and homemade hushpuppies.

"After the game, we gather back at our site and normally have desserts or other goodies, and hopefully celebrate victory. Several years ago our football win/loss ratio wasn't too good. Many times on Monday morning I was asked 'How was your weekend?' I would always respond 'food and fellowship was good, ballgame wasn't too sporty.' But Nick Saban changed all that.

"Sunday morning we get up early and normally travel back home in time for church, as there isn't much traffic at 6:30 in the morning.

"We always look forward to the next time. The song 'Sweet Home Alabama' works well with 'Roll Tide Roll.' Fortunately for us, we have been rolling quite well in recent years, and tailgating and enjoying our friends is part of the scene our group appreciates."

When tailgating in Tuscaloosa, make sure you go see the statue of coaching legend Bear Bryant.

DOMINATING THE
TAILGATE

We all know how dominant Alabama football has been the last half-dozen years under head coach Nick Saban. But Alabama tailgaters have been dominant for much longer than that. Here's a perspective from Crimson Tide tailgater Sharyn Nunn.

"In the early 1990s, my husband and I, along with a couple of friends, traveled to Ole Miss for a road game. It was our first time to attend a game at Ole Miss. We were amazed at their tailgating in The Grove. We were not sure if they even used the term 'tailgating' back then — maybe it was 'party.' Silver chandeliers. Recipes and dishes that would put *Southern Living* magazine to shame. Beautiful children playing around the magnolia trees. What was there not to be amazed about? For the rest of the trip, we talked about our experience in The Grove.

"The next year, our group of friends began to think about the possibility of us tailgating on our quad, certainly no Grove, but we would make it our own. The Limbaughs, Sissions and the Nunns decided it should be by invitation only. All good Southerners send invitations to parties. We picked a big-game weekend, LSU, had the invitations printed and mailed them to our friends.

"As we began to make plans for food and drinks, it occurred to us since no one tailgated on the quad, how were we going to actually pull it off? What if the campus police pulled up and asked, 'what do you think you're doing?' That became a big concern to us, so of course we turned to our husbands and asked them if they would accompany us to the quad to drop off the tables, setup supplies and such. Although they did not want to admit it, they were as much interested in seeing this event take place as we were, wanting it to be special for the invited guests. It will be hard for your cookbook readers to picture the quad without the circus atmosphere it is today — but the entire space was ours to have in 1995!

"The week of the game we still were not sure that even the husbands would be able to hold off the UA police. After all, it would be a gutsy move for someone to just pull up to the beautiful quad and start unloading a pile of stuff! The more we thought about it, there was only one thing we could do to ensure our first-ever tailgate on the quad, and that was to call our friend, the

Bart's Favorite Cucumber Dip

From Bart and Cherry Starr
Former quarterback at the University of Alabama, MVP of Super Bowls I & II with the Green Bay Packers

INGREDIENTS:

1 8-ounce package Philly Cream Cheese

1/2 cucumber (unpeeled), grated finely (pour off juice and reserve)

1/4 teaspoon dill weed

Garlic salt

1 heaping tablespoon Hellman's Mayo

DIRECTIONS:

• Blend all ingredients until creamy. If too thick, add reserved cucumber juice until right consistency for dip.

• Great dip to serve with chips or on crackers. Also makes nice spread for party sandwiches (open faced with a thin cucumber slice on top, or a sprig of parsley).

Cheryl E. Davis/Shutterstock

sheriff of Tuscaloosa, to come with his mounted horse patrol. Who would question us or him? It worked. I'm not sure we even saw the UA police at all that day.

"Let me say right up front, we didn't in any way come up to the standard of our Ole Miss brethren, but it was a start. We had a tablecloth, a beautiful flower arrangement in a carved-out pumpkin, one or two sliver chaffing dishes and, of course, our speciality drinks marked 'non-alcoholic' for the Baptists.

"Thanks to the sheriff, it was a great success. He even rode the kids on the horses and kept us guarded. We knew we had accomplished our goal when a passerby stopped, looked at our table and said, 'Are ya'll with *Southern Living?*'

"The next year we picked another big-game weekend, I think Tennessee, and sent out the invitations again. Another success. This is when the light bulb went off in our heads, and we decided to tailgate every home game, but to make it easier, we moved to Wood Square

so we had easy access to park our cars next to where we set up the tailgate. Next came tents, lights and TVs. But we were exclusive — not just anyone could join the group.

"As the years passed and the university decided they were sitting on a goldmine, our group moved to different parts of the campus trying to avoid paying for tents. My husband and I landed with The Hackberry HighTiders. Most everyone pays to park today. Our tailgating group is two blocks from the stadium. Our enormous red-and-white-striped tent has a TV, lights and long tables for the variety of food brought by tailgaters. Everyone brings his own chair and, yes, we are still somewhat exclusive. If you are having guests stop by, then you either have enough for them or tell them to bring something. And you must tell one of the founders of the Hackberry HighTiders that you are planning for a guest. It's just good Southern manners."

Roll HighTiders!

Pumpkin Rolls

From Terry (and Nick) Saban
Head coach at the University of Alabama

Particularly in the fall, we all get hungry for pumpkin rolls! Not only are they convenient to take to a tailgate party, but they also freeze well. Personally, I make several batches at a time and give them as gifts to neighbors. Try one with a hot cup of spiced tea during cold football season weather!

INGREDIENTS:

3 eggs

1 cup granulated sugar

2/3 cup canned pumpkin

1 teaspoon lemon juice

3/4 cup flour

2 teaspoons cinnamon

1 teaspoon baking powder

1 teaspoon ginger

1/2 teaspoon nutmeg

1/2 teaspoon salt

1 cup chopped walnuts

1 cup sifted powdered sugar

8 ounces cream cheese

6 tablespoons butter

1 teaspoon vanilla

DIRECTIONS:

• In a large mixer bowl, beat eggs with an electric mixer on high speed for 5 minutes until thick. Gradually beat in granulated sugar. Stir in pumpkin and lemon juice. In a separate bowl, stir together flour, cinnamon, baking powder, ginger, nutmeg and salt. Fold this mixture into pumpkin mixture. Spread in a greased and floured 15x10x1 jellyroll pan (I use a cookie sheet). Sprinkle with walnuts. Bake in a 375-degree oven for 15 minutes (I have found that 13 minutes is the perfect time for my oven). Immediately invert cake onto towel sprinkled with powdered sugar. Let sit for 4 or 5 minutes. Roll up cake in a dish towel, jellyroll style, starting from short side. Cool completely (I put it in the fridge for about 30 minutes). Unroll cake.

• For filling, in a small mixer bowl, beat the 1 cup powdered sugar, cream cheese, butter and vanilla with electric mixer on medium speed until smooth. Spread over cake, and re-roll cake. Cover and chill. To serve, cut cake into 1-inch slices.

• I put all of the dry ingredients into a Ziplock bag (flour, cinnamon, baking powder, ginger, nutmeg and salt). I make five or six bags so that the mixture is ready for when I want to make another batch of pumpkin rolls, and this really speeds up the process! Then all I have to do is beat the eggs, add sugar and pumpkin, pour in my Ziplock bag mix and pour onto my cookie sheet. Then add the walnuts and bake.

• Also, I spray my baking sheet with Pam cooking spray and then cover with wax paper. I then spray the wax paper with Pam. This makes it really easy to get the roll out of the pan when it is finished cooking. It may cause a little smoke in the oven, but don't be alarmed, this is normal!

Photo by Kent Gidley

LEE ROY LOVES COMING BACK HOME

Does a former player at your school, perhaps your favorite player, come back to tailgate with the fans and enjoy the traditions that the rest of your alumni do?

Archie Griffin does at Ohio State, but hey, he is head of the Buckeye alumni association, so it's part of his job. How often does Joe Montana go back to Notre Dame?

Terry Bradshaw is too busy on the weekends with his network responsibilities to return to Louisiana Tech. Mean Joe Greene, now that he has retired from the Pittsburgh Steelers' front office, may be able to take in a few games at North Texas. Earl Campbell has bad knees and gets about slowly, but lives in Austin so the campus is within reach. Roger Staubach returns to Annapolis occasionally. Archie Manning has a condo at Oxford, but its hard for him to get back to Ole Miss because he travels and spends time with his three sons, two of whom are in the NFL — Peyton with the Denver Broncos and Eli with the New York Giants.

Most former players who enjoyed long-term pro careers are not too keen on returning to campus and whooping it up with the alumni. Except Lee Roy Jordan, the All-American.

When there is a big game in Tuscaloosa, Lee Roy and his wife, Biddie, pack up and make the nine-hour drive from Dallas to Tuscaloosa — sometimes as many as six times a year. How many players with a fabled career at their alma mater exhibit that kind of loyalty to their favorite campus?

"It is fun and rewarding to go back to where I played college football," says Lee Roy, a 14-year NFL veteran with the Dallas Cowboys. "One of the reasons is the tailgating scene. I visit as many tailgate parties as possible. There are so many friends who have motor homes and specialized cooking equipment. I love walking around and seeing friends while they are grilling and preparing food. Only problem is that you visit one and then another and another….next thing you know, you will miss kickoff.

"Alabama fans travel well," he continued. "They crank up those motor homes and head down the road, wherever the team is playing." Roll Tide? The Alabama motor home fraternity embodies the phrase, literally.

Lee Roy Jordan looks like a football player ought to look. Rugged features with a chiseled visage, which would resonate if he joined the granite foursome at Mount Rushmore. If you were casting for someone to fit the image of the Marlboro Man, you couldn't do better than Lee Roy.

Some people have credentials that are worthy of ongoing review. Nothing wrong with restating the facts when there is such overwhelming credibility, as the case is with Jordan, the Excel, Alabama, farm boy whom Paul "Bear" Bryant idolized as much as the farm boy idolized his coach. It was the Bear who said that if the runners stayed between the sidelines, Lee Roy would "get 'em." Take the 1963 Orange Bowl, for example: Alabama versus Oklahoma in the pre-advanced technology days. They didn't keep statistics on such things as tackles for loss, assisted tackles, tackles while standing on your head, or any of the other media-spawned superlatives of today. Somebody, however, went back and checked the Orange Bowl film and discovered that Jordan made 31 tackles, and this was in the era when players played both offense and defense. If you consider that, in that game, Oklahoma ran 60 offensive plays, Lee Roy made over half the tackles.

Jordan's achievements in the golden era of the old Cowboys, those who established the Dallas dynasty, are as noteworthy as those of his Alabama career. He made 21 tackles in a game as a professional. Against the Cincinnati Bengals, he once intercepted three passes, and one went for a touchdown, in the space of five minutes. For 14 years, he was not only a performer, but he was a leader for the Cowboys.

Try to tell me of an All-American who goes home as much as Lee Roy Jordan. It'd be hard to find one!

Lee Roy's Favorite Cheese Ball

**From Lee Roy and Biddie Jordan
Former linebacker at
the University of Alabama**

INGREDIENTS:

1 8-ounce package of cream cheese

2 cups sharp cheddar cheese

1 or 2 tablespoons minced onion

1 can green chiles

1 tablespoon Worcestershire sauce

1 cup pecans, chopped

1 teaspoon to 1 tablespoon chili powder

1 teaspoon to 1 tablespoon cayenne pepper

1 teaspoon to 1 tablespoon paprika

DIRECTIONS:

• Mix everything together, roll into a ball and serve with Wheat Thins.

FLYING SUVS TO
HAWAII

When Dick Tomey, who finished his career as the head coach at San Jose State, was asked if he had a tailgate story, he paused for a moment and said, "When I found myself not coaching but doing some TV before joining Bill Walsh with the 49ers and subsequently Mack Brown at Texas, I was flabbergasted at the lengths people went to win the tailgate part of the game with great food and drink.

"During Dennis Franchione's tenure at Alabama, they played their last game at Hawaii. Three Alabama boosters flew their huge SUVs over to Honolulu with all the tailgating paraphernalia and put on a tailgate unlike any other. Hawaii won and Dennis took the Texas A&M job."

That's called taking "Roll Tide" to new heights!

Breakfast Casserole Muffins

From Bill and Mary Battle
Athletic Director at
the University of Alabama

INGREDIENTS:

1 1/2 pounds bulk sausage, brown and drain

6 eggs

1 cup Bisquick

2 cups Half & Half (or you could probably use milk)

1/2 teaspoon salt

1/2 teaspoon pepper

2 to 3 cups grated sharp cheddar cheese

DIRECTIONS:

• Spray muffin tins (if not using Teflon), and do not use paper liners. Place crumbled sausage evenly in muffin tins. Mix eggs, Bisquick, Half & Half, salt and pepper. Pour evenly over the sausage (I use a small ladle that works great). Top with grated cheese (be very generous with cheese). Bake at 350 degrees for 25 minutes. Allow muffins to slightly cool before removing from the tins. They freeze well and can be heated in a microwave or oven. I prefer heating them in the oven while wrapped lightly with foil. This makes 24 muffins. It doesn't work as well with miniature muffin tins.

ARIZONA'S RED-HOT TAILGATING

Arizona and the desert make tailgating hot in a variety of ways. The weather, of course, means that early in the season, tailgating is a hot exercise. Furthermore, there is the Mexican culinary influence on the tailgating, which can be jalapeno hot. Then sometimes you find a tailgater with a "hot" name, as is the case with Autumn Champion. What a name!

"I was born in autumn," says Autumn Champion, the All-America softball player at Arizona. "However, according to my mom, it would have been my name anyway . . . for no other reason than she liked it. And I just got lucky

with my last name. Now it is legally Schur, because I am married (oh how I pushed for him to take my name!), but I still use Champion often because . . . well, it sounds better and it is what I was known by in athletics."

Autumn is one of those students who enroll, find happiness and choose to reside within the confines of the address of their alma mater. Autumn gets high marks for her creative cooking, passion for the Wildcats and Arizona tailgating. The following is her testimony to an Arizona football game day.

"Arizona tailgating is unique in that we have some of the best weather one could ask for! It's always a beautiful day, which makes the entire experience even more enjoyable than it already is," says Autumn. "I also feel the setup for our tailgates is awesome in that we are right in the middle of campus in one long strip! It becomes one big alley to walk up and down and visit with other Wildcat fans. Most people wear red (unless it's a white-out game). Just before the stadium opens, the band marches in and plays. People can follow behind the

Pepperoni Chicken on a Stick

From Dick and Nanci Tomey
Former head coach at Arizona, Hawaii and San Jose State

INGREDIENTS:

1 pound of chicken breasts or tenders, trimmed

4 ounce block of sharp cheddar cheese

1/4 cup sun-dried tomatoes

1/2 pound wafer (sandwich) pepperoni

Basil, one large bunch

Marinara sauce for dunking (optional)

DIRECTIONS:

• Cut chicken into bite-sized chunks. Cut off 1/4-inch slices of the cheddar, then cut each slice into 4 or 5 narrow sticks. Slice the sun-dried tomatoes into thin strips. Preheat oven to 450 degrees. Place a sliver of sun-dried tomato on each large slice of pepperoni, then put a chunk of chicken over it. Tuck a piece of cheese against chicken on one side, then lay a basil leaf or two on top. Roll the chicken up in the pepperoni. Poke a skewer through, starting at the lose end of pepperoni, and right through. Skewer as you roll them, and lay out on baking sheet. Bake for 7 or 8 minutes, then remove and drain from oil. Serve with marinara if desired.

spirit," says Flip. "'Bear Down' and 'Go Cats' are common exhortations. Two hours prior to kickoff, the team rides in for the Wildcat Walk with a motorcade down the Mall. A sea of fans gathers and then parts to form a human tunnel from the buses to the locker rooms. Kids, alums and all fans have an opportunity to reach out in support of the team and favorite players as they enter the football facilities. You can count on seeing the band, cheerleaders, other student athletes, and the mascots Wilbur and Wilma visiting the entire tailgate area every game."

What are traditions one would not want to miss if tailgating at Arizona?

"In addition to the Wildcat Walk, homecoming just cannot be topped, with a parade through the Mall and tents for fraternities, sororities and student groups spanning the entire Mall, where nearly 80,000 fans and alums can be seen every game," says Flip. "After the game, the band plays a concert at Alumni Plaza, which ends with the ringing of the bell that hangs in the Union bell tower.

"Formal tailgating is supposed to end shortly after the end of the game," he continued. "Of course, the students are just getting started. Immediately following the game, the band, cheerleaders, students and alums head to Alumni Plaza to hear 'Bear Down,' 'All Hail' and ring the bell from the Union. The bell is the historic bell salvaged from the *USS Arizona*. This famous bell was actually featured in a Hyundai commercial with the story of Bill Bowers and how he made sure the bell found its home at the Arizona campus."

Bowers lived to be 100 years old. When he learned that the bell — from the battleship *Arizona* that was sunk during the Japanese attack on Pearl Harbor on Dec. 7, 1941 — was headed for salvage and meltdown, he initiated a move to save the bell, which is now located in the clock tower of the Student Union Building where it is rung on special occasions like the Sunday before Pearl Harbor Day in memory of the 1,177 men who lost their lives at Pearl Harbor. It also rings after UA victories, except when the Wildcats defeat other Arizona teams.

"The sun makes tailgating at Arizona special," says Flip. "To be surrounded by an oasis of green in the heart of the Sonoran desert is a wonderful scene. We call the place and time the 'Arizona Experience.' It is accompanied by wonderful food spreads and variety: Carne Asada, favorite salsas and guacamole — countless Mexican-influenced foods. When it comes to barbecue, Arizona gives up nothing to the South. We know how to cook, eat and drink!"

band to get the game started. At the beginning of the game, when the Wildcats are announced, fireworks go off. With every kickoff, everyone shakes their keys until the kick sails away."

For Flip May, tailgating at Arizona means relaxing on "the Mall," a lush strip of grass that runs about a half a mile through the core of campus with the stately and historic Old Main at the western end. Tailgaters line up hours in advance of the official on-campus tailgating start, which commences six hours prior to kickoff, he says.

"There is a sea of Wildcat faithful donning the cardinal and navy in celebration of 100-plus years of school

Photo courtesy of Autumn Champion.

Autumn and Flip were moved to invoke the name of John "Button" Salmon, the famed football player who, on his death bed, asked his coach, Pop McKale (of McKale Center fame), to tell the team to "Bear Down!"

When it's time to "Bear Down" at Arizona, do as many Wildcat fans do: reach for a Sonoran hot dog!

(Top) Autumn Champion with a Sonoran hot dog (above).

Arizona Champion-Style Sonoran Dog

From Autumn Champion
Former UA athlete

INGREDIENTS (FOR 4 PEOPLE):

3 Roma tomatoes

2 avocados, peeled & diced

1/4 cup red onion, diced

2 tablespoons cilantro, chopped

2 limes, cut in wedges

1/4 cup mayonnaise

1 teaspoon Tabasco sauce

1 lemon, cut in wedges

1/2 cup pineapple, diced

4 hot dogs

4 slices of bacon

1 15-ounce can ranch-style beans, drained

4 hot dog buns

Grill & grilling tools

1 medium bowl

1 small bowl

Pastry funnel*

24 wooden skewers

DIRECTIONS:

• Preheat grill to medium heat. Combine tomatoes, avocados, onions and cilantro in a medium bowl. Squeeze limes over the combined ingredients and mix together. In a separate small bowl, combine mayonnaise, Tabasco sauce and squeeze the lemon juice into the mixture. Transfer mayonnaise mixture into a pastry funnel*. Poke wooden skewers through pineapple (as many pineapple pieces as you can per skewer). Grill pineapple skewers until lightly browned on each side. Wrap each hot dog in a piece of bacon. Grill hot dogs until bacon is brown and crispy. While hot dogs are grilling, warm the beans over the grill. Put the hot dog wrapped in bacon in the bun, add pico de gallo, pineapples and/or drizzle mayonnaise mixture on top!

(*In place of a pastry funnel, you can use a plastic Ziplock bag and snip a tiny hole in one corner.)

WOOOOOOOO, PIG! SOOIE!

Before the University of Arkansas, there were the Razorbacks, a feral hog, which has become a menace in a lot of places across the South. That is the way Arkansas Razorback fans want it to be for their football team. Before the University of Arkansas became the Razorbacks, the official mascot was the cardinal, the bird. By 1910 the Cardinals gave way to the Razorbacks.

Today, Tusk is the official name of the Arkansas mascot, and he lives in hog heaven near Dardanelle, Arkansas, in a spacious 9,000-square-foot facility, a hog-friendly place complete with a mud hole for Tusk IV to take a daily mud bath.

"Seeing Tusk in the Tusk wagon circling the stadium while the band plays the fight song is something everybody should experience," says Wade Jones, who has to be a world-class tailgater with more credentials than any football fan who has ever lit a fire.

"It's special on game day to bond with same-interest fans, reconnecting with your friends," Wade continued. "Tailgating in The Pit and The Gardens, well, there's nothing like it. When we play night games, tailgating becomes an all-day affair. An interesting tradition at Arkansas is the naming of our tailgates like Pickled Pigs, Hogapolooza and Razorback Rednecks. At each game, a winner is honored on the Jumbotron. We often try to have themed tailgate parties. When South Carolina comes to town, low-country boils are popular. With LSU, it's Cajun cooking and Po' boy sandwiches."

With Wade and his friends, there is nothing like a home game in the fall in Fayetteville when everybody calls the hogs. "Wooooooooo, Pig! Sooie!" can be heard across the campus with the greatest of enthusiasm and energy. This is one of the most distinctive yells in all of college football. Wade, like many Arkansas fans, can't wait until game day as his following account reveals:

It's 6 a.m. on a crisp, cool Saturday morning in October and alarm clocks are going off all over the state of Arkansas, waking men and women alike who share a common thread. They aren't going into the office or

The Sooie Shuttle is ready for action. Photo by Michael Jones.

the job site today to work overtime nor are they headed to the deer woods or the nearest lake for a fishing trip. This is October, and Saturdays in October are reserved for one thing in Arkansas: Razorback football. In the Southeastern Conference, you don't show up on campus for a home game an hour before kickoff and walk straight into the stadium. You are tailgating by early morning, even for a 7 p.m. kickoff. It is a major social event. It is an all-day affair complete with great food, drink and socializing with friends and acquaintances from all over the state, many of whom you may only see on those home dates in the fall.

By 7 a.m., we are on the road with our Sooie Shuttle loaded and prepped, headed for Reynolds Razorback Stadium and our reserved tailgating spot in The Pit, or the parking lot just north of the stadium. Or if the game happens to be in Little Rock that weekend, we head for the War Memorial Golf Course to claim our spot amongst thousands of other tailgaters all across the course. The course is a most unique tailgating atmosphere, where you may be parked next to the 17th green or set up your grill just off of the 14th tee box. A sea of red and white clad fans line the entire golf course with their tailgating canopies, with the smell of grills cooking all kinds of food as people reunite with old friends and make new ones at the biggest party in Little Rock.

When we reach our spot, the set up begins. John, Berry and I have this part choreographed like the halftime performance by the Razorback dance team. It is best, at this point, for others just stand clear as the three of us know exactly what has to be done and how to do it with the most efficiency. Within 20 minutes, the empty spot of asphalt is transformed into what could be an outdoor wedding. We set up two 12-foot by 12-foot canopies, three large conference tables clad with custom

Pigskin Nachos

From Jimmy Johnson
Arkansas football letterman,
former head coach at Oklahoma State
and University of Miami

INGREDIENTS:

10 pound pork butt
1 red onion
1 white onion
Carrots
Celery
2 red peppers
2 yellow peppers
2 pablono peppers
Sliced jalapenos
Banana peppers
Pico de gallo
Shredded Monterey jack cheese
Shredded cheddar cheese
Sour cream
Guacamole
Diced scallions
Barbecue sauce
Tri-colored tortilla chips

DIRECTIONS:

• Slow roast the pork for 6 hours in a deep pan filled with onions, carrots and celery in a beef base, filled about halfway up the pan with about 22 ounces of your favorite beer. After cooking, let it rest and cool while you dice peppers, onions and scallions. Place tri-colored tortilla chips on a platter. Add pulled pork, peppers, onions, shredded cheeses and BBQ sauce. Layer with more chips and repeat step above. Top with pico de gallo, sour cream, guacamole and a touch of chopped scallions. Enjoy the game! Serves 15 to 20 people.

Razorback tablecloths, outdoor cooking station, 20 Razorback folding tailgating chairs and the rear door of the Sooie Shuttle open to one end of this spread. From the shuttle, the first thing I do is to play my "game day remix" that is piping from the outdoor speakers. Berry is connecting the outdoor 50-inch flat screen as well as the 32-inch TV that is mounted above the driver's seat inside of the shuttle. He has synched the monitors so both are tuned to ESPN, and we are ready for "College Game-Day." John is the resident chef and has already started the day's breakfast offering.

As the day goes along, The Pit swells with people and their outdoor parties are in full swing. If you are an out-of-town guest, we recommend you visit the Broyles Center and the football museum located under the massive Jumbotron scoreboard just outside the north end of the stadium, and the Bud Walton Arena, the basketball palace of Mid-America and the museum of Razorback history located on the first floor. As you exit the Bud Walton Arena, a short walk to the south will take you to The Gardens, which is the tailgating area to the south of the stadium and where you will find corporate sponsored parties and live music along with another sea of those red-and-white canopies.

Back over at The Pit, it's just a few hours before kickoff and the party is picking up steam. You can feel the electricity in the air, and the excitement of the Razorback faithful starts to bring about a loud buzz throughout the campus.

As it gets closer to kickoff, the Tusk bus — which is a huge open-stock trailer occupied by Tusk himself, a 500-pound live Razorback hog — makes its way around the

Sausage Dip

From Bret and Jen Bielema
Head coach at Arkansas,
former head coach at Wisconsin,
University of Iowa football team captain

INGREDIENTS:

1 16-ounce roll of regular Jimmy Dean Sausage

1 10-ounce can of regular Rotel

2 8-ounce blocks of cream cheese

DIRECTIONS:

• Brown the sausage in a pan over medium heat. Drain grease. Soften two blocks of cream cheese in the microwave for 1 to 2 minutes. Combine browned sausage, can of Rotel (do not drain) and softened cream cheese in a crockpot/slow cooker and mix. Serve with Tostitos Scoops.

Note from Jen: A crockpot/slow cooker will keep the dip warm. For added spice, you can use Jimmy Dean "Hot" Sausage and/or "Hot" Rotel.

Randy Lann at the smoker before an Arkansas game.

BROYLES ON GOLF

Frank Broyles, an outstanding quarterback at Georgia Tech, became an assistant coach at his alma mater and ultimately landed in Fayetteville where he became the leader and developer of a winning football tradition and enjoyed a head-turning experience as the Razorback athletic director.

Before he engineered the move for Arkansas' admission into the Southeastern Conference, Broyles' teams enjoyed ongoing success in the old Southwest Conference.

His biggest rival, Texas, was coached by his best friend, Darrell Royal. They had a relationship that should have been a model for all coaches to emulate — fight it out on the field Saturday afternoon and then enjoy dinner afterward. "It was the way coaching should be," Broyles says today. "We had a rule. We never talked about any of our games."

They often socialized together. In the offseason, they played golf frequently. A member of the Augusta National Golf Club, Frank delighted in hosting his friend Darrell at the home of the Masters. They would often play 36 holes a day.

"We weren't scratch golfers," Broyles says, "but our wives were scratch shoppers."

BB'S FABULOUS FUDGE

From Frank and the late Barbara Broyles
Former head coach and
athletic director at Arkansas

INGREDIENTS:

3 cups sugar
5 tablespoons cocoa powder
1 1/4 cups milk
3 tablespoons white Karo Syrup
3 tablespoons butter
1 teaspoon vanilla
1 to 1 1/2 cups chopped nuts

DIRECTIONS:

• Mix sugar with cocoa powder, and then add 1 1/4 cups milk and mix in a saucepan over high heat. Bring to a boil. Add white Karo Syrup and butter, stir, and then boil for 2 minutes. Reduce to simmer for 15 to 20 minutes, stirring frequently. Remove from heat, and add vanilla and chopped nuts, according to taste. Beat mixture until smooth. Pour into a buttered 9-inch by 12-inch pan, and let cool. Cut when cooled, and enjoy!

stadium and the tailgate areas. Atop the Tusk trailer is a platform with the pep band and cheerleaders leading cheers and, of course, "calling the hogs." Sirens wail as the team buses approach the north end of The Pit and the players and coaches exit into a human walkway of fans to make their way to the stadium.

* * *

"Having fun and making people and friends happy has always been my way of life," says Randy Lann, a passionate Razorback tailgater with regional cooking credentials. "What a better way to do that than grilling all kinds of food? In 2006, my family, Beech Creek Farms, won the World Championship Steak Cook-off and was featured on the Food Network Show 'Steak Challengers.' In 2010, I started grilling for the Dallas Cowboys, doing special events and grilling some Fridays at practice for the team and staff. I soon was named the 'grill master' for the Dallas Cowboys and Cowboys Tailgate Nation. I now promote tailgating for the Cowboys by shooting commercials, promo spots and entertain guests such as Commissioner of Tailgating Joe Cahn. Our very close family is known to many as Beech Creek Farms, named after my wife's grandparents, E.E. and Selma Franks. All three of their children — Peggy, Polly and Larry — attended the University of Arkansas, which turned our family into huge Razorback fans.

I may have the title of grill master for the Dallas Cowboys, which I love and cherish, but it's all about family and friends and doing something you love and have fun doing it. Arkansas Razorback tailgating allows our family and friends to gather on what we call an Arkansas Natural High. Go Hogs!"

That, my friends, is one serious tailgater!

LACEWELL'S TAILGATING MOMENT

Arkansas State, which competes in the Sun Belt Conference, is a small school of just over 13,000 students but has enjoyed success on the football field.

One of the Red Wolves' former coaches is Larry Lacewell, who developed dominating defenses at Oklahoma for Barry Switzer during the era of the Selmon Brothers. Lacewell was a wishbone offense advocate, which got the attention of Gus Malzahn, one of the many "name" coaches who have passed through Jonesboro on the way to a more prestigious job opportunity.

When Lacewell was the head coach at Arkansas State, he tried to balance the budget by playing Division I schools, like Texas A&M and Ole Miss. When he took his team on the road, he tried to expose them to different experiences — like having team buses ride by fraternity and sorority houses and by well-known campus landmarks. "Places they would likely never see if they were not college football players, traveling across the country by bus," Lacewell explained.

At Ole Miss in 1986, Lacewell decided he would have the team bus park as close to "The Grove" as possible. He let his team off the bus and allowed them walk through the popular tailgating enclave and the Ole Miss campus.

"They had never seen anything like that," Lacewell said with a laugh. "It almost backfired on me. The Ole Miss fans were cheering us and welcoming us with the greatest of hospitality. Some of our players stopped and began eating that good food and didn't want to leave. I worried that they were eating so much that they wouldn't be in condition to play. You talk about an experience! Jonesboro, Arkansas, is a far cry from the atmosphere of The Grove."

When the game was over, Lacewell and the Red Wolves had the last laugh. They tied a good Ole Miss team, 10-10, which put a damper on postgame tailgating at The Grove, which Ole Miss fans believe is the "tailgating capital of college football."

Simple Salsa

From Larry Lacewell
Former head coach at Arkansas State,
and assistant coach at Oklahoma,
Wichita State, Iowa State and Tennessee

INGREDIENTS:

5 or 6 tomatoes
5 or 6 peppers (jalapeño or habanero)
Garlic pod
Cilantro
Salt

DIRECTIONS:

• Boil tomatoes and peppers until tender. Put cilantro and garlic pod into a blender. Once tomatoes and peppers are soft, put them in the blender and blend until it still has some thickness. Salt to taste, and do not add sugar.

TAILGATING ON THE PLAINS

"Auburn University is located on a beautiful campus in the heart of the town of Auburn in Alabama," says Grant Harkness, an outdoorsman from Mobile.

Grant is one of those who tailgates with the bounty that comes from his hunting and fishing activity during the year. He might bring quail, dove or duck, red snapper or venison. Or he might bring a bushel of oysters from the Gulf. You never know what to expect when you tailgate with Grant. If there is anything that surpasses his love of the outdoors, it would be his affection for tailgating. Driving up to Auburn for home games brings about the greatest anticipation for him. He never tires of tailgating, and he forever enjoys paying tribute to Saturdays in Auburn, "the loudest village on the Plains."

"Auburn," he says, "is situated amongst large old oak trees, historical- and traditional-style architectural buildings, small shops and boutiques, and sports bars and restaurants all emulating a collegiate atmosphere with a small-town ambiance. Game day at Auburn begins on the Plains where everyone is scurrying around to prepare their ultimate tailgate area. The Plains is the area right outside the stadium where multiple tents and canopies are placed in rows with banners, signs and flags displayed to show their Tiger spirit. This is one of the most exciting places to experience Auburn tailgating in its truest form. It is in the center of the game-day madness. Not a stranger is in sight because on our campus we are all Auburn and welcome everyone with a loud and hearty greeting of War Eagle! This is the battle cry and motto of Auburn University, the Auburn football team and its Auburn family.

"Auburn games and the grand pageantry of its pregame show and the famous Tiger Walk are tremendous sights to see. The players are escorted from their state-of-the-art athletic training facility to the Jordan-Hare Stadium and are immersed in the Tiger spirit created by fans going wild with cheers and chants. The marching band leads the way blasting the fight song 'War Eagle' as they prance onto the football field in all their glory, followed by the dance and cheer teams parading large Auburn flags. Before all Auburn games, the traditional War Eagle Flight takes place. A golden eagle named Nova and a bald eagle named Spirit perform the War Eagle

Flight. Watching the two soaring eagles is an experience that stirs the Tiger pride felt by all present. Whether the Tigers win or lose, the show must go on. Anyone who has the love for football, good times, marching bands, soaring eagles, cheer and dance teams, friends and family, Southern hospitality and, of course, awesome tasting food need to experience Auburn's tailgating experience.

"Growing up and living in Alabama, my memories and love of Auburn football began as a young child watching Auburn football every Saturday. Tiger fever runs rampart in my blood. Obviously, it was only natural to raise my five daughters as Auburn fans. Any college campus has its unique way of tailgating, but nothing beats the Auburn family distinctive blend of traditions and unique atmosphere of southern comfort. I made my family a part of the Auburn family, and welcome anyone to come tailgate with the Auburn Tigers on our beautiful campus surrounded by old oak trees and a memo-

Grilled Dove Wraps

From Grant Harkness, Auburn Superfan

INGREDIENTS:

Fresh deboned dove breasts

Vegetable oil

Vinegar

Fresh jalapeno, sliced vertically

Water chestnuts, sliced

Monterey jack cheese, sliced

Bacon, cut into half slices

Round toothpicks

DIRECTIONS:

• Marinate fresh deboned dove breasts in oil and vinegar dressing with spices. Wrap the breast around the pepper, chestnut and cheese slice with a half slice of bacon. Hold the bacon in place with a moist round toothpick (be sure to wrap tightly to hold the cheese in place). Baste the wraps with marinade (to help cook the bacon faster and keep the meat from drying out). Only grill for 3 or 4 minutes on each side. Dove cooks quickly and will get tough if overcooked. Enjoy!

rable atmosphere of good ole southern charm that only a small town can offer.

"When my oldest daughter Paige became a freshman at Auburn in 2007, my Auburn tailgating experience was ready to go to a whole new level! As I am always up for an Auburn tailgate party and had been a part of many tailgate parties as a guest, I embraced the opportunity to host my own tailgate party in 2007. I gathered together my most trustworthy allies to prepare and implement a tailgate party strategy. Our goal was to throw a kick butt tailgate party like no other and provide the most unforgettable tailgate event for all of my Auburn friends.

"Owning and operating an event and equipment rental company, Blue Rents in Mobile, allowed us to plan and utilize my catering and rental items that many of my clients use to have spectacular events. My Blue Rents crew does a lot of the preparation, with my wingmen and longtime friends, Dan Elcans, Rick Saliba and the comptroller at my company, Hunter Swanzy. They came together to organize, plan and host a tailgate party using all my favorite recipes and the freshest meats available. Being a Gulf Coast angler who also loves to hunt, I wanted to share some of my favorite recipes and southern dishes at our tailgate party. Game and seafood for our tailgate is always better if you know you caught it or hunted it. Fortunately, I deep-sea fish out of Orange Beach and hunt on my farm, Blackwater Farms, located in Loxley.

"Fresh-caught red snapper or fresh large Gulf Coast shrimp grilled or fried, shucked oysters served on the half shell and roasted, dove or quail wraps, roasted pig and venison burgers are served with their flavorful condiments to enhance the menu at our famous tailgating parties.

"Usually during open snapper season on the Gulf Coast in Alabama and Florida, we fish off my 28-foot Contender. We fish all day until we reach our limit. As we grill burgers or fry our freshly caught fish, we bag up our snapper filets and store them for our parties. Snapper throats of fileted fish are awesome smoked or grilled. Hot off the grill, the tender fish meat falls off the bones and is the freshest and tastiest fish you could ever have.

"During hunting season, I enjoy hunting dove, quail and deer. My wing-dog and best friend Max is always right by my side and poses great for pictures. He wears his orange and blue well during his days off. My daughters have also hunted the farm and shot their first deer there, and Max contributes to the tailgate party by fetching up dove from our hunts. Wild pigs are abundant on

"Hurry Up, No Huddle" Buffalo Chicken Dip

From Gus and Kristi Malzahn
Head coach at Auburn, former head coach at Arkansas State

INGREDIENTS:

2 cooked boneless chicken breasts, shredded
1 8-ounce package cream cheese
1 12-ounce bottle hot wing sauce
1 cup ranch dressing
2 cups sharp cheddar cheese, shredded

DIRECTIONS:

• Mix all ingredients in a bowl. Place in baking dish. Bake at 350 for 25 minutes. Serve with tortilla chips or crackers.

the farm, and many nights are ended with a pig hunt. Great for roastin' at a tailgate!

"My tailgate crew also consists of my five daughters (Paige, Courtney, Julianne, Margret and Katie) who are all Auburn Tigers — except for the track star who is a an Ole Miss Rebel. Our famous outdoor menu items have become a tradition at our Auburn tailgate parties.

"As the years have progressed, my daughters have always shared and been a part of the tailgate tasks and experience. Paige, my oldest, was followed by my triplets, Courtney, Julianne and Margret. One of my triplets is not an Auburn Tiger. She yells 'Hottie Tottie' and 'War Eagle' at the same time. My last daughter, Katie, is now an Auburn student.

"Anticipation for our group begins on Friday before the big game and multiplies throughout the campus as the Auburn chants and cheers grow and do not stop until Sunday. My daughters make a nice contribution by staking out the territory for our tailgate area on Friday and to make sure the reservation for our tailgate area is obtained.

Tailgate Campfire Breakfast

From Pat Dye Sr.
Former Auburn head coach and
Georgia alum

INGREDIENTS:

1/2 pound bacon

2 pounds potatoes, diced

1 medium onion, diced

6 ounces shredded cheddar cheese

1/2 teaspoon salt

1/4 teaspoon pepper

12 large eggs

Salsa or catsup

DIRECTIONS:

• Cook bacon in a large skillet until crisp, then remove and drain on paper towels, while reserving 2 tablespoons of drippings in the skillet. Crumble bacon and set aside. Saute potatoes, onion, salt and pepper, and pour beaten eggs over potatoes in skillet. Cook over medium heat 4 minutes or until eggs are set, stirring if necessary. Sprinkle with bacon and cheese. Serve with salsa or catsup. Makes six hearty servings.

Spinach Cheese Squares

From Pat Dye Sr.
Former Auburn head coach and
Georgia alum

INGREDIENTS:

4 tablespoons margarine

3 eggs

1 cup milk

1 cup flour

1 teaspoon salt

1 teaspoon baking powder

1 pound (16 ounces) grated sharp cheddar cheese

1 tablespoon chopped onion

1 10-ounce package frozen spinach, chopped and drained

DIRECTIONS:

• Melt margarine in a 13-inch by 9-inch roasting pan in a 350 degree oven. Beat eggs, and then add milk, flour, salt and baking powder. Add cheese, onion and spinach last. Bake for 35 minutes and then cool for 45 minutes. Cut and freeze, or reheat at 325 degrees for 15 minutes. Makes 2 to 3 dozen squares. Great as an appetizer!

"Early on Saturday morning around 7 a.m., the setup begins and grills are fired up. My wingmen take charge and organize the setup efforts. The morning is faced a little easier with some grilled Conecuh sausage and a Bloody Mary loaded with pickled okra, celery, Worcestershire and hot sauce.

"Our tailgate area includes tables and chairs, large grills for roasting and grilling oysters on the half shell, specially prepared pig or other game, a beverage station outfitted with a game specialty drink or hot chocolate bar, and a fixins table with a variety of southern and coastal prepared appetizers and side dishes. We also provide an area with seating and plantation-style rocking chairs and a large flat-screen television to monitor all the SEC games scheduled for that day. At the beginning of the season, the weather is fairly hot, so oscillating fans and cold drinks are essential to our tailgate party.

"Some of our famous main course menu items include a fresh 'kill,' smoked and roasted, fried fresh Gulf Coast shrimp and fresh red snapper, West Indies salad, shucked oysters grilled on the half shell with special seasonings, shrimp kabobs, grilled dove wraps, spiced-up grilled chicken wings and gourmet beef or venison burgers. You hungry yet? Be sure to stop by!"

JIMMY RANE ON AUBURN'S TRADITION

Jimmy Rane, CEO of Great Southern Wood Preserving, Inc., in Abbeville, Alabama, may be the best-known Auburn graduate outside those who win the Heisman Trophy and make the All-America Team. His company for years sponsored coaches' shows in the South, principally the Southeastern Conference. He is still doing those clever commercials promoting pressure-treated lumber. A member of the Auburn University Board of Trustees, Rane takes Auburn football seriously, and that includes tailgating.

"In a lifetime of tailgating at my alma mater, Auburn University, I've had so many wonderful memories that it's hard to know where to start," says Jimmy.

"In looking back over the years, I especially remember the times I spent on the Plains in the early 1980s when I was introducing my young children, Ashleigh and James, to the traditions of tailgating at Auburn and cheering on the Orange and Blue," he continued. "This was long before our company became such a visible supporter of collegiate athletics and long before the days when generators, big-screen TVs and satellite dishes became a part of tailgating.

"We'd start our day out early, packing our car with a cooler of cold drinks, a well-stocked supply of snacks and a very special black-bottom pie. This pie was so good that we often wondered if it'd make it out of the driveway before we dug in — much less all the way from our hometown of Abbeville to Auburn. But even more than delicious, it was like a taste of family history.

"The black-bottom pie was something my mom made for the day from a recipe she had been given back in the late 1940s or early 1950s by Mrs. Frances Murphy. Mrs. Murphy (Miss Frankie to her friends) managed the Hotel Frances in Abbeville, which was located next to a res-

Bo Jackson's Favorite Mac & Cheese

Provided by Auburn Tigerettes Cookbook

INGREDIENTS:

2 1/2 pounds macaroni

4 tablespoons salt

2 gallons water (for boiling)

12 ounces butter or margarine

6 ounces flour

3 quarts milk

3 pounds shredded cheddar cheese

12 ounces bread crumbs

DIRECTIONS:

- You will need two 12-inch by 20-inch baking pans that are at least 2 inches deep, as this serves a lot of people! Preheat oven to 375 degrees. Cook macaroni, drain and pour into the two pans. Mix butter, flour, salt and milk, and make into a sauce. Add cheese to sauce. Pour sauce over macaroni in the pans. Sprinkle with bread crumbs and bake at 375 degrees for 35 minutes.

taurant that my father, Tony Rane, owned and operated — The Village Inn Restaurant. In fact, when my parents were first married, they lived at the Hotel Frances for a while, and it was during that time that they first tasted Miss Frankie's black-bottom pie. They loved it so much that when dad opened The Village Inn he made sure to have it on the menu, and it's been a favorite of my family as long as I can remember.

"Needless to say, we loved having this special pie along for the ride to Auburn," Jimmy continued. "Of course, we also loaded up the car with all the usual fan gear — stadium seats and shakers were always a part of our trips — and headed out on beautiful fall Saturdays.

"Back then, our route took us from Abbeville to our first stop at the Holiday Inn in Eufaula. This had nothing to do with an overnight stay but everything to do with what else we'd be chowing down on that day. My father

Black-Bottom Pie

From Jimmy Rane, Auburn Board of Trustees president pro tempore

INGREDIENTS:

1 cup finely crushed ginger snap crumbs (14 ginger snaps)

5 tablespoons of melted butter or oleo

Filling:

1 envelope of unflavored gelatin

1/4 cup of cold water

2 cups of milk

1/2 cup of sugar

1/8 teaspoon of salt

1 1/4 teaspoons of corn starch

4 eggs, separated

Chocolate custard layer:

1 1/2 squares of unsweetened chocolate, melted

1 teaspoon of vanilla

Rum-flavored chiffon layer:

1/2 cup of sugar, or 1/3 cup light or dark syrup and 2 teaspoons of sugar

1/4 teaspoon of cream of tartar

1 teaspoon of rum extract

Topping:

2 tablespoons semi-sweet chocolate, shaved

1 tablespoon of nuts finely chopped, or 1 cup of cream, whipped

2 tablespoons of sugar

1/2 square of bitter chocolate, shaved

DIRECTIONS:

- Mix ginger snap crumbs and melted butter or oleo. Press into a 9-inch pie plate with back of spoon dipped in water. Bake 10 minutes at 300 degrees then let cool.

- Soften gelatin in cold water. Scald the milk. Combine sugar, salt and corn starch. Beat egg yolks and add scalded milk very slowly, stirring constantly. Stir in sugar mixture. Cook over simmering water for 20 minutes, stirring almost constantly. Remove from heat and take out 1 cup of custard. To this add melted chocolate, and beat with rotary beater. Cool, add vanilla and pour into crumb crust. Chill. To remaining hot custard add the softened gelatin, stirring until dissolved. Cool but do not chill. Beat egg whites until frothy, add cream of tartar and continue beating until stiff. Add sugar (or corn syrup and sugar) slowly in three additions, beating between each addition until whites are very stiff. Add rum extract to custard and fold in the egg whites. Pour over chilled chocolate custard layer. If whipped cream topping is omitted, garnish with shaved semi-sweet chocolate and chill, or top with sweetened whipped cream, garnished with shaved bitter chocolate just before serving.

was a great entrepreneur, and, at this time in his career, he owned several Holiday Inns, and his restaurants were the best in the franchise. So I would ask dad to call the hotel restaurant in Eufaula and place a special order for fried chicken and Diplomat and Club sandwiches for us to take to the game.

"The Diplomats were one of dad's specialties — a triple-decker sandwich with turkey, ham, Swiss cheese and slaw, grilled and served on pumpernickel bread.

The whole family loved them, so we made sure we had enough for tailgating before the game, plus some for after the game, too. Just knowing they were in the trunk, ready and waiting, kept us focused on getting to Auburn and getting ready for a delicious tailgate meal.

"After leaving Eufaula, we'd wind our way up Highway 431 before turning onto 169 and finally to Auburn. This being Alabama, the weather from September to November varied a lot. It could be hot, cold or rainy. But

Black Bean & Corn Dip

From Pat Dye Jr. and wife Barbara
1984 Auburn grad

INGREDIENTS:

2 cans black beans, drained and rinsed

2 cans white shoepeg corn

2 bunches green onions, sliced

1 avocado, diced

2 4-ounce packages crumbled feta cheese

The dressing:

1 cup extra virgin olive oil

1 cup apple cider vinegar

1 cup sugar

3 shakes garlic powder

Salt

Pepper

DIRECTIONS:

• Mix everything together and refrigerate. Serve with Fritos Scoops.

Extra-Point Italian Chicken

From Al and Lisa Del Greco
Kicker on AU's Team of the Century

INGREDIENTS:

6 boneless chicken breasts

1 cup bread crumbs

1/4 cup margarine

1 15-ounce jar Prego meat-flavored sauce

1/2 cup Half & Half

1 pound shredded mozzarella cheese

Italian seasonings

Rigatoni noodles, cooked

DIRECTIONS:

• Cut the chicken into bite-sized pieces. Bread the chicken and brown it in margarine in a large skillet. Add Prego sauce, Half & Half and cheese. Add Italian seasonings to taste. Lower temperature to simmer for 30 minutes. Toss into cooked noodles and serve.

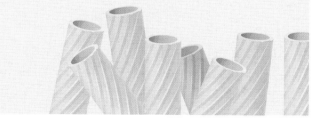

nothing dampened our Auburn spirit. As any Auburn fan will tell you, any day on the Plains is a great day.

"Once we got to campus, we'd park in the same general area where all our friends were. Then we'd pop open the trunk and enjoy some cold beverages, fried chicken, my dad's sandwiches and some of that black-bottom pie while the kids would play. They really loved tossing the football around and making new friends with the other children who were there.

"This was such a great bonding time with my kids, and the memories will stay with me forever. Anybody who knows me knows that I love Auburn, and I love my family. So now I'm thrilled that another generation of Ranes will come to understand just how great it is to be an Auburn Tiger!

"Today, my children have their own families, and I'm delighted that they've continued the tailgating traditions we started so many years ago by sharing those same traditions with my grandchildren.

"You know how those small things that your grandkids do just tug at your heart? Well, I get a feeling of pride every time I hear them say it. Because they know like I do, when you're tailgating on the Plains, the only words you need to make a new friend or to spur the team on to victory are 'War Eagle!'"

BAYLOR GETTING INTO THE TAILGATING GAME

According to John Garrison, associate athletic director for marketing at Baylor, the school hasn't had a long tradition of extensive tailgating. "However," he says, "over the past half-dozen years, or more, it has grown into a thriving game-day experience. The tailgating locations at the new McLane Stadium are on the Brazos River and are unique: electricity and a cable hookup are provided for most spots.

"A not-to-be-missed tailgating tradition at Baylor is the Bear Walk, which happens two and a half hours prior to kickoff when the team buses drop off the players and coaches to walk through the tailgate area as they enter the stadium," he continued. "Fans and alumni start setting up the day before, when RVs begin arriving. On game day, some people arrive before 8 a.m. no matter when kickoff is scheduled. For the occasional 11 a.m. game, the lots open at 6 a.m., and tailgaters are already lined up to get in."

Garrison added that "tailgating spots are presold, so there is no rush to the spots. Fans stay to tailgate after the game. One fan in particular has a huge postgame spread. His ribs and smoked tenderloin are in high demand. And since we moved into our new on-campus stadium in 2013, his tailgate continues to be the main attraction for people to visit."

With McLane Stadium's proximity to the Brazos River, one can only reflect on the past when the Chisholm Trail gained popularity as the route of the big cattle drives to the northern stockyards. Cowboys and their herds crossed the Brazos in Waco, accompanied by chuck wagons and campfires. Based on that, you could say that Baylor has had a link to some form of tailgating as long as any college in the country!

"Hobby" Howell was born in Waco and has lived there for all but three years of his life. He is co-owner of Academy for Creative Learning and the owner of Source Access, Inc.

"I began tailgating at Baylor games when I moved back to Waco from St. Louis in 1999," says Hobby. "Back then we only had RV parking spots and regular parking spots to tailgate in. It is very different today. Tailgating is a great way to extend the football game-day experience and get together with friends and meet new friends. When I started tailgating, Baylor football was not as exciting as it is today. Tailgating provides another reason to go to the stadium. I think there may have been instances where we had a larger crowd at the tailgate than were actually inside the stadium during the time before Art Briles took over.

"Several years ago Baylor — most notably John Garrison, associate athletic director for marketing — realized the importance of the game-day experience and the part tailgating could play in that experience. A special area was designated for tailgating, complete with cable TV and electric outlets. Since that time the atmosphere at BU games has really improved. Beginning three to four hours prior to game time there is an excitement that begins to build and leads up to the kickoff, and then carries over several hours after it is over.

"The introduction of electricity and cable expanded the number of activities that may be incorporated to enhance the tailgate experience," Hobby continued. "Most football fans are interested in more games than the one they are at the stadium to watch. I bring a 60-inch flat-screen TV, shade structures and chairs so we can comfortably watch other games when we are not in the stadium.

"A successful tailgate requires a good deal of effort prior to, during and after the game. I am very fortunate to have a son, Clark, who helps with the preparation and has also helped with the cooking for the past several

A Vitek's Gut Pak®. Photo courtesy Vitek's BBQ.

BBQ Brisket Bear Cups & Dr Pepper Floats

From Rusty and Lindy Parker
Baylor Superfans

In Waco, the most famous game-day meal is the Vitek's Gut Pak®. Winner of the Cooking Channel's 2013 Best College Eats bracket, Baylor fans pick up their styrofoam containers filled with smoked brisket, Fritos, cheese and all the fixins at Vitek's BBQ restaurant before boarding the shuttle to the game, or they grab theirs from the Gut Pak Shak food truck parked in the tailgating area of the stadium before each home game.

At our recent Tostitos Fiesta Bowl appearance in Arizona, Baylor fans were thrilled to see that the Gut Pak Shak had made the long drive from Waco to hand out free Gut Paks to traveling fans tailgating in the desert.

But when it's game day and we're away from Waco, with the Gut Pak Shak nowhere in sight, we do our best to create convenient tailgating Bear Cups inspired by our hometown favorite. These savory cheddar corn muffins topped with BBQ brisket and sauce provide a perfect treat as a sort of Waco, Texas, cupcake. And we always serve them with hometown Dr Pepper floats.

Sic 'em Bears!

INGREDIENTS:

BBQ Brisket Bear Cups:

1 package of Jiffy corn muffin mix

1 egg

1/3 cup milk

2 tablespoons melted butter

1 cup grated mild cheddar cheese

1 pound hand-chopped, fully-cooked, smoked and untrimmed brisket

1 jar of your favorite barbecue sauce

DIRECTIONS:

• Preheat oven to 400 degrees. Line a muffin pan with foil baking cups. In a mixing bowl, blend corn muffin mix, egg, milk, melted butter and cheddar cheese. Batter will be slightly lumpy. Spoon just 1 tablespoon of batter into each foil cup (cups will only be about 1/3 full). Bake 15 to 20 minutes, or until golden brown, and allow muffins to cool. Top each muffin with about 1 ounce of chopped brisket. Finally, drizzle about 1 teaspoon of your favorite barbecue on top of the muffins.

Dr Pepper Floats:

Created in Waco, Dr Pepper can be found at all Baylor events. And nearly every week during the semester, the Baylor community gathers for Dr Pepper floats. We like to bring this tradition to those hot Texas early season game days.

3 scoops vanilla ice cream (preferably Blue Bell Homemade Vanilla)

1 bottle of Dr Pepper

Optional toppings: whipped cream, green and gold sprinkles

Place 3 scoops of vanilla ice cream in a large cup. Slowly pour Dr Pepper over the ice cream. Top with whipped cream and sprinkles, if desired. Enjoy with a straw and spoon

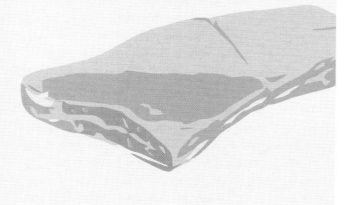

Fire & Ice Salsa

From Art and Jan Briles
Head coach at Baylor University

INGREDIENTS:

Dice into small pieces:

4 or 5 cups watermelon or ripe strawberries

1 bunch of green onions

1 small green bell pepper

1 jalapeno, corded and seeded

1/2 teaspoon garlic

Juice from 1 or 2 limes

DIRECTIONS:

• Combine all ingredients and then add the 4 or 5 cups of diced watermelon or fresh strawberries. Serve with tortilla chips.

Buffalo Chicken Wing Dip

From Art and Jan Briles
Head coach at Baylor University

INGREDIENTS:

3 pounds chicken tenderloins

2 8-ounce packages of Philadelphia Cream Cheese

1 16-ounce bottle ranch or blue cheese dressing

1 12-ounce bottle of Frank's Hot Sauce

2 pounds shredded cheddar cheese

DIRECTIONS:

• Boil chicken and shred into 9-inch by 13-inch pan. Spread softened cream cheese and dressing over chicken, and mix together. Pour hot sauce on top. Bake for 25 minutes at 350 degrees. Layer top with shredded cheese for last 5 minutes. Serve with tortilla chips.

years. I bring a smoker to the games and will go through about 36 racks of ribs, 36 pounds of beef tenderloin and 20 pounds of sausage each game. We serve several hundred people each game.

"The preparation begins the day prior when we season the meat and put it in the coolers. This takes about five hours. We also load the smoker with wood, knives and other things we will need while we are cooking and serving the next day. On game day we begin about six hours prior to game time by loading the smoker and beginning to smoke the meat. The ribs take around four hours to smoke and the beef about one hour. I like to serve the first round an hour and a half prior to game time. That is when most people begin to arrive. The smoking of the meat is staged so it will be ready to serve prior to the game, at half time and after the game.

"I only smoke the meat for the tailgate and am lucky enough to have teamed up several years ago with Brett Beene, who takes care of all of the beverages," continued Hobby. "You can't overestimate the importance of good beverages at a tailgate! I guess ribs would have to be my signature dish. I get the dry rub in bulk from a company in El Paso. The ribs are served from a cutting board and usually disappear as soon as they are sliced.

"Having a great tailgate is no different from hosting a great party. Have plenty to eat and drink in a place that is comfortable and enjoy the people you are with."

Have you ever seen a Bear who wasn't hungry? Nobody feeds more hungry Bears than Hobby Howell!

Cranberry Coffee Cake

From Grant Teaff, Executive Director of the American Football Coaches Association and former head coach at Baylor University; and his wife, Donell Teaff, former member of the Baylor University Board of Regents and "The First Lady of Football"

INGREDIENTS:

2 cups fresh cranberries

1/2 cups nuts, chopped

2 eggs

1 1/2 cups sugar

1 cup flour

3/4 cup butter, melted

DIRECTIONS:

• In an 8-inch by 8-inch dish, sprinkle in the cranberries, nuts and 1/2 cup of the sugar, and set aside. In a bowl, mix together the eggs, 1 cup of the sugar, the flour and the melted butter, and then pour this mixture over the ingredients in the dish. Bake 1 hour at 325 degrees. This is a great treat for fall football and the holidays, and you can even have it for breakfast! It's also very good when warmed up and topped with ice cream.

Dutch Babies

From Grant Teaff, Executive Director of the American Football Coaches Association and former head coach at Baylor University; and his wife, Donell Teaff, former member of the Baylor University Board of Regents and "The First Lady of Football"

This is perfect for breakfast or brunch when entertaining a large football crowd. It's fast, easy and yummy!

INGREDIENTS:

1/3 stick butter

1 cup milk

1 cup flour

Salt

3 eggs

Sour cream

Fresh strawberries or strawberry preserves

DIRECTIONS:

• Melt the butter in a 9-inch by 9-inch dish. In a blender, mix together the milk, flour, a pinch of salt and the eggs. Pour the blender ingredients over the butter and put the dish in the oven at 350 degrees for 15 to 20 minutes, or until brown. Serve immediately with sour cream and fresh strawberries, or strawberry preserves.

BOISE STATE
DUO TAKES IT SERIOUSLY

Every campus has its established tailgating personalities, the "cooking stars" you might say. But then there are the next generation of tailgaters like Micah Cranney and Darryn Corburn of Boise State. They are new at it, but their reputation is growing faster than a Broncos wide receiver.

"We are learning and we are enjoying ourselves as we go," says Micah. "Neither Darryn or I have any background in cooking for big groups, but we're having fun and learning a lot!"

After hearing Micah describe their cooker and grill, you may conclude that if they were to buy an airplane, it would likely be an Airbus A380.

"Our trailer-smoker was conceptualized by both Darryn and myself," says Micha. "Darryn researched it and designed it. We had a local trailer company fabricate the design. The smoker and grill box components were built by Meadow Creek of New Holland, Pennsylvania,

Micah Cranney and Darryn Corburn are prepared to tailgate.

shipped to Idaho and assembled. The smoker is a 250-gallon chamber, with three slide-out grill trays (we estimate that we could fit as many as 11 racks of pork ribs on each tray, allowing us to smoke as many as 33 racks of ribs at any one time). The grill box comes with a grill, flat top and has rotisserie capability. The trailer has two gas burners (if I remember correctly, 40,000 BTU each), a sink with three basins, and storage tanks for fresh water and for gray water. It is wired for audio, and includes additional lighting on the inside. The sides of the trailer have hydraulic lifts so that they open to become canopies. This is nice for the cookers as a protection from the sun (early season) and from rain. It also holds in heat a little bit in late season.

"Attached to the sides of the frame are trailer hitches (receivers)," he continued. "These hitches are used for bar stools that attach and add more seating. The back of the trailer has a firebox, connected to the smoker. It uses indirect heat to cook/smoke. Attached to the top of the firebox is a heating box. We often use that to slow cook beans, or as a warming chamber for leftovers. We use lump charcoal as our main cooking fuel, supplemented by smoking woods, which will vary between mesquite, hickory, cherry, apricot, peach and oak, depending on our particular tailgating food.

"Darryn arranged with the BAA (Bronco Athletic Association, which manages and sells tailgating spots for the university) for multiple spots for the trailer and for the truck required to pull it. For 2013, the BAA put our tailgating spots in the middle of the aisle, but close to the stadium. We burst at the seams on most days with the people we entertain. Boise State's tailgating scene is nascent when compared against most tailgating environments in the SEC, Big 12 or Big Ten, but while it is a small tailgating culture, it is vibrant and adds to the overall atmosphere at the stadium.

"Our trailer, to our surprise, has been quite a hit. We do grab a pretty large amount of attention, which neither of us anticipated. We easily spend as much time talking to strangers walking by as we do cooking or eating. We can't possibly share food with everyone who stops by, but we do share with some. We always cook for more guests than we are expecting, knowing that we'll have plenty of opportunities to serve others.

"Since Boise State has become a marketable brand, our football team gets a lot of television coverage. This is a blessing and a curse with tailgating. With television, the kickoff times are often at the mercy of the network. We may have a kickoff at noon local time, or at 8:30

p.m. The start time of the game has a huge impact on our menu. Because a lot of what we do will take six or more hours to cook, if we have an early kickoff, we may just serve hamburgers and brats, and probably chicken drumsticks, chicken thighs or 'chicken bombs' (which is a cream cheese-jalapeno pepper mix wrapped in chicken thighs, wrapped in bacon and smothered in barbecue sauce) prior to the game, and have ribs or brisket after the game. If the game is a late start, we'll get to the stadium early and start cooking at 9 a.m. for ribs and/or brisket, and then feed ourselves with hot dogs, snacks

Jalapeno Shrimp

From Bryan and Kes Harsin
Head coach at Boise State

INGREDIENTS:

1 pound shrimp

Skewers

1 package bacon

1 can jalapeno peppers

1 bottle of barbecue sauce

DIRECTIONS:

• Clean the shrimp. Cut bacon package in half. Cut up jalapenos. Take a piece of bacon, lay jalapeno down and put shrimp on top. Roll up tight and place evenly on skewers until filled up. Place on grill and cook until the bacon is done. Put on a plate next to the barbecue sauce for dipping. This is easy and very good! Go Broncos!

BOB BEHLER MAKES
THE CALL

Bob Behler, the Boise State play-by-play announcer, like the team, does a game-day walk through. But Bob does his walk through in the parking lot, surveying the tailgating scene.

"Boise State football," says Bob, "is big time. From the wins to the atmosphere. Most people recognize the blue field immediately and know that when they see it. It is a Boise State game they are watching. Bronco Stadium is great spot to watch a game. It seats around 35,000, and there isn't a bad seat in the house. The stadium is right on campus, set against the Boise River, overlooking downtown and the foothills.

"There is plenty of room for tailgating," he continued. "As the Broncos play-by-play announcer, I arrive at the game about five hours before kickoff, and many of the tailgaters are going strong by then. People have tents on grass areas on campus. Others do it by their cars in the parking lot. Some tailgaters have elaborate setups, while others might just have card table and chairs. But the best thing walking from my parking space in the Lincoln Garage across campus is the smell. The grills are going and you can smell and see the smoke wafting in the air.

"Unfortunately, I can't stop to sample the fare. I know if I did, I would never get to the booth on time. One of these days, I'd like my pregame assignment to do a report on the best food. It sure looks to me like there is a lot to choose from."

and hamburgers along the way, usually serving the majority of our guests a couple of hours before kickoff.

"Our tailgating started out relatively small, with our two families and two or three sets of good friends. By the end of the season, we were entertaining 50 to 70 invited guests at each home game. By the end of the season, we were also feeding the staff of the football team's equipment managers. These are typically students who are either volunteers or receive minimal stipends for their respective positions. They have to be fed and ready for their work assignments four hours before kickoff, so we have to go through two different shifts of food preparation for tailgating — one for the equipment managers and one for our guests. They enjoyed the food and we had a great time getting to know some of the guys. We normally feed 12 to 15 guys as part of the first shift. Some of the passersby we've met include players' families, photographers, reporters, media personalities and university administrators — and all have become new friends.

"As early as the spring game, we are collecting new recipes and practicing our regular menu items. Early on, we are thinking about our next tailgating season."

A BEAUTIFUL SCENE IN BOSTON

"**B**oston College, with its soaring stone towers, majestic collegiate Gothic architecture and pristine campus grounds, is nestled into a parcel of land that spans the city of Boston's western border and the picturesque Newton village known as Chestnut Hill," says Reid Oslin, who was associate athletics director for Sports Media Relations at Boston College from 1974 through 1997. Reid is the author of two books on the history of Boston College football — including the *Boston College Football Vault: The History of the Eagles.* He saw his first game at BC's Alumni Stadium in 1963 and hasn't missed one since. Nobody knows the Boston College scene better than Reid.

"On football game days," he explains, "every available inch of BC's lower campus — the area around Alumni Stadium that is located within Boston — is transformed into a tailgate heaven by Eagles' alumni and fans who travel by automobile, trolley, bus and foot to enjoy an afternoon or evening of picnicking and watching the region's top college football team.

"It is a choice and beautiful locale," Reid continued. "BC's Shea Field, for example, offers vistas of the campus towers to the west and the Boston skyline to the east. But since this area is within Boston's city limits, the city's licensing board regulates tailgating time limits. With a three-hour timeframe placed on pregame festivities, BC fans must do a little extra planning to fully enjoy the tailgating experience.

"No Eagle does a better job of this than Bob 'Pops' LeBlanc, who graduated from BC with a degree in chemistry in 1971 and has rarely missed a Boston College football game, home or away, since he was a student," says Reid. "LeBlanc now lives in North Carolina after retiring as a senior executive in the chemical and manufacturing industries, and he travels to Boston — or wherever his beloved Eagles may be kicking off — with his wife, Peggy, and longtime friends and fellow BC diehards Rick and Cilla Gagne of Beverly, Massachusetts.

THINGS TO SEE

When Doug Flutie threw his "Hail Mary" touchdown pass to lead Boston College to a 47-45 victory over Miami in the Orange Bowl in 1984 — one of the greatest plays in college football history — all of Boston celebrated. It was like the Red Sox winning the World Series, which they hadn't done lately in those days. Part of the fun of tailgating at Boston College is strolling over to the statue of Doug Flutie for a photo op.

Tony Williamson, Boston College class of '72, enjoys returning to campus for the tailgate scene when autumn peaks. "There is active tailgating around the stadium. Beans — what did you expect in Boston? — and lobster rolls are popular with BC tailgaters, but you can also find burgers and hot dogs."

An enterprising visitor with a historical bent can enjoy Boston on game day and catch the "T," Boston's rapid transit system out to the BC campus, which features Gothic buildings and the Golden BC Eagle, as Tony points out, "flying high in front of Gasson Hall."

Of course, you may want to head over to Comm Avenue and visually peruse the statue of Doug Flutie, who gave BC its "greatest moment to remember."

Depending on kickoff, you can visit the Union Oyster House for lunch or dinner. You get more than a filling and fulfilling meal at the Oyster House, where Daniel Webster ordered oysters on the half shell at the downstairs bar, and John F. Kennedy dined in his favorite booth on the second floor. In fact, you can call ahead and get a reservation for the Kennedy booth, if you are lucky. The Oyster House is where toothpicks were first used, and also where the first woman was employed as a waitress.

A Boston College football game and a glimpse of Boston's appealing history is a fine game-day opportunity. For BC fans, the memories of Doug Flutie's Heisman Trophy year in 1984 linger like the palatable aftertaste of an expertly cooked lobster at Ye Olde Union Oyster House.

Italian Meatballs

**From Gene and Anne DeFilippo
Former athletics director at
Boston College**

INGREDIENTS:

1 pound ground beef
1 egg
1/3 cup Italian-style bread crumbs
1/4 cup cold water
2 tablespoons chopped onion
1 teaspoon salt
1/4 teaspoon basil (optional)
Oil
Marinara sauce
Pasta or sandwich buns

DIRECTIONS:

• Combine all ingredients except oil and mix well. With well-oiled hands, shape into 1 1/2-inch balls. Place on foil-lined pan. Bake in preheated 375 degree oven for 12 to 15 minutes or until done as desired. When done, add to marinara sauce and serve with either pasta or as a meatball sandwich.

"Tailgating at BC is pretty much unlike tailgating at any other college I have ever been to,' says LeBlanc, whose Eagle Tailgater Team undoubtedly is the royalty of this culinary art form in Chestnut Hill. 'It has to be significantly more coordinated, and you have got to want to do it.'

"To 'do it,' Gagne has a fully outfitted maroon pickup truck pre-positioned at his home on Boston's North Shore for games at Alumni Stadium; LeBlanc keeps a similar pre-stocked vehicle in the Carolinas ready for ACC road contests. Each vehicle is carefully pre-packed with a specially made and logo-embroidered BC tent, poles with American and BC flags, a full array of cooking and barbecue gear, serving dishes, plates, utensils, Eagle Tailgater logo glasses, folding tables and chairs, ice storage and, of course, a well-stocked bar.

"When the tailgate area opens on game day, LeBlanc and his Tailgater Team unpack the truck and set up the pregame spread with military precision. 'Everybody has a specific assignment,' LeBlanc says. 'It's like an army in full operating mode in order to get the gear ready. I call it 'Operation Tailgate' when we are at the Heights.

"LeBlanc's tailgate menu for big games features a New England 'turf-and-surf' entrée, usually sautéed lobster tails and grilled filet tips. Otherwise, the food varies game by game but includes a specially chosen item in the general theme of the day's football opponent: freshly

Bob LeBlanc's Tailgater Team.

made crab cakes for games against Maryland and Navy; deep-fried turkey legs for Virginia Tech; Cuban sandwiches for Miami; or perhaps a delicious peach cobbler dessert when Georgia Tech comes to town. 'This is not a hamburger and hot dog tailgate,' LeBlanc insists. 'But we have a lot of fun.'

"Sometimes, such tailgate elegance has its pitfalls. 'Back in 2006, we were playing Clemson at Alumni Stadium and we said 'Let's cook live lobsters,' LeBlanc recalls. 'We had the pot with the BTU heater, the boiling water, the whole thing, and the lobsters were great. Then it was time to go into the game. We had to pour out the hot water and we accidentally dumped it on the new sod in front of Yawkey Center. It killed the grass in the whole area for the entire season,' he says with a laugh. 'It did recover, though.'

"LeBlanc and his friends have another special tradition prior to each game. About 30 minutes before kick-off, when the truck is repacked, the group doles out rations of 'maroon and gold' liquors — anything from cherry brandy to lemon cello to flavored vodka shots. 'Everybody collects together, we play the BC fight song, we take a picture of the group with our glasses held high, and we toast the BC team,' he says. 'We call it 'Eagle Up,' and we have done it all over the country. It's a tradition. It's what we do.'"

DAN
HENNING'S
BC FLASHBACK

Dan Henning, who was a respected head coach in the NFL with the Atlanta Falcons and San Diego Chargers, later became the head coach of the Boston College Eagles.

His athletic director suggested that Henning go meet all the department heads on campus and articulate the values and importance of football on campus. Henning did. When he met with the head of the English Department at BC, he got this assessment/question.

"Mr. Henning, I am head of this department, and I have been a tenured faculty member for over 20 years. This is your first year at Boston College, and you make more money than I do. Why is that?"

Without hesitating, Henning poignantly replied, "It's like this. When your students fail, you get rid of them. When mine fail, they get rid of me."

PAPPY WALDORF: A SON OF A BISHOP

Old-timers enjoyed Lynn Osbert "Pappy" Waldorf, who was a raconteur with a colorful vernacular that led to a speaking career after a College Football Hall of Fame coaching career in which he posted a record of 157-89-19. A native of Clifton Springs, New York, he played at Syracuse but was the head coach at Oklahoma A&M (now Oklahoma State), Kansas State, Northwestern and California. For years he was the winningest coach in Cal history until being passed by Jeff Tedford in 2010. Pappy's father was a bishop.

When Pappy worked in the personnel office for the NFL's San Francisco 49ers following his collegiate coaching career, he often made speeches as he traveled. One of his favorite stories had to do with making a speech with a retired football official in attendance. The old official, afflicted with hearing loss as he aged, leaned over to a guy beside him when Pappy was introduced and said, "Who's he?" The guy beside him said, "Pappy Waldorf. Football coach. Son of a bishop."

The old official responded, "That's certainly no surprise to me."

Cheesy Chicken Spaghetti

From Sonny and Kate Dykes
Head coach at Cal, former head coach at Louisiana Tech

INGREDIENTS:

1 chicken (cooked, deboned and shredded)

2 cups shredded cheese

4 sticks celery (leaves removed)

1 onion

Mushrooms (optional)

1 can diced pimentos

1 jar Cheese Whiz

1 can cream of mushroom soup (or cream of chicken)

1 can of milk (use the empty soup can and fill with milk)

Spaghetti noodles

DIRECTIONS:

• Bring a large pot of water to a boil on stove. Chop onion, celery and mushrooms finely and saute in a pan. Use any seasonings you prefer (I use season salt, garlic salt and pepper). Cook spaghetti noodles in boiling water. Drain noodles and place back in pot. Add soup, Cheese Whiz and milk to noodles, and stir until completely mixed. Add pimentos, sauteed onions, celery, mushrooms and chicken, and stir until thoroughly mixed. Place in a 9-inch by 13-inch casserole dish and sprinkle with 2 cups of shredded cheese. Bake at 350 degrees for 30 minutes. Serve with biscuits and green beans or a salad. Note: you can also use a rotisserie chicken instead of cooking chicken to make the recipe even easier!

IT'S A GERMAN HERITAGE THING

Tailgating at a Cincinnati Bearcat game might make you think you have happened upon a beer hall somewhere in Germany. Cincinnati's German heritage is such a part of the tradition of Bearcat game day.

"Tailgating at Cincinnati is very popular and enthusiastic," says J.C. Carletti, class of '81. "Cincinnati is steeped in German heritage, and on game day, there are copious amounts of beer and plenty of brats, but we are also fond of our metts (minced port meat with hot cheddar). It is an exciting atmosphere. Our stadium in and of itself is museum-ish, sitting cozily in the center of the campus. It is a unique sight. Night games are special."

Nippert Stadium, named for a great grandson of a co-founder of Proctor & Gamble, is nestled into the center of the campus. Tailgaters like Carletti find their way to the "Grid," which is near the stadium and where the "Cat-walk" takes place. The Cincinnati team walks though the Grid, evoking an emotional response from fans that have gathered to tailgate as many as five hours before kickoff.

"I do an Oktoberfest theme once a season," says Carletti. "It features brats and metts along with sauerkraut and potato pancakes."

Carletti is a creative tailgate host. He will have an Italian theme and a breakfast entrée for the early kickoff games. Other menu items include chicken and home-made pulled pork, and, of course, deep-fried hamburgers and meatball sliders. "These items," he says, "are simple to handle and people can eat as little or as much as they choose."

Lest we forget, an abundance of locally brewed beer. It is not only a German heritage thing, it's a Cincinnati Bearcat thing.

Buffalo Chicken Wing Dip

From Tommy & Suzanne Tuberville
Head coach at the University of Cincinnati, former head coach at Texas Tech, Auburn and Mississippi

INGREDIENTS:

2 bricks of cream cheese
1 small bottle of hot sauce
1 regular bottle of ranch salad dressing
1 stalk of celery, chopped finely (optional)
2 large cans of chicken breast
1 pack of shredded sharp cheddar cheese

DIRECTIONS:

• Put all ingredients in a skillet, excluding the bag of shredded cheese (we use an electric skillet). Stir continuously until all ingredients are melted and mixed together, and hot. Pour mixture in a 9-inch by 13-inch pan. Top with bag of sharp cheddar cheese. Bake at 350 degrees until cheese is melted. Serve with tortilla chips or Fritos Scoops.

AN ELEVATED PASSION AT CLEMSON

Passion for the home team is as elevated as the temperature when Clemson fans gather for anything Clemson in late summer — actually any time of the year — but with football being the centerpiece of the community with paws-painted-in-orange on every building, every street and every flag flying, it is hard to beat the love of alma mater by Tigers fans.

Some observers have long felt that Clemson wears underdog chip-on-the-shoulder emotions and feelings for the agricultural and engineering school, located hard by Lake Hartwell on the southwest side of diamond-shaped South Carolina.

A longtime military college, which admitted coeds in 1955, Clemson, through the years, didn't enjoy access to the best talent but always clawed, scratched and fought fiercely and Tiger-like in the image of its mascot.

When coeds were admitted, you immediately found becoming beauty with brains and charm. Like Sherry Thrift, Miss South Carolina 1985, and Nancy O'Dell, who won the same beauty title in 1987 and is now host for "Entertainment Tonight." You see Sherry Thrift Bradshaw at all Clemson home games carrying on a family tradition, which began when she was a kid growing up in Westminster, just 21 miles from the campus. And whenever she can come across the country to see her beloved alma mater in action, you see Nancy tailgating with family and friends about half a football field away from Memorial Stadium.

Nacho Casserole

From Sherry Thrift Bradshaw
Former CU cheerleader, Miss South
Carolina and first runner-up Miss America

INGREDIENTS:

1 10¾-ounce can cheddar cheese soup

1/2 cup low-fat (1 percent) milk

1 16-ounce jar mild or medium-hot salsa

1 7-ounce bag baked, unsalted tortilla chips

1 16-ounce can fat-free refried beans

2 jalapeno chiles, thinly sliced

1 cup shredded cheddar cheese

DIRECTIONS:

• Preheat oven to 400 degrees. In a 13-inch by 9-inch ceramic or glass baking dish, stir undiluted soup with milk; spread evenly. Top with half of salsa and half of chips. Carefully spread beans over chips. Top with remaining chips and salsa. Sprinkle with chiles and cheddar. Bake 20 minutes or until hot.

Nancy O'Dell and author Loran Smith get together before a Clemson game. Photo by Sherry Thrift Bradshaw.

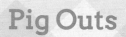

Pig Outs

From Dabo and Kathleen Swinney
Head coach at Clemson University

INGREDIENTS:

2 sleeves of Saltine crackers

2 sticks of butter

1 cup of light brown sugar

6 Hershey bars

Chopped pecans

DIRECTIONS:

• Preheat oven to 375. Line a jellyroll pan with aluminum foil. Spray foil with a nonstick cooking spray. Line crackers on pan. On the stovetop, melt the butter and then add the brown sugar. Bring to a medium boil for 4 minutes, stirring constantly. Pour hot mixture of crackers and spread until even. Then place pan in the oven for 7 minutes. Meanwhile, break Hershey bars into small pieces. After 7 minutes, remove pan from the oven and immediately drop chocolate pieces all over the hot crackers. Let stand for several minutes until chocolate melts and then spread the chocolate evenly. Add chopped pecans. Put pan in fridge for about 30 minutes or until the chocolate hardens. Then break into pieces and enjoy!

"Clemson is 'baptized' in tradition when it comes to tailgating," says Sherry, the former Tiger cheerleader who was first runner-up Miss America 1985. "On any given game day if you stroll by orange and purple tailgates, you will be offered anything from a fried apple pie with sweet iced tea and fried chicken to a hot Mexican dip with a cold beer and lime. If you are not a hostile visitor, you are able to wander around empty-handed and be welcomed at almost any 'Saturday spread' and experience true traditional Southern hospitality.

"Growing up just miles from the Clemson campus, I have found there are hundreds of Clemson fans who support the program and tailgate but who never actually attended Clemson, or any university for that matter, including my parents," Sherry continued. "The local citizens from neighboring communities participate with as

Barbecue Beef or Pork Roast

From Elizabeth Douglas
Secretary for coach Dabo Swinney

INGREDIENTS:

1 beef roast or pork roast

2 teaspoons black pepper

1 teaspoon granulated garlic

1/2 teaspoon celery salt

1/2 cup finely diced onions

1/4 cup finely diced celery

2 tablespoons molasses

1 small bottle Figaro liquid smoke

1 small bottle Worcestershire sauce

1 small bottle KC Masterpiece Barbecue Sauce

DIRECTIONS:

• Place roast in a shallow roasting pan. Rub with spices and sprinkle with onion and celery. Mix together molasses, liquid smoke and Worcestershire sauce, and pour evenly over roast. Cover tightly with foil and refrigerate overnight. Next morning, put roast (still covered) in 250-degree oven for 5 hours. Remove foil and coat with barbecue sauce. Cook for an additional hour at 300 degrees. Let stand about 20 minutes before slicing.

Easy Brisket

From Danny Ford
Former Clemson University head coach

INGREDIENTS:

1 large oven bag

1 large brisket

2 tablespoons all-purpose flour

1 cup water

2 packs Lipton Onion Soup Mix

DIRECTIONS:

• Trim fat off brisket. Rub brisket with favorite dry rub, but also add salt and pepper. Refrigerate for 1 hour or longer. Put brisket in oven bag, add flour, water and soup mix. Slit top of bag and bake at 500 degrees for 1 hour, and then 350 degrees for 3 hours. Optional: Add potatoes, carrots and onions on top of brisket

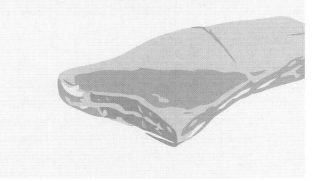

much enthusiasm as the alumni! Clemson is a school that has always embraced its alumni, students and the community and culture that surrounds it. Many have joked about the farmers and rednecks, and I am proud to say I am one of the alumni and a local. I wear the reputation proudly because of the down to earth and simple warm and loyal culture that surrounds the school.

"Tailgating is a social event in the fall for all Clemson fans. It is planned out, valued and, most of all, enjoyed by most who choose to participate. It has even been a place where people have met and fell in love, and where major business deals have been birthed. Tailgating at Clemson is best described as the 'epitome of Southern hospitality and home-cooked food.'"

Sherry has learned to control her emotions on some Saturday game days after marrying a former South Carolina player, Bill Bradshaw. Her two sons, Brewer and Thomas, played golf for Clemson, and her daughter, Collins, enrolled on golf scholarship at Georgia, which is only 80 miles away.

Another loyal Clemson graduate who loves to speak up for her alma mater, Nancy O'Dell, can often be found tailgating at Clemson home games, just a few first downs from Frank Howard Field.

"Tailgating at Clemson brings back so many fond memories from when I was a student there," says Nancy. "I remember being so excited about Saturday football games as my parents would come in for every game and

it was such a wonderful time to see them! Seems as if my whole family went to Clemson. My dad, my sister, my brother-in-law, my uncle, my cousins, my nephews are all Tigers! No question our family blood truly does runneth orange! So tailgating was actually a family reunion, of sorts, for me. And that is one reason my favorite tailgating recipe is one from my family — my mom's favorite homemade biscuits, called Betty's Biscuits after her, of course! And boy, they sure do go well with my other favorite tailgating food — southern fried chicken! I love getting back to Clemson from Los Angeles as often as I can, not only because of my extreme love of the university, but it also gives me an excuse to eat all these 'guilty-pleasure' foods!"

Danny Ford, who coached Clemson to a national championship in 1981 and is a cattle farmer in nearby Central, shows up to tailgate with his friends and countless other luminaries like Lucas Glover, who won the 2009 U.S. Open. "Clemson fans love football, they love Clemson and they love each other," says Ford. "You see great spirit at other schools, but I don't think anybody has more passion for their school than Clemson fans."

Clemson fans take their tailgating seriously. Photos courtesy of Sherry Bradshaw.

Betty's Biscuits

From Nancy O'Dell
Clemson alum,
"Entertainment Tonight" anchor

Note from Nancy: "Betty's Biscuits is my mom's recipe, my favorite holiday recipe and my favorite tailgating recipe. The biscuits go great with southern fried chicken, my other fave tailgating food. Betty's Biscuits are delicious."

INGREDIENTS:

2 cups self-rising flour

2 teaspoons baking powder

2 tablespoons confectioner's sugar (10x)
   or granulated sugar

1/3 to 1/2 cup solid Crisco

1 cup buttermilk

DIRECTIONS:

• Mix flour, sugar, baking powder and Crisco (crunch it up with your hands). Add buttermilk and stir. Roll out on wax paper with a rolling pin. Cut with cutter. Bake on greased sheet in preheated oven at 400 to 425 degrees until brown.

HOWARD WAS A COLORFUL GUY

There was a time when you didn't think of Clemson without recalling the Tigers' colorful former coach, Frank Howard. Perhaps you know about Howard's Rock, which the players rub for good luck before each game.

A friend of Howard's brought the rock from Death Valley, California, as a gift. Howard used the 2½-pound rock as a doorstop for years but stumbled over it one day while cleaning out his office and demanded to friend and booster Gene Willimon to "get rid of it."

Willimon did "get rid of it" but his disposal was not what the coach expected. Willimon put it on a pedestal that the players would pass by on the way into the stadium. They would rub the rock for good luck. In a game against Virginia when the Tigers were behind by 18 points, a stunning rally ensued, and Clemson won the game 40-35. Howard told his team afterward, "Give me 115 percent, or keep your filthy hands off my rock."

Coach Howard was a colorful character whose girth was expansive. He was balding and always had a plug of tobacco in his cheek. However, it was his colorful, homespun vernacular that everybody remembered him for. Following Jess Neely's decision to leave Clemson as head coach to take over the same position at Rice, the Clemson athletic council met in an open session. When a member of the council, Sam Rhodes, nominated Howard to replace Neely, a booming voice in the back of the room shouted, "I second the motion." That booming voice belonged to Howard.

There are countless colorful stories about Howard, who always enjoyed a good joke, even if it was on him. He took special delight in poking fun at the coach of the rival South Carolina Gamecocks. When Jimmy Carlen became the South Carolina coach, he was given the rights to his TV show, which was novel for the times. Howard would say on the banquet circuit that this favorable TV arrangement could make Carlen a lot of money. "He already has two really big sponsors signed up — Kentucky Fried Chicken and Schick Razors," Howard would grin and then add, "They're gonna call his show the 'Chicken Schick Show.'"

BOB CASCIOLA ON THE EAST

Bob Casciola, longtime executive director of the National Football Foundation and College Football Hall of Fame, played football at Princeton and has experienced the colorful atmosphere of Ivy League and Eastern football for years.

The following from Bob reminds us that with the passing of time, a lot of things change with respect to the college football scene, but the game itself and the alumni spirit will forever remain a staple of campus Saturdays.

"My experiences were at two Ivy League schools (Princeton and Dartmouth, 15 Years) and four years at the University of Connecticut," says Bob. "Tailgating in the 1950s and '60s in the Ivy League was a 'big' thing. Returning alumni and friends usually gathered in assigned parking areas, many times with classmates or fellow teammates.

"They used the trunks of their cars (no SUVs in those days) to carry the food, spirits and beverages. Many had cooking (ensembles) stores. Others would have prepared catered dishes — from hors d'oeuvres to the main course. The spread was very elaborate and well presented.

"This all started at least 2 to 2 1/2 hours prior to kickoff, usually 1 p.m. or 1:30. Most provided seating (folding chairs). The drinks included everything, including

Hall of Fame Burgers

From John and Megan Stephenson
CEO of the College Football
Hall of Fame in Atlanta

INGREDIENTS:

1 pound ground beef

1 cup shredded cheddar cheese

1 package Lipton onion soup mix

2 to 3 packages low-fat crescent rolls (Pillsbury tubes)

Sandwich slicers and dill pickles (optional)

DIRECTIONS:

• Brown ground beef and drain. Over low heat, add onion soup mix and a teaspoon of water, mix until well combined. Still over low heat, add cheese and stir until melted. Remove meat from heat. Unroll crescent rolls and smooth over the perforations to make a solid sheet of dough. Cut dough into rectangles and add 1 large spoonful of meat on one half of the dough rectangle. You can also add a dill pickle slice if you desire. Fold the other half of the dough rectangle over the top of the meat, making a mini-sandwich. Repeat until meat is all used up. Place sandwiches on a cookie sheet and cook according to directions on the crescent roll package or until bread is golden brown.

THE NEW COLLEGE FOOTBALL HALL OF FAME

The College Football Hall of Fame is now located where many more fans will have an easier time getting to the shrine.

In the fall of 2014, a 94,000-square-foot, state-of-the-art attraction opened its doors in downtown Atlanta. With the College Football Hall of Fame as its anchor exhibit, the Hall attraction is an immersive and entertaining experience for fans of all ages and levels of fandom, as well as unique meeting and event space.

Just steps away from Centennial Olympic Park, the Georgia Aquarium, the Georgia World Congress Center, the Georgia Dome, the World of Coca-Cola, the National Center for Civil and Human Rights, CNN Center and numerous other attractions, the Hall's new home presents the ideal location for a college football-themed "museum." This experience will redefine how people think of halls of fame, and will provide a "home away from home" for college football fans from across the country.

Previously, the College Football Hall of Fame had been located in South Bend, Indiana.

rye, bourbon and scotch, with the ability to make mixed drinks if requested. Beer, although available, was not as prominent except among perhaps the younger members and students.

"Remember, too, that through the '60s, most male fans came dressed in jackets and ties, with the women wearing dresses. Fashion was an important part of the whole scene. As time progressed, tailgating is still a part of the Ivy League scene, but it is far less formal. Today, clothes are very casual — jeans, shorts — a much more everyday look!

"In addition, more people use fashionable grills — and much simpler preparation. The hot dogs, hamburgers and hors d'oeuvres of yesteryear have been replaced by deli-bought chips and dips. Beer has become the popular beverage, plus diet sodas.

"At the University of Connecticut, they tailgate in the normal parking lots set aside for all attendees. Although it is very basic, it is a definite part of football weekend, and fans gather at every home game in the same location — sharing time with friends and teammates.

"I would say that 'tailgating' in the East is still a colorful part of the football weekend, but it is not necessarily as elaborate as in the past."

Rice University Sugar Cookies

From Matthew Sign, National Football Foundation and Rice University

INGREDIENTS:

1 1/2 cups powdered sugar
1 cup margarine (softened)
1 teaspoon vanilla
1 egg
2 1/2 cups flour
1 teaspoon baking soda
1 teaspoon cream of tartar

DIRECTIONS:

• Cream sugar and margarine together. Add vanilla and egg to mixture. Sift together flour, baking soda and cream of tartar, and then add to the cream mixture. Refrigerate 3 to 4 hours. Roll out dough and cut to desired shapes. Spray cookie sheets or cover with parchment paper. Bake at 350 degrees for 8 to 10 minutes.

Blow Your Mind Baked Chicken Wings

From Steve Hatchell President of the National Football Foundation and the College Football Hall of Fame

INGREDIENTS:

2 teaspoons cornstarch
3 tablespoons coconut oil
3 cloves garlic, minced
1 tablespoon fresh ginger, grated
3 scallions, sliced, with whites and greens separated
1/4 cup low-sodium soy sauce
1/2 cup honey
2 limes, juiced
2 tablespoons chili flakes
2 pounds chicken wings, separated and tips removed
Salt
Pepper

DIRECTIONS:

• Preheat oven to 350 degrees. In a small bowl, make a slurry of the cornstarch and a tablespoon of cold water, and set aside.

• Heat the coconut oil in a wok or saucepan. Toss in the garlic, ginger and scallion whites. Cook for 30 seconds until fragrant. Stir in the soy sauce, honey, lime juice and chili flakes. Add in the cornstarch slurry and bring to a boil. Reduce to a simmer and cook 3 to 4 minutes until the sauce slightly thickens. Remove from heat and allow to cool to room temperature. The sauce can be made in advance and stored in a refrigerator or cooler.

• Season the chicken wings with salt and pepper, place in a rimmed baking pan and bake for 20 minutes. Pour the sauce over the wings and return to the oven for 20 minutes or until the wings are cooked through and the sauce is sticky. Remove from oven and allow to cool slightly before serving. Garnish with reserved scallion greens.

RAM-TOUGH TAILGATING

"Colorado State," says Tiffany Wuthrich, "has an interesting history, dating back to the time when we were known as Colorado Agricultural College (1870) and Colorado A&M (1935).

"The Aggie 'A' is painted on the hill behind the stadium, creating a lot of interest," she continued. "Greek pledges are required to paint the rocks on the hill. It always stimulates great pride when you attend Hughes Stadium, which is nestled into the foothills of the Rocky Mountains.

"Due the unique location against the foothills, on colder game days, a strange phenomenon happens where the hot air from inside the stadium rises and meets the cold air coming over the foothills and causes a cloud to form over the stadium.

"We also seem to get a lot of attention because we tailgate in snow! Most of football season in Colorado is cold. We wear sweatshirts, jackets and even sometimes stand in sleeping bags to cheer on the Rams in a blizzard. Cooking brats and burgers in the snow is a lot of fun. Nothing keeps us from enjoying our tailgates at CSU.

"Our campus is in one of the most beautiful settings you could ever find. And The Oval is the prettiest place on campus. The Oval drive is lined with elms that are more than a century old. It is home to the oldest buildings on campus. If you visit our campus, you can enjoy a beautiful setting and you can enjoy cooking out in a snowfall. Nothing like it, and there is nothing better."

Roasted Salmon & Red Cabbage With New Potatoes

From Tyler and Katherine Schermerhorn
Former letterman at Colorado State

INGREDIENTS:

4 cups shredded red cabbage (half a small head)

10 new potatoes, cut in half

Olive oil

Salt

Fresh ground pepper

1 pound skinless salmon filet

2 tablespoons grainy mustard

2 tablespoons horseradish

1 lemon

DIRECTIONS:

• Preheat over to 400 degrees. Toss shredded red cabbage and 10 halved new potatoes with olive oil. Season with coarse salt and fresh ground pepper. Roast for 25 minutes. Smear skinless salmon filet with a mixture of grainy mustard, horseradish and the zest of 1 lemon. Nestle in a pan and roast 15 minutes

THE RIVALRY WITH COLORADO

Katie Schermerhorn is a graduate of Colorado, and is married to a Colorado State football letterman, Tyler Schermerhorn. They have enjoyed the Rocky Mountain Showdown for several years, although they don't always have the same rooting interest.

The game takes place at Authority Field at Mile High Stadium where the Denver Broncos play.

Buffalo Chili

From Tyler and Katherine Schermerhorn
Former letterman at Colorado State

INGREDIENTS:

2 tablespoons vegetable oil

4 pounds ground buffalo

4 cups yellow onions, chopped

3 tablespoons chili powder

1 tablespoon ground cumin

2 teaspoons cayenne pepper

1 teaspoon ground cinnamon

1/4 teaspoon crushed red pepper

1 bay leaf

2 tablespoons minced garlic

4 12-ounce bottles dark beer

2 28-ounce cans whole tomatoes, crushed

2 tablespoons tomato paste

1 tablesoon salt

1 tablespoon plus 1 teaspoon dark brown sugar

1 ounce (1 square) unsweetened chocolate

6 cups cooked red kidney beans (or four 15-ounce cans, drained and rinsed)

1 cup grated cheddar cheese, for garnish

1 cup finely chopped green onions, for garnish

1/2 cup chopped fresh cilantro, for garnish

DIRECTIONS:

• Heat oil in large heavy pot over high heat. Add the buffalo and brown well, or about 10 minutes. Add the onions, chili powder, cumin, cayenne, cinnamon, crushed red pepper and bay leaf, and cook, stirring often, until the onions soften, or about 8 minutes. Add the garlic and cook until fragrant, or about 30 seconds. Add the beer and cook until the foam subsides, or about 1 minute. Add the tomatoes, tomato paste, salt, brown sugar and chocolate to the pot. Stir well and bring to a boil. Reduce to a simmer and cook until slightly thickened, or about 1 hour, while stirring occasionally to prevent the chili from sticking to the bottom of the pot. Skim off as much fat as possible. Add the beans, return to a simmer, cover and cook until thickened, or about 1 1/2 hours longer. Serve with the cheese, green onions and cilantro as garnish.

"The students are bused down from each school, and everyone tailgates in the parking lots around the stadium," says Katie. "CSU and CU have become bitter in-state rivals within the last 15 years. CSU has upset CU several times during this period, but prior to that, CU always dominated. The tailgating feels intense because the fan bases for both teams are present and tailgating amongst each other. There is lots of taunting and trash talking during the tailgates."

The Rocky Mountain Showdown is unique in that this game has traditionally become the seasonal kick-off for each team, while most rivalry games take place at the end of the season. But it is no less intense.

Shutterstock

CUMBERLAND'S INTERESTING HISTORY

Cumberland, which lost to John Heisman's Georgia Tech team 222-0 in 1916, still plays football in Lebanon, Tennessee. Today, the Bulldogs are better known for their baseball success under Woody Hunt — who has won two NAIA national championships — than their football, which is played on a nearby high school field. Therein is an interesting story.

Believe it or not, during Heisman's time on the Tech campus, baseball was the bigger sport. Cumberland had defeated the Golden Tornado, which is what Tech was called before being named the Yellow Jackets, in a spring baseball game but Tech claimed Cumberland used "ringers" — several professional players — to embarrass them 22-0. Heisman, by the way, was also Tech's baseball coach. Tech (mainly Heisman) wanted revenge and would not let Cumberland, which had a two-year contract to play Tech, out of the game.

"The story goes," says coach Hunt, who is very familiar with the details, "that Cumberland had to coax players on the way down to Atlanta to get enough players to field a team. If you know the details, you can easily understand what a mismatch it was."

Heisman, leading 126-0 at the half, is supposed to have said, as he made plans to pour it on, "We're ahead, but you just can't tell what those Cumberland players have up their sleeves. They may spring a surprise. Be alert, men."

Ham & Swiss Delight

From Woody and Irma Hunt
Cumberland University

INGREDIENTS:

2 packages of Hawaiian King Rolls
1 8-ounce package Swiss cheese
1/2 pound deli baked ham
Sauce:
1 stick margarine
2 tablespoons Worcestershire sauce
2 tablespoons minced onion
2 tablespoons prepared mustard
1 1/2 tablespoons poppy seeds

DIRECTIONS:

• Slice rolls in half, and place bottom half in a large glass baking dish. Put the ham and cheese on top of bottom piece of the roll. Place top half of roll on the top. Prepare sauce in pan and heat until margarine melts. Pour sauce over rolls and bake at 350 degrees for 10 minutes.

In addition to having lost a football game by the largest score in college history, Cumberland's once highly regarded law school was sold to Samford University in Birmingham.

Matriculates and school officials have ambiguous reactions about the 222-0 point loss to Georgia Tech. "Well," says Jo Jo Freeman, Cumberland's sports information director, "people still remember us."

On football game day when fall colors are resplendent in Lebanon, Cumberland's tailgating scene is no different from those of Alabama, Ohio State or Texas. Those serious about tailgating arrive early with their smokers and set up for the day. "Just like any other school, except on a smaller scale," says Freeman, a graduate of Mississippi State.

Coach Hunt summarizes the ignominy of the record 222-0 loss to Tech this way: "It is embarrassing to a lot of people, but it is part of our history, and I don't really get mad about it. I think what upsets most of our alumni and friends is that we sold our law school, which had an outstanding reputation."

DUKE FOOTBALL GOES BIG-TIME

Even a serious Blue Devil fan might have to enjoy a drink with a seasoned Duke historian to become familiar with the days in Durham when Wallace Wade fielded powerhouse teams and played in the Rose Bowl. Then there was a consistency of split-T success under coach Bill Murray in the 1950s and '60s — six ACC titles, 93 victories — and a brief spell when Steve Spurrier won 20 games in three years along with one ACC Championship. There has been a latent comeback under head coach David Cutcliffe, and nobody appreciates that more than Dave Miller, class of '77.

Most people know about Duke's prolific basketball program, but with Duke's football program on the upswing, tailgating should continue to grow. In 2012, Duke played in a bowl game for the first time in 18 years. The year 2013 had Duke playing in the ACC Championship Game and an exciting bowl game against Texas A&M and Johnny Manziel in the Chick-fil-A Bowl.

Dave Miller is one proud alumnus, as is his friend, Bill Miller, who is a past president of the Duke Alumni Association. Here is Bill's alumnus-tailgating-speak with an undercurrent of enthusiasm that would make the taciturn William D. Murray smile:

"The Gothic architecture featured on the Duke main campus makes for a beautiful tailgating backdrop. Tents and tailgaters line up on grass-covered fields and parking lots. Fans gather along Blue Devil Alley, between Cameron Indoor Stadium and Wallace Wade Stadium, awaiting the band, mascot and team. Duke tailgaters celebrate a new football excitement.

"Duke allows ticket holders to leave and re-enter WW (Wallace Wade Stadium) by getting your hand stamped and showing your stub, so tailgating continues at halftime and beverages can be refreshed, as most Iron Duke lots are adjacent to the stadium. The president's house (Hart House) is next to the stadium and the visitor's

Duke fans tailgate prior to the 2013 ACC Championship Game in Charlotte. Photo courtesy of KathyMillerTime.com.

Pineapple Cream Cheese Ball

**From David and Karen Cutcliffe
Head coach at Duke University**

INGREDIENTS:

2 8-ounce packages of cream cheese, softened

2 teaspoons finely chopped onion

1 teaspoon seasoning salt

2 cups chopped pecans

1/4 cup chopped green pepper

1 small can crushed pineapple, drained

DIRECTIONS:

• Combine cream cheese, onion, salt, green pepper and pineapple with 1 cup of nuts. Chill and then roll into a ball. Roll the ball in remaining nuts. Serve with crackers.

locker room. President Richard Brodhead and wife Cindy host wonderful pregame events with a constantly changing tailgate menu.

"Wallace Wade Stadium was the first facility constructed on Duke's West Campus and opened in 1929 when Duke hosted Pitt. Notably, it was the site of the 1942 Rose Bowl game between Oregon State and Duke after all large public gatherings were banned on the West Coast in the aftermath of the Pearl Harbor attack. Multiple-year renovations have been announced, which will remove the track, lower the field, and add a new press box, club seating and luxury boxes, along with new amenities and restrooms, and increased seating capacity.

"To confirm the re-emergence of Duke's football program, ESPN scheduled a game between Duke and archrival North Carolina in 2014. That was a big deal in Durham.

"While there is not tailgating in the quads other than living groups grilling out, many parking lots adjacent to the dorms, Cameron Indoor Stadium and other Gothic architecture does create a true campus feel. The barbecue is all pork. A big debate begins with, 'Which is better: western (Lexington, North Carolina) or eastern (Wilson, North Carolina) style?' This BBQ rivalry is almost as big emotionally as Duke-Carolina."

THERE'S NOTHING LIKE FALL SATURDAYS IN GAINESVILLE

By Therese Lau, Serious Gator Fan

A fall Saturday in Gainesville, Florida, completely revolves around Gator football.

Every Gator fan knows tailgating starts at 7:30 a.m. You can hear the UF fight song playing from every car. It's important to claim your tailgating spot early, because once your spot is claimed, it is yours for the whole day.

Then the smell of the grills cooking hot dogs and hamburgers starts to fill the air along with the cheers of "Go Gators." As the bell chimes from Century Tower, fans know it's time to hit Stadium Road to cheer on the football team as it enters "The Swamp."

After another round of hot dogs everyone heads over to Emerson Hall, which is home to the Alumni Association. While there, fans are greeted by mascots Albert and Alberta, and the Gator cheerleaders, as they help get the Gator Nation pumped up for the game. Waves of fans then head over to the stadium where they take pictures in front of statues of UF's three Heisman Trophy winners: Tim Tebow, Steve Spurrier and Danny Wuerffel.

After the game – win or lose – the party doesn't stop. Everyone heads back to their spot to have a postgame tailgate and talk about the game, and start making plans for the next tailgate!

Sisters Wendy Donato, Therese Lau and Amy Czerniewski enjoy a pregame get together in Gainesville.

A SOUTHERN TAILGATING PERSPECTIVE

Kathy Miller is what college football and its attendant traditions — from school spirit to affection for alma mater to appreciation for tailgating traditions of other campuses — should be. Root, root for the home team, but be civil to the visiting team and its fans. Kathy has an interesting "Tailgating Through The South" football blog at KathyMillerTime.com, which includes her paintings of the campuses she has visited over the years.

Enjoy this narrative about her from her website, and see how geography can also affect where one chooses to enroll:

"Kathy Lovett Miller — born and raised in Knoxville, Tennessee. Growing up in Knoxville was like growing up in a world where the color wheel only had two colors: orange and white. Although my father graduated from the University of South Carolina, there was no chance of me becoming a Gamecock fan. I was destined to become a Tennessee Volunteer. My two sisters and I spent our childhood listening to radio sportscaster John Ward's play-by-play calling of the Tennessee games. John would say, 'It's football time in Tennessee,' and everything else stopped. I felt cold chills from head to toe when John exclaimed, 'Give him 6! Touchdown Tennessee!'

"Driving across the Henley Street Bridge on crisp, fall Saturdays, looking at Neyland Stadium, hearing the roars and cheers echoing from the sold-out crowds, I couldn't

---

7 Layer Tailgate Dip

From Therese Lau and sisters Wendy Donato and Amy Czerniewski, Gator Superfans

INGREDIENTS:

1 can refried beans
1 cup sour cream
1 cup guacamole
1 cup salsa
1 can olives, sliced
1 cup lettuce, shredded
1 cup cheese, shredded
Tortilla chips (for dipping)

DIRECTIONS:

• In a glass bowl, layer in each ingredient in the following order: refried beans, sour cream, guacamole, salsa, olives, lettuce, cheese. Serve with tortilla chips. Go Gators!

Kathy Miller, right, gets interviewed by niece Kelly Hawkins for The Tailgate Tour. Photo courtesy of KathyMillerTime.com.

Carla's Gator Eggs

From Carla Spalding, Gator fan

INGREDIENTS:

1 dozen hardboiled eggs, peeled

3 tablespoons Duke's mayonnaise

1 1/2 teaspoons prepared mustard

7 shakes of Crystal Hot Sauce

4 teaspoons Wickles Relish

1/4 teaspoon Tony Chachere's Creole Seasoning

Olives, cut in half for topping

Small sprigs of fresh dill

DIRECTIONS:

• Cool eggs completely and peel, then cut carefully in half. Scoop yolks onto plate or low-edged bowl, mash until fine. Set whites aside. Add each of next five ingredients one at a time, mixing thoroughly with egg yolks. Generously fill white halves with yolk mixture. Add olive half to top of each egg. Finish with dill sprigs. Makes 24.

help but think, 'I can't wait to go to school at Tennessee.' And go I did. All of my UT experiences were memorable, but ranking at the top was a Saturday football game with 100,000-plus fans wearing orange and white, singing Rocky Top. I graduated from UT with a B.S. in Textiles and Clothing/Fashion, Merchandising. After working with Proffitt's Department Store as a buyer, I became a women's divisional merchandise manager. After nearly 10 years, I resigned and began my second career raising our two children.

"Our family, as it turns out, became a Tennessee/Florida family. We moved from Knoxville to Jacksonville, Florida, when our children were very young. Even living in Florida, they remained avid UT fans — at least until they reached college choosing time and they decided, 'We want to be Florida Gators!'

"After years of following and rooting for my favorite team, the Tennessee Volunteers, attending Florida football games as a Gator Mom, and traveling around the SEC going to away games, I began painting each school's unique tailgating experience. The paintings celebrate special traditions, landmark buildings and intense rivalries.

"Kathy Miller Time's 'Tailgating Through The South' has been a most exciting project. I have had the time of my life traveling to SEC tailgates with family and friends, talking with hundreds of fans, gathering recipes, exploring the best tailgating spots on each campus, and composing paintings depicting these moments."

Living in Jacksonville would figure in the decision making of her children when it came to enrolling in college, so Kathy enjoys multiple loyalties. Her husband, Dave, is a Duke man, which enabled Kathy's college football exposure to expand into the Atlantic Coast Conference.

She continues to return to Knoxville, but most often can be found on game day at "The Swamp" in Gainesville. There's nobody better with her Southern taste, good sense and good manners with a deep and abiding love of college football to tell you about tailgating at the University of Florida.

"Tailgating Florida Gator-style is similar to tailgating at many other campuses," she says. "Tailgaters stake out their locations and arrive early on game days to claim these coveted spots. In Gainesville, many fall days are still hot and humid. The Florida campus uniquely has many stately oak trees throughout. These provide welcome shade for fall football tailgaters.

"A popular tailgating spot is along the Plaza of the Americas," she continued. "Because the campus is so large and the weather so hot, tailgaters will set up anywhere they find shade. Many fans like to tailgate beside Lake Alice. Florida's signature building, Century Tower, watches over many tailgaters.

"My 'Tailgating In The Swamp' painting gets its inspiration from the stately oaks and palm trees around Lake Alice, along with oranges as the state fruit. Look closely. Is that Mr. Two Bits under one of the tents? Mr. Two Bits is a special tradition at Florida. He is George Edmondson

A&E Grill

Chan Gailey, the former Florida quarterback and former head coach at Georgia Tech and the NFL, retired to his grandparents' home in Clarkesville, Georgia, where he frequents the nearby A&E Grill — a hamburger emporium that serves the best hamburger in North Georgia. Allen and Ellen Browning not only cook the best burger for Chan, they also accommodate Chan's sweet tooth, and his desire for pepper hash. Ellen's cakes are as big of a hit as her hamburgers to Chan and the A&E customers.

Pepper Hash

INGREDIENTS:

12 large green sweet peppers
12 large red sweet peppers
2 small jalapeno peppers
5 small onions
1 pint boiling water
1/2 cup vinegar
2 cups sugar
3 tablespoons salt

DIRECTIONS:

• Remove the seeds from the peppers, rinse and finely chop. Pour boiling water over them and let set 10 minutes. Drain and add finely chopped onions, vinegar, sugar and salt. Cook for 30 minutes and then seal in sterilized jars.

Black Walnut Cake

INGREDIENTS:

2 sticks butter
1 stick margarine
1 box light brown sugar
1 cup sugar
5 eggs
1/2 teaspoon baking powder
1/2 teaspoon salt
3 1/4 cups plain flour
1 cup milk
1 cup black walnuts

DIRECTIONS:

• Cream butter, margarine and sugars, and add eggs. Sift flour, salt and baking powder together, and add to mixture. Add milk and black walnuts. Bake for 1 1/2 hours in tube pan, starting with a cold oven.

Jr., and he led the Two Bit Cheer during the 'Florida Pre-game Show' for 59 years. He always wore a yellow shirt with orange and blue striped tie, blue and white seersucker slacks, and usually with saddle oxfords.

"He has retired and is dearly missed. In 2013 a new tradition was born. Celebrity Gators, such as Heisman Trophy winner Danny Wuerffel, now lead the Two Bit Cheer dressed the same as George Edmondson.

"Many tailgaters set up on the campus side of University Avenue. Tailgating tents line the street from the east corner of campus to the stadium. The opposite side of University Avenue houses lots of bars, restaurants and shops. Many fans decide to tailgate at The Swamp Restaurant. The Swamp is the happening place on University, and visiting fans join Gator fans to grab a bite, some liquid refreshment and some friendly banter.

"The time of the game also determines where people tailgate. They may hit The Swamp first and then later join their tailgates. Many times we tailgate at my father-in-law's house. 'Pops' bought a house on University a couple of blocks from the stadium to have a place to stay on game weekends. With a large deck and music from parties next door, we manage to set up a fun tailgate. The nice part is not having to worry about bathrooms!

"One of the most endearing traditions at Florida is the singing of 'We Are The Boys of Old Florida' between the third and fourth quarters. The entire stadium stands, wraps their arms around their neighbors and sways, singing the song with 'Hey!' and 'Go Gators!' yells at the appropriate moments. It is a special feeling watching 88,000-plus people swaying and singing together.

"Probably the most famous tradition (and the most annoying for visiting fans) is the Gator Chomp. Florida children learn early on how to place their hands just so and CHOMP. The marching band plays a two-note music sequence from 'Jaws' and everyone chomps. The Chomp is a syncopation thing, and the fans do it very well. And they do this all game long."

FSU FANS GET ROLLING ON FRIDAY

I n Tallahassee, tailgating is highlighted, as one Florida State fan says, by cold beverages. But after head coach Jimbo Fisher, in 2013, took FSU to its first national championship since the days of Bobby Bowden, tailgating — like the Seminole offense — has left FSU fans calling for more roasting of opponents on the field.

"Sometimes food can be as basic as football fundamentals like blocking and tackling," as publisher Carrol Dadisman points out. "My successor as publisher of the *Tallahassee Democrat*, FSU grad and huge fan Mike Pate, said only that he would describe FSU tailgating as typical of other regional schools — with barbecue, burgers and beer being favorites, so non-stop eating and drinking.

"FSU fans get a head start on tailgating with a Downtown Getdown in Tallahassee on the eve of all home games," Carrol continued. "From 6 p.m. Friday until late in the evening, two major downtown streets are blocked and turned into a kind of carnival filled with restaurant tents offering favorite foods, other tents offering peanuts, popcorn and cotton candy, merchants selling FSU memorabilia and other souvenirs — accompanied by a large bandstand and sound equipment for music and street dancing. It's a 'happening' all built around a run-up to FSU's game the following afternoon or night.

"I've been to Friday night pregame parties in private homes and elsewhere that featured such regional specialties as Apalachicola Bay oysters — raw or fried, or both — and sausage from an iconic area store and food producer, Bradley's Country Store," says Carrol.

Ruth Peterkin/Shutterstock

Chocolate Chip Pie

From Bobby and Ann Bowden
Former coach at Florida State University

INGREDIENTS:

1/4 cup margarine/butter

1 cup sugar

2 cups chocolate chips

3 eggs

3/4 cup white corn syrup

1/4 teaspoon salt

1 teaspoon vanilla

1/2 cup chopped pecans

9-inch unbaked piecrust

DIRECTIONS:

• Cream margarine; add sugar gradually. Add beaten eggs, syrup, salt and vanilla. Add chocolate chips and nuts; stir well. Pour into crust and bake at 375 degrees for 40 to 50 minutes.

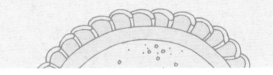

Macaroni & Cheese

From Charlie Ward
Former FSU quarterback and
1993 Heisman Trophy winner

INGREDIENTS:

2 cups macaroni

1 stick butter or margarine

3 cups of cheese (sharp, cheddar, gouda or cream, depending on your taste)

2 eggs

2 cups of milk

1 teaspoon salt

1 teaspoon pepper

Dash of hot sauce (optional)

DIRECTIONS:

• Preheat oven to 350 degrees. Boil water for macaroni and cook until tender. Drain and pour into mixing bowl. Add butter, milk, eggs and 2 cups of cheese, and then add salt, pepper and hot sauce to taste (optional). After mixing, pour 1/2 macaroni mixture into lightly sprayed casserole dish and then sprinkle with 1/2 cup of cheese; pour remainder of macaroni mixture in dish and add 1/2 cup of cheese on top. Bake for about 25 or 30 minutes, or until bubbly. Let stand for 10 minutes before serving.

Bradford Lewis, a loyal Seminole, captures the flavor of Florida State tailgating in this essay, excerpted from a Tallahassee magazine:

"Boiled peanuts, cornhole boards, the occasional ice luge, beer and lots of satellite TVs so people can watch games from around the nation. Our tailgating normally opens hours ahead of kickoff, so we are somewhat limited as to what we can do on site due to the time constraint. Cowboy Caviar is one thing we always have at our tailgates, and pigs in blankets are another favorite.

"(The fall means) football is back in 'Tallaclassy' and that means it's time to dust off the war wagons and extra-long barbecue tongs and head for our local Mecca, Doak Campbell Stadium. Tailgating is one of my favorite parts of an FSU game, right up there with Chief Osceola planting the spear and a four-touchdown victory margin. Nothing can replace a bit of smoke bellowing from under a stainless steel smokestack with the heavenly aroma of the Other White Meat basted with a savory secret sauce. Be careful here . . . smoke is for veteran tailgate warriors. So if this is your first buffalo hunt, don't get rushed and wind up choking down a charred Bubba Burger. We all know people eat with their eyes first, so put out a good spread of bait, lots of colors and shapes, go heavy on the dips and lots of finger-type stuff to keep them distracted in case the smoke needs a bit more time, or your ex-grillmaster gets distracted by the ice luge next door (YouTube can verify this). Watch out for that species of tailgater that has a sense of smell to make a buzzard envious; they will come and patiently wait for a moment when you let your guard down to lighten your load.

"At most tailgates, there is one standout Tomahawker who exudes what we are all about . . . Seminole spirit. When you see that warrior on site three hours before

Strawberry Delight

From Brad and Nikki Johnson
Former FSU quarterback

INGREDIENTS:

20 whole large strawberries

1 16-ounce tub of cream cheese frosting

1 1/2 cups of chopped pecans or pecan chips

DIRECTIONS:

• Wash strawberries, with stems, thoroughly and pat completely dry. If the strawberries are not completely dry, the cream cheese frosting will not adhere. Open tub of frosting and stir until smooth. Pour pecan chips on a plate. Take one strawberry by its stem and dip into cream cheese icing, and then roll frosting-covered strawberry into pecan chips. Place finished strawberry on a platter. Repeat until all strawberries are completed, then cover the platter and refrigerate until ready to serve.

Crab Spread

From Nan O'Leary, daughter of
Jack Nicklaus, mother of
FSU's Nick O'Leary

INGREDIENTS:

1 6-ounce can of crabmeat

1 medium onion, minced

1 1/2 teaspoons milk

1 teaspoon horseradish

Garlic salt, to taste

Pinch of sugar

Parsley, for color

DIRECTIONS:

• Mix all ingredients together, but add the crabmeat last. Bake at 375 degrees for 15 minutes. Serve with crackers.

kickoff icing coolers, staking claim to turf with a malfunctioning pop-up tent, keeping the vultures at bay until kickoff, and then emerging from the post-victory fireworks haze with an elbow slung close to their side nursing a sprained Tomahawk Chop tendon — and they *still* help you load the truck, you know you have the winner of the Golden Coozie."

Obviously, Bradford is a serious tailgater. Perhaps some perspective from an academic is in order.

"Florida State has had a dramatic increase in the quality of its football teams, the size of its stadium and its tailgating since Bobby Bowden arrived as the head coach in the 1970s," explains Chuck Ehrhardt, law professor and longtime chair of the FSU Athletics Board. "Those years under Bowden featured two national champions and 14 straight years with top-five finishes in national rankings. At the same time, the stadium grew from a 40,000-seat

steel-beam structure to the present modern, attractive brick stadium seating over 80,000.

"The pre-kickoff pageantry of Chief Osceola charging down the field and planting his flaming spear at midfield astride Renegade, the Appaloosa horse, and the crowd breaking into the War Chant cheer began in those years and adds much to the game-day experience," continued Chuck. "The past few years have marked a resurgence of enthusiasm for the program, an undefeated season, and a third national championship and third Heisman Trophy quarterback.

"The success of the team has led to a dramatic increase in the fervor of the fans and their interest in tailgating. One unique feature is the dining club and sports grill located atop the stadium in the south end zone. On game days, it is open for tailgating, and the adjoining decks are full of tailgaters overlooking the stadium

Hot Chicken Salad

From Nan O'Leary, daughter of
Jack Nicklaus, mother of
FSU's Nick O'Leary

INGREDIENTS:

3 cups cooked chicken breast

1 cups slivered almonds

1 can water chestnuts, sliced

1 small red pimento, drained

2 cups celery

1 teaspoon salt

1/2 teaspoon pepper

1 tablespoon lemon juice

1 1/2 cups Hellman's Mayonnaise

1 cup cheese

1 can cream of chicken soup

1 can onion rings

DIRECTIONS:

- Bake 45 minutes at 325 degrees in a 13-inch by 9-inch baking dish, putting in the onion rings with 10 minutes remaining. Remove from oven and let stand 10 minutes before cutting into squares.

and enjoying the scene below. Because of the stadium's location, the nearest parking and tailgating is available through the Seminole Boosters, with student parking in lots around the campus.

"Most of the culinary tailgating favorites are accompanied by beer. A variety of smoked meats and ribs top the list. Of course, fried Gator tail is always on the menu when the University of Florida comes to town."

If Jack Nicklaus succumbed to tailgating, you can only imagine the scene. Photo ops and autograph requests would mean that if he really wanted to sample the food, he would have to relegate himself to taking a doggie bag with him. He obviously is not a tailgater, but appreciates the fun that fans get from tailgating. There are times when he and his wife, Barbara, find a way to meet up after the game with grandson Nick O'Leary, who plays tight end for the 'Noles. Postgame reunions are important to the Nicklauses, who might very well be America's No. 1 fans when you consider all the sporting activities involving their 22 grandchildren.

"Our entire year is dictated by the schedule of our grandchildrens' teams," says Jack. It was the same when his children — Jackie, Steve, Gary, Nan and Michael — were coming along. Their teams' schedules sometimes influenced Jack's playing schedule on the PGA Tour. It was not uncommon for him to finish a round in the afternoon somewhere on Tour and then fly home to North Palm Beach for one of Nan's volleyball games, for example. Jack also caddied for his sons in golf tournaments. Now his grandchildren caddie for him at the Par 3 tournament at the Masters each spring.

A graduate of Ohio State, Jack is a big sports fan. He often shows up at Wimbledon, for example. He has always been a college football fan, dating back to his college years in Columbus. When FSU won the national championship in 2013, Jack did not miss a single game. Always in control of his emotions, just like it was when one of his putts curled into the cup for a major championship victory, Jack doesn't whoop it up during the game. But as you might expect, he is a serious student of football. His daughter, Nan, however, says, "he was pretty proud to see Nick and the Seminoles win in the Rose Bowl."

The victory brought about one of the greatest Jack Nicklaus smiles ever. "I'm a grandfather, you know," says Jack. Greater than winning his last major, the 1986 Masters? "Close," he said with a grin.

HAVING FUN IN THE SUN

By Jan Outlar Edwards, Fresno State professor

The temperature is anywhere from 98 to 105 degrees when the Fresno State Bulldogs descend on Bulldog Stadium to open their college football season every August. But sweltering temperatures don't deter the thousands of tailgating fans who have fun in the sun. After all, this is the San Joaquin Valley — the single richest agricultural region in the world — and heat can't stop the tailgating frenzy that accompanies all things Fresno State football.

Located in the center of California, Fresno is the fifth-largest city in the Golden State. This city of a half-million-plus is just hours away from the celebrated beaches of Carmel and Monterey, the giant Sequoias of Yosemite National Park, Los Angeles, San Francisco and nearby ski resorts for later in the fall. There is a lot to do on a Saturday in the Valley, but for the thousands of Red Wavers — as Bulldog fans are called due to their penchant for dressing in red — there is no place to be other than Bulldog Stadium at Jim Sweeney Field.

California State University, Fresno is home to over 23,000 students. The richness of Valley agriculture brings people here from all over. The Valley is home to one of the most diverse populations in the world, and this is mirrored in the student body at Fresno State and at Bulldog tailgates. This gift of diversity can be seen and smelled in the vast array of foods, tailgate setups and people.

Bulldog tailgating began in the 1970s when the Dogs played at Radcliff Stadium. Hundreds picnicked around their cars and trucks. But the festivities changed when Bulldog Stadium opened in 1980. There are still plenty of pickup trucks — agriculture drives the economy — but many of them are customized with Bulldog-painted themes. High-priced custom trailers and buses designed exclusively for tailgating abound, too, and some feature generators, granite countertops, running water and even air-conditioning. Folks party under elaborate shade structures, pop-up tents or umbrellas to ease the sweltering heat. They are from very different walks of life, but they are all brought together by the love of the Fresno State Bulldogs.

Fresno State tailgaters enjoy traditions and a unique landmark. There are the red-and-white checkered end zones, and there's the marching band and cheerleaders weaving in and out of tailgaters' parties. There is also a tunnel that the players run through when entering the field. But the vistas provide the most unique landmark of Fresno State tailgating. Attendees enjoy the expanse of grape vineyards and other magnificently planted fields nestled around Pete Beiden Baseball Field.

When walking through Fresno State tailgating lots, you'll see a glimpse of what America is all about. You'll see folks dressed in traditional Native American garb with delicious tandoori chicken cooking. You'll hear Tex Mex playing on the radio with carne asada sizzling on the grill. You'll see folks dressed from head to toe in Bulldog Red with radios blaring pregame buzz, and hot dogs and hamburgers grilling. You'll see elegant linen-draped tables of food displayed like a wedding, but with homemade pasta, stuffed peppers and grapes freshly picked on game-day morning. You'll see friends sipping sake and dining with chopsticks seated by a portable flowing fountain. Next to that you'll see folks sitting on the beds of their trucks crunching on chips and enjoying Subway sandwiches. You'll see a lot of different kinds of people, setups and food, but everywhere you look, you'll see love — a love within each tailgate circle of friends and a love of the Dogs!

Tri-tip steak is popular at Fresno State tailgates. Photo by Katie Eleneke/Sportspoint.com

Fresno State's loyal Red Wave family includes multi-generations of people scattered in the Red, White, Purple and Blue lots surrounding Sweeney Field. Many tailgaters boast of attendance from four generations, from babies to great grandparents. Attendees say this is their connection and reconnection time. Rather than wait for a wedding, christening, funeral or family reunion, they tailgate because they can laugh and enjoy their family and friends while supporting Fresno State at the same time. They plan menus and themes often a year in advance, and spread the word for folks to mark their calendars to come and relish this fun time.

Fresno State head coach Tim DeRuyter's wife, Kara, hosts tailgate parties at all home games for the coaches and their families. It's a time when they relax and enjoy themselves before the whistle blows. "I have to tell you," she says, "I go big on my tailgates. My brother-in-law has a trailer and does all of my cooking. My sister does all of the centerpieces. All of the coaches' wives, family and friends are invited. We pick a theme, and go with it for the food and decorations." Two of Kara's favorite themes are "Dog-to-ber-fest" and "Play for the Ring."

Her favorite recipe is the accompanying Red Wave Eggs & Sausage on page 62.

In 2006, the California State University System enacted a rule prohibiting all 23 campuses from selling alcoholic beverages at any intercollegiate athletic event held at university-owned or operated facilities. But Fresno State tailgaters have embraced the BYOB doctrine. There is even a wine named "Tailgate Red" to quench your thirst before entering Bulldog Stadium. Tailgate Red is made by the Fresno State winery, which is the first commercially bonded university winery in the nation. This wine is a blend of 15 different varieties all grown on the Fresno State campus. Once harvested, grapes are crushed, fermented and bottled by Fresno State enology students. About 3,000 cases are bottled annually. Of course, the peak season is football season! Marketing students sign up to pour the wine at the Foundation Tailgate venue before each game. You can hear corks popping open in the warmth of fall days near Bulldog Stadium.

Although all Valley folks know food choices have to work around the stifling temperatures of 100-plus degrees throughout much of tailgating season, the favorite

Herb Spice Tri-Tip Steak

From the Fresno State
Alumni Association

INGREDIENTS:

Tri-tip roast

1/4 tablespoon paprika

1/2 teaspoon onion powder

1 tablespoon kosher salt

1/2 teaspoon dried oregano

1 teaspoon garlic powder

1/2 teaspoon dried thyme

1 teaspoon ground black pepper

Olive oil

DIRECTIONS:

• In a bowl, mix together all ingredients except the olive oil. Stir in the olive oil until it forms a paste. Trim excess fat and skin from the roast. Rub the paste all over the tri-tip. Let it sit at least 30 minutes. Some prefer overnight refrigeration to bolster the flavor. Heat charcoal or gas grill to high heat. Sear the roast 2 to 3 minutes on each side. Reduce the heat to low. Grill until cooked to your preference. About 20 to 30 minutes is best for medium rare (you can use a meat thermometer, as tri-tips seem less done than they really are, so overcooking can happen). Remove the tri-tip and let it sit for a minimum of 10 minutes while covered with tented foil. Cut into thin slices and serve with salsa or horseradish.

Jalapeno-Stuffed Tri-Tip Sandwiches

From the Fresno State
Alumni Association

INGREDIENTS:

1 whole white onion

3- to 5-pound tri-tip roast

Red wine (any kind, but beer can also be used)

5 to 7 whole jalapeno chilies

Jalapeno juice from can

Peppers (embasa canned or pickled jalapenos)

DIRECTIONS:

• Cut into the interior of the roast from the smallest end with a long sharp knife without piercing the outer wall of the roast, making a cavity from side to side through the entire roast. Stuff the cavity with whole jalapenos, quartered onion pieces, wine and jalapeno juice. Tie the opening of roast with sterile string (sterilize by boiling any string). Using heavy-duty foil, form a loose airtight covering around the roast. Add more wine (or beer), onions, jalapenos and jalapeno juice around the roast in foil covering (this creates a steaming effect). Seal tight and place on an old cookie sheet or other pan to keep the roast off of the direct flame when barbecuing. Barbecue 2 to 3 hours over a charcoal grill. Check every 30 minutes for liquid content around the roast; add more wine as needed, because you do not want to burn the roast. When finished cooking, the roast should fall apart like deep-pit barbecue. This is delicious hot or cold as a sandwich.

Red Wave Eggs & Sausage

From Tim and Kara DeRuyter
Head coach at Fresno State

INGREDIENTS:

1 1/2 pounds ground Italian sausage

2 quarts of your favorite marinara sauce (I use my grandmother's recipe)

12 eggs

Red pepper flakes

Hearty Italian bread, sliced

Olive oil spray

Portable gas grill

Foil pan

Aluminum foil

DIRECTIONS:

• Spray the foil pan with olive oil, and then brown the Italian sausage. Pour in the 2 quarts of marinara and let it simmer. When the sauce is nice and hot (bubbling), crack and drop the eggs into the sauce. Cover with a piece of foil. Let the eggs simmer for approximately 3 to 5 minutes (until the eggs whites are firm; don't overcook them, because some folks like the yolks runny). Then scoop the eggs onto the plate, making sure not to crack the yolk! Spray your bread slices with olive oil spray and grill/toast your bread while the eggs are cooking. You can use the bread to dip into the eggs and sauce. This recipe is my good luck and always brings a win!

Stuffed Sheepherder's Bread

From Tim and Kara DeRuyter
Head coach at Fresno State

INGREDIENTS:

8 ounces cream cheese

1 pint sour cream

1 jar dried chipped beef, sliced

1 7-ounce can chopped green chilies

1 cup sharp cheddar cheese

1 round loaf of sheepherder's bread, scooped out (slice off and save the top)

DIRECTIONS:

• Mix the first five ingredients and put them in the scooped out bread. Put the bread top back on and wrap in foil. Bake 1 1/2 hours at 350 degrees. Serve with crackers. This will serve eight people.

dish is "tri-tip." Often called "Santa Maria steak," tri-tip is a cut of beef from the bottom sirloin cut. It usually weighs 1.5 to 2.5 pounds. The roast is very popular in the Central Valley. Aficionados say tri-tip has full flavor, lower fat content and is priced lower than other cuts. Tri-tip, a popular cut of meat for producing chili con carne on the competitive chili cooking circuit, is big at Bulldog Stadium. The favorite way to prepare tri-tip is to barbecue it, slice it and eat it while it's warm. The accompanying two tri-tip recipes on page 61 are from *Bon Appetit:*

The Fresno State Cookbook prepared by the Fresno State Alumni Association.

Fresno State has great hometown fans. Win or lose, the tailgating goes on. For six Saturdays in the heart of California, Fresno State sports zealots discuss the game, kids toss footballs at Bulldog Lane and dream of one day playing for the Dogs, friends connect with friends over good food and laughter, and the sun shines brightly on the San Joaquin Valley.

Special thanks to Peter Robertson, Vinci Petrosino Ricchiuti, Keeley Bramer, Judge Brant Bramer, Steven and Cindi Lee, Kara DeRuyter, Paul Ladwig, Dianna Conaway, Kevin Smith, Stephen Trembley, Shenee Sanchez, chef Steve Fernandez, sous chef Bryan Kramer, catering manager Karen Focarazzo, Jim and Lisa Scroggin, Molly Watson, Bruce Farris, Betsy Hays and the Fresno State Alumni Association.

A FEW PERSPECTIVES FROM ATHENS

Tailgating at Georgia, depending on the authority, dates way back.

Naturally, when Sanford Stadium hosted its first game in October 1929 — when the famous privet hedges were in their infancy — it was a hot day as the Georgia Bulldogs lined up against the Yale Bulldogs, the scourge of the East. A record number of Coca-Colas in the traditional 6.5-ounce bottle were sold. Legend has it that the other drink of choice — white lightning, also known as moonshine — was abundantly available.

UGA has a beautiful campus in the northern part of Georgia, whose geography connects with the foothills of the Blue Ridge Mountains — but the topography is hilly. Athens, home of the oldest chartered state university in the country, has a short supply of flat acreage. There is charm and beauty reflected by the 93,000-seat stadium, which was built on two natural hillsides. Before construction of Sanford Stadium, the area was known as "The hollow at the foot of Lumpkin Street."

There are many parking lots — used by the faculty during the week — that become prized tailgating places on game day. You can walk from North campus to South campus and find hospitable tailgates on lawns where luminaries from the past hung out at landmarks that are rich in tradition and lore. Some even tailgate where the first Garden Club of America was formed. Tailgate clubs and parties flourish all over campus.

* * *

Every school has a favorite fan. Whatever school is your alma mater, there will be countless graduates and aficionados who will brag on who they consider the school's greatest fan. When it comes to the University of Georgia, there could be very few Bulldog fans who could rival the passion and commitment of the late John "Kid" Terrell. Kid, in my view, was Georgia's greatest tailgater, and that won't change, at least in the short term. Even in death, he remains the quintessential Bulldog tailgater. His friends carry on. His tailgate remains the "Kid Terrell

Meat Pies

From Vince and Barbara Dooley
Former head coach at the University of Georgia

INGREDIENTS:

1 pound ground beef

1 medium onion, chopped fine

1/4 cup pine nuts

Juice from 3 lemons

1 tablespoon Laban or plain yogurt

1 teaspoon salt

1/3 teaspoon pepper

DIRECTIONS:

• Saute meat and onions lightly. Remove from heat and drain off liquid. Add remaining ingredients, stirring mixture well. Using basic dough recipe or canned biscuits, center each round of dough with filling. Place on a greased cookie sheet and bake in preheated oven at 400 degrees for 20 minutes or until lightly browned.

Hot Dawg Delight

From Mark and Katharyn Richt
Head coach at the University of Georgia

INGREDIENTS:

Bread of your choice

Hot dogs

Sliced cheese

Baked beans

DIRECTIONS:

• Toast the bread on both sides in oven. Slice hot dogs on bread, cover with sliced cheese. Melt the cheese under the broiler and then add as many baked beans as possible. Throw a little ketchup on top. Serves as many as you want. You must use a fork and also plenty of napkins.

John Culpepper, pictured with his wife Katherine, carries on the Kid's Tailgate tradition with John Barrett.

Tailgate Club," all remembering his deep and abiding love of alma mater. Kid tailgated with warm feelings in his heart.

John Culpepper carries on the Kid Terrell tailgate tradition, in concert with John Barrett, who has helped orchestrate a merging of tailgates that brings over 200 tailgaters to a parking lot near the stadium on many game days.

"In the mid-60s, John 'Kid' Terrell, Terry Wingfield, Bob Poss, Bob Argo, my late father E.H. Culpepper and a few more diehard Bulldog fans joined together to form a small tailgate group in the parking lot outside the west end of Sanford Stadium," says John Culpepper, class of '96. "The ringleader was Kid Terrell. Poss, a letterman on Georgia's Rose Bowl team and stadium concessionaire, provided parking. Every family brought their favorite tailgate dish. In 1980 our group move up the hill behind Clark Howell Hall, about two football fields from the entrance to Sanford Stadium. This was the perfect setting for a classic tailgate. By then the group had grown and was a little more organized. They pooled their resources to purchase a huge red and black tent to host their tailgate and provide shelter from the hot Georgia sun. In 1981 following a national championship, Bulldog tailgating fever became epidemic. To kick off the inaugural season in their new tailgate spot, the group rented a piano from a local music store, and advertising executive and Georgia graduate Clisby Clarke played his infamous Bulldog tunes ('Bulldog Bite') for the tailgate group before the game.

"In 2007 John Barrett and I took over the weekly operations," Culpepper continued. "The founding members were still active in the tailgate, but they had paid their dues and did not need to work so hard. We named the group Kid's Tailgate in honor of founding member John 'Kid' Terrell. We still tailgate in the same spot.

"Kid's Tailgate has been a part of my life since I was a child, and I am honored to carry on the tradition that Kid Terrell and my father started so many years ago. There no other place I'd rather be on a Saturday afternoon in the fall."

* * *

"If anything is certain from one autumn to the next in Athens, it is that about 6:45 a.m. on home football Saturdays, a white cargo truck will make its way to the parking lot beside Dawson Hall on the University of Georgia campus," says UGA history professor Dr. Jim Cobb, a member of the Bulldawg Tailgate Club, organized by alumnus and insurance executive Jimbo Laboon Jr. "Within a few minutes, several other vehicles will join it, their occupants fixed on their watches, awaiting the precise stroke of 7 a.m., the magical hour when they are allowed to unload the van, set up tables and tents, position the coolers and the satellite dish, and generally make ready for yet another day of pregame and postgame food, drink and frolic. This detailed preparation

Bulldog Cheese Ball

From Ann Hunt
Administrative associate to
head coach Mark Richt

INGREDIENTS:

16 ounces cream cheese, softened
8 ounces sharp cheddar cheese, grated
1/2 teaspoon sea salt
1/2 teaspoon cayenne pepper
2 tablespoons pimento, chopped
2 tablespoons green pepper, finely chopped
2 teaspoons sweet onion, finely chopped
3 tablespoons Worcestershire sauce
2 teaspoons fresh lemon juice
1 cup pecans, chopped

DIRECTIONS:

• Beat cream cheese and cheddar cheese with electric mixer until smooth. Blend in salt, pepper, pimento, green pepper, onion, Worcestershire sauce and lemon juice. Shape into a ball and roll in chopped pecans. Chill for at least 6 hours and serve with your favorite crackers.

Fresh Pesto Linguine

From Fran and Linda Tarkenton
Former quarterback at
the University of Georgia

INGREDIENTS:

2 cups fresh basil, cut into strips
5 ounces Parmesan cheese, cut into very
   small cubes
1/2 cup toasted pine nuts
6 cloves fresh garlic, crushed
2 1/2 cups high-quality virgin olive oil
1 pound linguine, or your choice of pasta
1 cup cherry or grape tomatoes, halved

DIRECTIONS:

• Combine the basil, cheese, pine nuts and garlic in a bowl. Pour the oil over all. Season to taste with salt and pepper. Let mixture stand at room temperature for about 3 hours. Cook the linguine in boiling salted water until just tender (do not overcook). Drain and toss immediately with the sauce. Mix in the tomatoes. Place in transportable container and serve at game-day temperature. Makes approximately 6 servings.

BBQ Pork Butt Roast

From Herschel Walker and Julie Blanchard
Former running back and Heisman Trophy
winner at the University of Georgia

INGREDIENTS:

4-pound Boston butt roast at room
   temperature

Dry rub ingredients:
2 tablespoons salt
2 tablespoons black pepper
2 tablespoons dark brown sugar
2 tablespoons paprika
1/2 tablespoon cayenne pepper

Liquid ingredients:
2 cups apple juice
1 cup apple cider vinegar
2 tablespoons Worcestershire sauce
1/2 tablespoon garlic powder

DIRECTIONS:

• Mix rub together very well. Press into roast and cover the roast with plastic wrap for 2 to 4 hours.

• Preheat oven to 325 degrees.

• Prepare the liquid ingredients in a large Dutch oven.

• Place the pork roast in Dutch oven with liquid ingredients and tightly cover pot with foil and then the lid. Roast for 4 hours, carefully basting the pork with the liquid every 1/2 hour. Remove pork from Dutch oven, let it cool, then shred it while also removing the fat. Serve with buns and cole slaw.

for merrymaking is no offhand effort, but rather the work of G.A.T.A., LLC, whose title may represent either the 'Greater Athens Tailgate Association' or the group's motto: 'Get After Their A___.'

"Suffice it to say, G.A.T.A. is no bunch of Bulldogs-come-lately," Cobb continued. "It began in 1986 under the leadership of a trio of young Athenians, honchoed by one Jimbo LaBoon, a.k.a. 'The Fireman,' who remains to this day the heart and soul — not to mention the secretary, purchasing agent, parliamentarian and benevolent despot — over all things G.A.T.A. In a town and a culture where tailgating is as sacred a custom as church on Sunday, the G.A.T.A. pioneers wanted to follow in their parents' footsteps while putting their own generational stamp on this hallowed tradition. The group itself has remained remarkably stable across a 28-year span that has seen it ranks swell from approximately 30 people in 1986 to roughly 120 families today, most of them Athenians, but with a healthy sprinkle of Atlantans and others spread across the state. G.A.T.A. has also maintained a continuing balance between new blood and old even though its locations have changed with the times. For 20 years, it was a fixture in UGA's Tate Student Center parking lot, immediately adjacent to the main gate to Sanford Stadium. This was a great place to see and be seen, perhaps too much so, for it became a standard pausing spot for dozens of non-G.A.T.A. folks eager to score one last free adult beverage before entering the stadium. In 2006 when expansion plans for the Student Center threatened to devour the G.A.T.A. staging area, the intrepid LaBoon scoured the entire campus before settling on the current grassy, shady patch on the South campus, which is ideal for kids and tucked well away from the major flows of foot traffic on game day.

"Although G.A.T.A tailgates seem utterly relaxed and freewheeling, they actually reflect a highly organized and closely supervised operation," says Cobb. "Dues are modest and convey a generous option to invite guests at no additional charge, but all members are assigned to teams responsible for providing and serving food for a particular game. Over the season, G.A.T.A. dining options are likely to include the traditional tailgate fare, such as fried chicken, deviled eggs and pimento cheese sandwiches, along with hot dogs and burgers. As the weather cools down, however, ribs and pulled pork barbecue, as well as chili (meat and vegetable varieties) become centerpieces of game-day offerings. Recent culinary innovations include jalapeno-stuffed bacon-wrapped quail served in a yeast roll. Not surprisingly, these mouth-watering two-bite morsels do not last long. Finally, as all such classic social happenings must, a G.A.T.A. tailgate also boasts a truly iconic bartender in the laid-back and friendly Tamarious Hill, who dispenses both spiritual and liquid good cheer (as appropriate) to young and old alike.

"G.A.T.A. may not be the only tailgate group with its own truck (which is actually the property of one Greg Irvin, whose nickname 'Hog' pays tribute his prowess as a preparer of pork in his own right), but it may well be the only such entity with its own formal running event.

Breakfast Shrimp & Cheese Grits

Terry and Jennifer Hoage
Former defensive back at
the University of Georgia

INGREDIENTS:

Shrimp:

4 large vine-ripe tomatoes

1 stick of butter

1/2 cup chopped onion

1/3 cup chopped red bell pepper

2 cloves garlic, finely minced

2 pounds peeled and deveined shrimp

1 teaspoon paprika (or 1/2 teaspoon paprika and 1/2 teaspoon smoked paprika)

1/2 teaspoon sea salt

1/4 teaspoon cayenne pepper

Fresh ground black pepper, to taste

1/4 cup chopped parsley

Cheese Grits:

3 cups water

1 cup milk

1 cup quick grits

1/2 teaspoon salt

1 cup extra-sharp grated cheddar cheese

DIRECTIONS:

• For the shrimp, dip tomatoes in hot boiling water, peel, seed and chop, set aside. Melt butter in pot, add onion, bell pepper and garlic; saute until onions are clear. Add diced tomatoes, shrimp and spices, and saute until shrimp are done, or about 10 minutes.

• For the cheese grits, bring water and milk to a boil, while being careful to not boil over with the milk. Add grits and salt, and cook about 2 to 4 minutes, add cheese and stir until melted. Place in greased baking dish at 350 degrees for 5 minutes. Enjoy with a bottle of Terry Hoage Vineyards' Picpoul Blanc!

Stuffed Piquillos

From Richard and Joanna Tardits
Former defensive lineman at
the University of Georgia

INGREDIENTS:

12 sweet red peppers
Garlic
Olive oil
4 cod steaks
6 medium-sized potatoes

DIRECTIONS:

• Marinate the sweet red peppers in garlic and olive oil. Cook 4 cod steaks in the oven and debone them when cooked. Make mashed potatoes from 6 medium-sized potatoes. Put potatoes and the cod in a blender and mix them until there are no big pieces left. Stuff your red peppers with the potato/cod mix. You can serve the piquillos warm or cold, depending on how much time before kickoff!

Dippin' Ritz

From Jon & Ali Stinchcomb
Former offensive lineman at
the University of Georgia

INGREDIENTS:

16 ounce jar of crunchy peanut butter
7 ounce jar of marshmallow fluff
1 box of Ritz crackers
20 ounces chocolate-flavored almond bark

DIRECTIONS:

• Stir marshmallow fluff and peanut butter together in bowl. Put about a tablespoon of mixture in between two Ritz crackers to make a sandwich. Do this until all mixture is gone. Heat almond bark in separate bowl as directed. Dip sandwiches into chocolate and set on wax paper to dry.

Pat's Jerk Chicken

From Pat and Mary Ann Hodgson
Former Georgia lineman

INGREDIENTS:

2 packages family-size wings or drumsticks

3 or 4 heaping tablespoons of jerk sauce/rub (Busha Browne's is excellent and available at Fresh Market)

3 or 4 ounces olive oil

3 or 4 ounces bottled Italian salad dressing

Dash of Chinese chili oil or Tabasco

1/4 cup red or white wine for additional liquid (optional)

Salt

Pepper

DIRECTIONS:

• I use an ice pick or fork to poke holes in the chicken so the marinade seeps into the meat. Place the chicken in a large Ziploc bag. Add all of the above ingredients into the bag and mix well with the chicken. Marinate overnight, 8 to 10 hours — the longer the better — and flip the bag occasionally.

Grilling with direct heat:

• Oil the grill (so the skin doesn't stick), place chicken on grill and cook on very low (250 to 300 degrees) heat for at least an hour, turning every 7 to 8 minutes. It will burn if you cook on high heat. It smokes a great deal due to the jerk sauce, so I would not recommend an oven.

Grilling with indirect heat:

• Oil the grill. You can cook the chicken indirectly by turning off the back burner of the gas grill (if you have that option) and using the front burner(s) for heat. I turn off the back burner and stack the chicken toward the back. I keep the front two burners on low to medium (around 300 degrees) with the lid down, and I turn the chicken about every 20 to 25 minutes. It takes about an hour and 20 minutes for the wings and drumsticks at that rate.

The 'Game-Day Run' typically attracts about two-dozen participants who head off shortly after tailgate set up is complete and pass straight through the heart of prime campus tailgating activity. Though outsiders may find the fixed rituals of G.A.T.A. a bit quaint, for those who observe them religiously, they offer vital reassurance of friendship and belonging as well as a mighty good reason to count off the days until fall," concluded Cobb.

* * *

Robert "Bob" Martin's history with Georgia football began back in the mid-1950s when he owned Seagraves on the Old Atlanta Road. Every Thursday night he had an all-you-can-eat special, and the UGA football players would take full advantage. He said it seemed a lot of them ate enough to last several days.

Bob has been an avid Georgia football fan for over 60 years, attending home games, out of town games and bowl games. In 1978 the tailgating changed in that he purchased a motor home that became the headquarters for 30 to 40 tailgaters.

Bob and his wife Helen arrive for tailgating in early morning on game day, and after getting the motor home set up, they settle in to "people watch," read or do crossword puzzles until their crowd slowly starts to congregate, bringing side dishes to share.

For early games, Bob prepares a breakfast casserole and the "best in the South cheese grits." Helen always has several homemade desserts for those with a sweet tooth. Regardless of the menu, there is always a lot of food, and Bob invites everybody to come share — including the opponent's fans.

Bob is now a very young 87 years old. Perhaps tailgating is his fountain of youth.

* * *

Jarrell Greene of Gray, Georgia, is living proof that if you run a super tailgate party, you are recognized and

GOOD OLE
APPLE KNOCKER

Robert Westmoreland is a longtime Bulldog supporter from the mountain town of Elijay, which is known for producing some of the best apples in North Georgia, from which a tasty and warming libation is called an "Apple Knocker."

"Our best producers can make it to where it will literally knock your socks off," Robert says with his drawl. "Legally, most Apple Knocker is treated like moonshine by law enforcement. If you know somebody who can make the good stuff, you don't just walk up to his door and ask for it. Unfortunately, the guys who can really make the best Apple Knocker are beginning the pass on, but there are a few guys around who can make it the old-fashioned way."

Robert found an Apple Knocker recipe to share.

"First, you need a clean 55-gallon drum. Pour a gallon of 'rye feed' into the bottom, then add six to eight bushels of mashed/hammered apples. Add 10 to 15 pounds of sugar. Next, fill the drum almost full of water. Allow this mixture to 'work off' (ferment) for several days until the odor seems right. Next, all the liquid is drained and poured into the cooker equipment of the still, using only the finest copper lines. The finished product can cure almost any known ailment."

Robert Westmoreland is also a fan of Jarrell Greene's tailgate.

"Jarrell is a close friend and is a true legend in tailgating on the Georgia campus," says Robert. "His tailgate is appropriately named 'Tailgreat.' Typical of the way he does things came about 20 years ago when I heard music at his tailgate on Hull Street. My wife and I walked over to see what was going on, and Jarrell's brother invited us to participate the next home game. We've been going to Jarrell's tailgate ever since.

"You can't imagine better food or a greater host, and he treats the fans of opposing teams as if he is cooking just for them. He gets the hospitality award on the Georgia campus."

* * *

There are countless moonshine stories. One of my favorites came from the late Fred Russell, longtime sports columnist with the *Nashville Banner*. He came to Athens one Friday afternoon before a Georgia-Vanderbilt game and met up with three sportswriters from Atlanta. They had spent the afternoon with a jug of moonshine. Fred said they were playing an interesting game. "One would leave the room," he said, "and the other two would try to guess who had left."

appreciated just like those who run and pass for touchdowns are.

"Tailgating started kind of slow but gained momentum pretty fast," Jarrell remembers. "It was so much fun. A couple of buddies and I started in the early '80s taking in some away games. That was fun, too. By 1985, we were the three amigos with a boom box and two speakers in the trunk — listening to all of the great songs that we grew up with and enjoying adult beverages. The 1985 season began a 25-year stretch where I did not miss any Georgia games played in the continental USA. Food wasn't the big thing in the beginning, just some grocery store cookies and adult beverages. My friend David attracted everybody with his music. Whether we were

home or away, the music began to get us invited to other tailgates for food in exchange for our music.

"Perhaps the birth of my tailgate experiences happened in 1990 at Commonwealth Stadium in Lexington, Kentucky," he continued. "We always were big on 'come early, stay late,' and on this date, we were one of the first to show up. We saw a UGA flag in the lot, drove over and asked if we could park there. We were told it was a UK priority lot but since it wasn't a basketball game, it would probably be fine. We parked, raised the trunk, and started the music and the adult beverages. As they say, the rest is history.

"Following the 'Commotion at Commonwealth,' the tailgate got bigger, as grills and cooking became a part of home games. Initially, 10 or 12 people soon became

Curried Chicken Salad

From Pat and Mary Ann Hodgson
Former Georgia lineman

INGREDIENTS:

8 cups cooked chicken, cubed

1 No. 2 can water chestnuts, drained and sliced

2 pounds seedless grapes, halved (white or green)

2 to 3 cups celery, diced

2 1/2 cups almonds, sliced

3 cups mayo (1 1/2 cups regular and 1 1/2 cups light, if desired)

1 tablespoon curry powder (or more if desired)

2 tablespoon soy sauce

2 tablespoon fresh lemon juice

12 mini croissants

DIRECTIONS:

• In large bowl, combine chicken, water chestnuts, grapes, celery and 1 1/2 cups almonds. In a smaller bowl, mix remaining ingredients and add to chicken mixture. Toss to mix well. Chill several hours before serving. Add remaining 1 cup almonds. Serve with mini croissants. Serves 12.

Charley's Chops

From Charley and Peggy Trippi
Two-time All-American at Georgia

INGREDIENTS:

6 pork chops (boneless center cut loin 1/2 inch or so)

6 medium potatoes

2 large onions (sweet is best)

1/2 cup Italian bread crumbs

1/2 cup grated parmesan cheese

1 egg

Salt

Pepper

DIRECTIONS:

• Peel and cut potatoes into quarters. Brown lightly in small amount of oil. Place into lightly greased baking dish. Slice onions thinly, and saute' until tender. Place onions on top of potatoes. Salt and pepper chops according to taste, and dip each chop into egg. Dredge chops in small amount of olive oil. Place chops on top of onions and potatoes. Bake in 325 degree oven about 45 to 60 minutes.

• Chicken may be used instead of chops, and the recipe may be prepared a day or two ahead of baking. (Men love this dish!)

30 or 40. Within a few years, it was not unusual to feed 125 to 150 football fans. My tailgate experience is now much a part of me.

"Our favorite tailgate food is barbecue and country-style ribs. Boston butts are the staple for large tailgates. We have cooked a whole hog. We stuff the hog with 'turduckin' — a turkey and a duck. The low-country boil is always a big favorite at the LSU game. A chili dump has been a big hit the past few years. A chili dump is where each person brings a large family portion of their favorite recipe of chili and dump all into one pot. Then, it is heated and served. I'm happy to say I'm the guy who would rather serve for 20 or 30 people rather just serving a single person. I have had tailgate food for Sunday lunch on many occasions."

Now that's a good Bulldog!

GEORGIA-FLORIDA RIVALRY GAME

The Georgia-Florida game — or the Florida-Georgia game, depending on the colors you wear — settled permanently in Jacksonville in 1933, owing to the view that there was a more attractive gate when played at this neutral site. Geography naturally had its influence in that it became an opportunity for more people in south Georgia and north Florida to drive to the annual game.

There was no special attraction to Jacksonville except it was the largest population base north of Orlando and

Vidalia Onion Delight

From Billy and Martha Payne
Chairman of the Augusta National Golf Club, former UGA football player and CEO of the Atlanta Committee for the Olympic Games

INGREDIENTS:

4 or 5 large Vidalia onions, sliced into thin rings (or a different sweet onion, if you must)

2 cups sugar

4 cups water

1 cup white vinegar

1/2 to 3/4 cup mayonnaise

2 to 3 teaspoons celery salt

DIRECTIONS:

• Dissolve sugar in water and add vinegar. Put onion rings in mixture and marinate for at least 4 hours. Drain and coat with mayonnaise. Add celery salt and toss. Serve on crackers as an appetizer, or in salads, or on sandwiches.

Savannah Marinated Shrimp

From Sonny Seiler
Breeder of Georgia's white bulldog mascots named Uga

INGREDIENTS:

4 pounds shrimp, peeled and cooked

1 cup Wesson oil

1 cup tarragon vinegar

2 cloves garlic, crushed

2 medium onions, sliced

Salt

Black pepper

Red pepper

DIRECTIONS:

• Cook the shrimp and mix well with all other ingredients. Salt and pepper to taste. Marinate in refrigerator overnight. Serve on toothpicks with crackers. This also travels well in a wideneck soup-sized Thermos.

south of Macon and Savannah. The game, however, did not flourish until the 1960s when both teams became more competitive under Florida's Ray Graves and Georgia's Vince Dooley.

"Today, CBS's first schedule decision is to lock down this rivalry weekend," says Carl Parks, a Georgia graduate who never misses the Jacksonville classic. "Since the early 1980s, the networks have eagerly scheduled this game, which has become popular throughout college football. The fans gave it a thumbs-up, however, long before the network cameras came calling.

"With the tickets allocated with an even split, the game has been a scalper's dream for well over a half century. Fans arrive early in the day at EverBank Field, the site of the old Gator Bowl. It is a party scene that has endured for years. The intensity and the reverie, much of it induced by balmy temperatures, led to the game being described as the 'World's Largest Outdoor Cocktail Party.' Both schools have tried to tone down that image, but this game will always be a party scene for the fans.

"The game setting is a beautiful October fall afternoon on the banks of the St. John's River, a neutral field in this vibrant north Florida border town," muses Carl. He and his wife, Barb, are devout college football fans who wear red and black but find a good neighborly attitude of fans from both teams. "One of college football's greatest traditional rivalries, the Dawgs and Gators represent football talent-rich neighboring states with rabid SEC fan bases that focus on this game 365 days a year. Adding to the intense atmosphere is the unique circumstance with over 40,000 fans for each team resplendent in red and black or orange and blue.

"Truly more than a game, this three-day festival includes raucous beach parties, golf tourneys and fun in the sun along the Atlantic Coast from St. Simons Island to St. Augustine," Carl continued. "It's not unusual to get caught up in a cheering flash mob snaking through a fine restaurant, led by senior citizens celebrating their 50th consecutive Georgia–Florida weekend — and that's only Thursday night — 100 miles up or down the coast from the game site.

Carlene Talton and her brother Cully (on left) grill a pork shoulder before every Georgia-Florida game. Photo courtesy of Carl and Barb Parks.

Drought-Breaker Chili

From Theron and Kay Sapp
Former All-SEC fullback
at the University of Georgia

INGREDIENTS:

1 pound lean ground beef

1 onion, chopped

2 large cans Bush's Chili Beans

1 regular-sized can Bush's Chili Beans

1 can diced tomatoes

1 can tomato sauce

1 can Rotel tomatoes with chili peppers

1 can beef broth

1 tablespoon chili powder (add more if you desire)

3 shakes of Tony Cachere's Creole Seasoning

Black pepper, to taste

Salt (optional)

Garlic powder, to taste

DIRECTIONS:

• Brown together in a skillet the lean ground beef and chopped onion, then set aside. In a large pot, mix together all other ingredients, and then add the browned ground beef and onion mixture. Mix well and let it simmer. Serve with toasted pimento cheese finger sandwiches and crackers.

"Most surprisingly perhaps — beyond all the hype and hubris, team chants and cheers, and the electric atmosphere around and in the game itself — we found an amazing collegiality and respect among even the most zealously partisan fans in the tailgate lots nearest the stadium on game day. And day it is, as the lots are packed and partying in full swing by 10 a.m. for the 3:30 p.m. kickoff. Postgame revelry continues well past dark at the beaches and elsewhere until, well, whenever."

Buffalo Chicken Dip

From Matt Stinchcomb
Former offensive lineman at
the University of Georgia

INGREDIENTS:

2 cups chopped chicken

2 cups sharp cheddar cheese

1 package ranch dressing

3/4 cup buffalo sauce

DIRECTIONS:

• Mix it all together and bake at 350 degrees for 30 minutes. Serve with corn chips.

Sausage Balls

From Will and Karen Jones
University of Georgia alum
and Executive Director of the
Augusta National Golf Club

INGREDIENTS:

1 pound hot sausage (Tennessee Pride is usually the hottest)

1 pound extra sharp cheddar cheese (shred it yourself, don't buy pre-shredded)

3 cups Bisquick

Cayenne pepper

Red pepper flakes

DIRECTIONS:

• Mix all ingredients together. Use your hands and squish everything until it's combined. Roll out into balls, place on a cookie sheet and bake at 400 degrees for about 10 minutes. Keep them warm. Mustard goes well with these sausage balls.

REMEMBERING ERK

Erskine Russell became the "Bald Eagle" when he took over Georgia Southern's football program in 1981 after leaving the University of Georgia, where he had been the popular defensive coordinator since 1964.

Erk was a clever, funny personality. When Georgia Southern officials called for a press conference to announce Erk's hiring, they had to go out and buy a football for a prop. Erk said he knew that things were bad when the athletic director who hired him came to Athens and took him to dinner. "I got the check," Erk cracked, "and he stayed at my house."

There was a very limited budget, but Erk called on friends for donations. He was such a genuine and engaging person that it was hard not to do something for Erk. He remembered a farmer in overalls, slipping Erk a $100 bill periodically. Getting Georgia Southern re-started and kick-started required a village. One man, Gulfstream Chairman Allen Paulsen, built the stadium, but to make it happen, everybody had to pitch in. Erk's warm and engaging and selfless personality brought about football championships in Statesboro. Equipment managers, who were friends at colleges in the area, gave him used equipment and practice jerseys. The Eagles literally started from scratch, playing as a club team in 1982-83, but two years later in 1985, they won the national championship over Furman in a game that was played in Tacoma,

Erk's Favorite Cornbread

From Jay Russell, son of Erk Russell, the former head coach at Georgia Southern

INGREDIENTS:

1 cup rising cornmeal

1/2 cup sour cream

1 8-ounce can of creamed corn

1 stick oleo

2 eggs

DIRECTIONS:

- Mix and cook in heavy skillet.

Smoked Ribs & Chicken

From Tracy Ham,
All-American at Georgia Southern

DIRECTIONS:

When smoking ribs or chicken on an enclosed grill or smoker:

• Step 1: Season the ribs and/or chicken at room temperature with Season Salt and pepper, plus any of your favorite seasonings.

• Step 2: The most important part of cooking your meat is your fire. Before you start the fire, put your coals on one side so you can keep your meat away from the flames after you start it. Make sure all of your coals are in the fire zone.

• Step 3: Sear your meat on both sides before you move it to the "smoking side."

• Step 4: Add your favorite wood chips to the coals to enhance the special flavor from your meat.

• Step 5: Close the grill and smell your ribs and/or chicken smoke to perfection. Turn the meat every 20 minutes so it can smoke evenly.

Washington. Erk won three national championships in five years, and coaxed Paulson to build a classy stadium on the Southern campus. No coach has ever been more beloved in a community.

Erk and quarterback Tracy Ham arrived in Statesboro about the same time.

Tracy led the Eagles to their first national title. He was a whirring dervish at quarterback, running Erk's wishbone as a sleight-of-hand artist with the ball, with feet akin to Bojangles. When he reached the corner, he optioned countless defenders out of their shoes. Hambone, Hambone where you been? To the end zone and going again. That was the story of Tracy's life.

Tracy is as versatile in the kitchen as he was on the field.

"During the football season, I enjoy cooking because I get to enjoy the outdoors," says Tracy. "Being from a small town in Florida (High Springs) we were always outside cooking with family and friends. My brother Donald Ham was a military man, and while he was in the service, went from a guy in the field to a chef (due to an accident). He always talked about how he cooked for 800 soldiers. When they finished, nothing was left. I am not sure if the food was good or the soldiers were just plain hungry. I'm sure some of it was the result of my cooking tradition. I am a ribs-and-chicken guy. Love to cook the ribs and chicken to perfection. Remember, patience is important."

UPSCALE TAILGATING AT ITS FINEST

There was the time when Georgia Tech was the toast of Atlanta when it came to football, but today, Yellow Jacket fans have to compete with the presence of the Atlanta Falcons and games like the Chick-fil-A Kickoff Classic, the Chick-fil-A Bowl and the annual Southeastern Conference Championship Game.

None of that, however, bothers Robie and Adele Ogilvie and their colony of good friends who set up for passionate tailgating for Tech games just a few first downs from the Yellow Jackets' locker room.

"Robie," says Mindy Hyde, director of Development for Athletics at Georgia Tech, "is serious about what he cooks each home game. Sometimes he surprises his guests with something very special."

As food aficionados, Robie and Adele check out the best restaurants when they travel, and particularly enjoy Gallitoire's, perhaps the preferred restaurant of locals in New Orleans.

Robie, like the rest of the football tailgating world, began with burgers and hot dogs, but soon evolved into more sophisticated menu choices.

"I can do better than that," he said to himself one balmy autumn day. Affiliated with Home Depot, he cooks, among other choices, Chateaubriand lamb chops with mint jelly, stuffed port tenderloin, stuffed French

Buttermilk Fried Chicken

From Bill and Carolyn Curry
Former head coach at Georgia Tech,
Alabama, Kentucky and Georgia State

INGREDIENTS:

Buttermilk marinated chicken (already prepared for you)

2 cups flour

1 or 2 teaspoons cayenne pepper

2 tablespoons Old Bay Seasoning

2 teaspoons salt

2 teaspoons pepper

DIRECTIONS:

• Preheat oven to 350 degrees. Combine the flour, cayenne pepper, Old Bay, salt and pepper in a large bowl and mix well. Remove the chicken from the buttermilk recipe and drain well. Dredge the chicken in the flour mixture and let it sit for a few minutes. Dredge the chicken again just before frying. Working in batches if necessary, fry the chicken in a deep fryer until golden brown, or about 4 to 5 minutes. Drain the chicken on paper towels and then transfer to an oven rack. Finish the chicken in the oven until it reaches an internal temperature of 180 degrees, or about 25 to 30 minutes. Serve the chicken on a warm platter accompanied by the milk gravy.

Robie Ogilvie (front left) and his Georgia Tech tailgating gang.

Marchand de Vin Sauce

From Rob Ogilvie,
The Georgia Tech Tailgate Chef

INGREDIENTS:

6 tablespoons butter

1 medium onion, finely chopped

1 large clove garlic, minced

1/2 cup finely chopped green onions

1/3 to 1/2 cup extra finely chopped cooked ham

1/2 cup finely chopped mushrooms

1/3 cup all-purpose flour

2 tablespoons Worcestershire sauce

2 cups brown sauce

1/2 cup of Cabernet Sauvignon

1/2 teaspoon fresh thyme, finely chopped

1/2 cup finely chopped fresh parsley

Salt

Pepper

DIRECTIONS:

• Melt butter in a skillet. Sauté the onion, garlic, green onions and ham until onions are tender. Add the chopped mushrooms and cook for 3 more minutes. Blend in the flour and cook, stirring until smooth. Add the Worcestershire sauce, brown sauce, wine and thyme. Simmer over low heat, stirring occasionally to prevent scorching, until the sauce thickens — about 45 minutes to an hour. Stir in parsley. Season to taste with salt and pepper. Makes about 3 cups. Pour on beef tenderloin sandwiches or even eggs hussarde.

Tailgate Salmon

From Pepper and Livingston Rodgers
Former head coach at Georgia Tech,
UCLA & Kansas

Note from Livingston: We have dropped in on tailgate parties, especially some of Pepper's former players at Georgia Tech pregame tailgates, and we are always amazed at the variety of food that partiers put out for their guests. It is a great college tradition and everyone seems to have a great time sharing everything. I love to make salmon and serve it cold. Here's how I do it:

INGREDIENTS:

1 large salmon filet

Panko crumbs

Parmesan cheese

Salsa (optional)

Tartar sauce (optional)

Aluminum foil

DIRECTIONS:

• Place a filet of salmon, skin side down, on aluminum foil. Shake a lot of panko crumbs and parmesan cheese on the flesh of the fish, and press it with spatula to make it stick. Cover it with another piece of foil and fold it all up tight and then bake for 15 minutes. If you like it crispy, open the foil and broil for several minutes. This is very easy with no clean up. Put out some hot salsa or tartar sauce for topping choice for those who want it. As far as Pepper and I are concerned, everything goes well with salmon.

toast, steak, waffles, grilled shrimp, low-country boil, fresh-baked chocolate chip cookies, strawberry short-cake with homemade cream cherries jubilee — all on the latest grills and accompanying paraphernalia. He often likes to surprise his guests with something different, like his tailgate-made whipped cream, using a power drill. It would be a challenge to find a more creative college football tailgating chef than Robie.

With his location being so close to Bobby Dodd Stadium, many of Tech's former players and a lot of the coaches stop by after the game and sample Robie's cooking.

All food can be enhanced with herbs, spices and sauces. Rob's Marchand de Vin sauce is something that his friends rave about. "I serve it on a breakfast sandwich, which I call Egg McBuzz," Rob says. He has cultivated it to where it is, in Adele's view, "better than what you'll find at any super market."

Being the gentleman that he is, Robie doesn't like to talk about his role in, perhaps, Tech's best known tailgating club, noting that Tom and Polly Sapitowicz and Jared and Jinny Shope are just as central to the success of their game-day routine as the man behind the grill.

Come and get it! All of Robie's friends do.

Robie Ogilvie cooks up some steak.

PEPPER'S
COACHING TREE

The story about Franklin "Pepper" Rodgers, following a modest career at Brown High School in Atlanta, was that when several of his teammates showed up at Georgia Tech one day to sign grants-in-aid, Pepper went along and talked his way into a scholarship. That turned out to be as good of a deal for Tech as it was for Pepper, who was always finding a way to win games.

In addition to playing quarterback, he was also a kicker. His big game came in the Sugar Bowl in 1954 when he passed for 195 yards and three touchdowns, leading the Yellow Jackets to a 42-19 victory over West Virginia. Pepper was named the MVP. Playing for the Mountaineers was Sam Huff, who would become an NFL Hall of Fame linebacker. Huff said years later that he had a hard time with losing by such a lopsided score. "Hell," Huff said, "it took me a long time before I could get over it. When I sat down to eat and somebody said, 'Pass the pepper,' I wanted to get up from the table and fight."

Pepper would go on to head coaching jobs at Kansas, UCLA and back in Atlanta to coach at his alma mater. He enjoyed success everywhere he went. "You would have to say that Pepper hired good coaches and got out of the way and let them coach," said his friend, Jim Minter, former editor of the *Atlanta Journal and Constitution*. This is who Minter was referring to, Pepper assistants who became head coaches: Terry Donahue, Dick Tomey, Steve Spurrier, Homer Smith, Bill Curry, Ed Emory, Don Fambrough, John Cooper, Dick Bestwick, Barry Wilson, Jim Criner, Dave McClain, Charlie Taafe, Sandy Buda and Doug Weaver.

Pepper has an all-star cheerleader at home. He is married to former Hollywood actress Janet Lake, also known as Livingston Rodgers.

YES, THEY TAILGATE AT HARVARD, TOO

If you are a purist, you sometimes ponder the question. What would college football be like if Harvard-Yale and Army-Navy were still relevant? There are those who maintain that it is. It's just not on the same level as Oklahoma-Texas, Auburn-Alabama, Georgia-Florida, Ohio State-Michigan or USC-Notre Dame.

The Ivy League kids work just as hard, they compete just as keenly, and their fans are just as enthusiastic about tailgating as the fans are in Austin, Tuscaloosa, Gainesville, Ann Arbor or South Bend.

The big difference is obvious. Getting to the NFL is not the priority of the kids who matriculate at New Haven, Cambridge, West Point and Annapolis. Going to class and getting a degree is their priority. They play football on the side. As much as those who love King Football in the SEC, the Big Ten, the Big 12, the Pac 12, the ACC and other high-powered conferences, it is the other way around with most of their student-athletes. Becoming trained for the NFL is the priority, and their activity on the side is going to class — often wishing they were somewhere else. Reality is, there's no business like show business, which is why the cameras hunt the campuses where brawn often trumps brain when it comes to football.

Anyone with an exposure to campuses other than their alma mater comes away with the same conclusion — tailgating is as important on one campus as it is on another. That is why rivalry games have become so popular for the TV networks. Even if the two teams are not going anywhere when the final results are in, the level of intensity pregame and on the field is often akin to playing for the national championship.

I love seeing what it is like when Yale plays Harvard and Army plays Navy. I find it no different from the big games in the SEC and other conferences, which I have had the good fortunate to experience over the years. Observing the sea of tailgating tents at Cambridge, the teeming parking lots at Yale Bowl in New Haven, seeing the boats dock on the Chesapeake for Navy aficionados, and watching the Army tailgaters enjoying an autumn party near the Hudson offers an inspiration that is unsurpassed in pregame socializing.

These games are now played by teams that are no longer contenders for the national championship, but on game day when these rivals face off, you find the same relevancy in emotions and tailgating that you find Anywhereelse, USA.

A conversation with Clem McDavid from Sandersville, Georgia, about his Harvard experience reinforces what college football is all about. When it comes to tailgating and playing a big game, it is your alma mater that counts. Your campus and its traditions are what tug at the heart. Clem's perspective underscores the affection and feeling at Harvard, an attitude we all share about where we went to school.

What was it like, coming from a small town in Georgia and playing at Harvard?

I didn't find myself overwhelmed by the big city, but rather, I was underwhelmed by the lack of interest in college football. The SEC, which was part of my growing-up experience, is such a power, I just assumed everyone adored football as much as my family and I did — forgetting I was also around the top students and minds in the world. Once I set that and the lack of crowds at our games aside (I played before more people at the Georgia Dome for Washington County than I did most home games at Harvard), I began to appreciate the history of the program, the stadium and the game itself. I played on fields that presidents played on long before me. Our stadium was built to incorporate the forward pass, which is mind blowing.

What was the game-day fan experience in supporting the team at Harvard?

It is on par with any FCS school and many smaller FBS schools. There is tailgating and smoke-filled air. Autumn in Cambridge is second to none.

Did you do any tailgating, perhaps with family, after the game?

A unique aspect of the Harvard experience was the family atmosphere after the game. After our postgame meetings and showers, we'd join our families in the parking lots for food and fellowship. Unlike many other schools around the country, our players are from over half of the states in the country. Families made the trip to campus from all over, including Hawaii, for our games. I was fortunate enough to have a family member at every game my senior year and most every home game before my senior year.

What is unique about Harvard game day and tailgating?

There are many differences, but perhaps most unique is the stadium in which we play. Only three stadiums are listed in the National Historic Register, and Harvard Stadium is one. But tailgating is certainly unique as well, especially for Harvard-Yale when we attract a sold-out crowd at home of over 30,000 and nearly 60,000 when played at Yale. You really get the feel of a big-time college football game. When a stadium is sold out, it doesn't matter if there are 15,000 or 93,000 — it feels awesome. Alums in fur coats with cigars are right there with current undergrads. It's a sight to see.

What was a Harvard-Yale game like?

Aside from Army-Navy, this is college football at its purest. There are no scholarships, big TV contracts (though it is on national TV) or corporate banners. Just true student-athletes competing in basically the same game that was played there 100-plus years ago. It is always a sell-out, and as of late, it has huge conference implications on the line. But like most rivalries, throw the records out the window. I lost my last game at home to Yale, and I'll remember that forever, but I also started. We won the 2004 game, which capped off the first 10-0 season in nearly 100 years for Harvard. The pageantry certainly differed for this game, and the buzz truly takes over the campus for the one week of the year. Standing there singing the national anthem with both bands on the field prior to the game brought a tear to my eye every year.

As an alumnus, how often do you return to Harvard and do you tailgate?

I try and return for one game a year, most likely Harvard-Yale. We do not have a homecoming, so that is the de facto weekend. I certainly tailgate, but it's a little classier than I did it as an undergrad. More single malt scotch and less $1 beers.

Clem's mother, Missy, whose family made old-fashioned Southern Barbecue products, was raised on SEC football and became a passionate Ivy League fan.

"It is totally different at Harvard," she says. "As a parent, I miss it very much, especially for the Harvard-Yale weekend, and especially the old-timers in very old full-length beaver coats, the occasional set of candelabras and awesome food! I did bring barbecue (her family owned Castleberry Foods in Augusta, Georgia) on the plane. Also frozen barbecue ribs in sauce, which I took to a tailgate with other players' families for the last H-Y game. They were amazed. We ran out way too fast. From my point of view, the H-Y game is a tradition everyone should experience. Ivy League football, with the 'pep club' bands is just something totally unique. I grew up on SEC football, and I love it. However, I found that Ivy League football is just as much fun, and the tailgates are just as enjoyable, creative and varied as you would find anywhere football is played."

Marinated Vidalia Onion Dip

From Missy deSouza
Mother of former Harvard player
Clem McDavid

INGREDIENTS:

3 or 4 Vidalia onions

1 cup sugar

2 cups water

1 cup apple cider vinegar

1 to 2 tablespoons of Duke's Mayonnaise

2 teaspoons Jane's Krazy Salt

Premium Saltine crackers

DIRECTIONS:

• Cut in half and very thinly slice 3 or 4 Vidalia onions. Marinate overnight in 1 cup sugar, 2 cups water, 1 cup apple cider vinegar (two nights is even better). I use a resealable gallon plastic bag and turn occasionally. Drain and drain again until all of the liquid is gone. Stir in 1 to 2 tablespoons of Duke's Mayonnaise (you must use Duke's for the perfect flavor!) and toss well to coat all of the onion slices. Add Jane's Krazy Salt to taste (about 2 teaspoons). Serve on Premium Saltine crackers for a delicious taste!

FROM ALL-PRO TO AUTHOR

Jerry Kramer, perhaps the most famous male graduate of the University of Idaho, had the distinction of playing for Vince Lombardi's Green Bay Packers who won five NFL titles and two Super Bowls during his career. His fame as an offensive lineman ranked high on the recognition scale. Perhaps not like Jimmy Taylor, Bart Starr and Paul Hornung, but for a lineman, his star shone brightly, much like the aforementioned, in the Packer firmament.

Some of it had to do with his exceptional blocking for the backfield heroes. Then there was his career as an author that has segued into a speaking career.

He collaborated with Dick Schaap to write a best seller, *Instant Replay*, a diary of the 1967 season. After he retired, he authored *Farewell to Football*. When Lombardi passed away, Kramer wrote, *Lombardi: Winning is the Only Thing*. Lastly, he went back and visited his old teammates for a book called, *Distant Replay*.

When he is not out on the speaking circuit, he is usually back home in Idaho, and he is usually fishing. Jerry grew up fishing for his supper and is an accomplished angler — salmon, bass, crappies — but added, "I really am a rainbow trout guy."

He admits he is no match for his wife, Wink, who was popular on the racing circuit for years as Pure Oil's "Miss Firebird." Jerry then noted, "She can fish, and she can cook! When she was growing up in Mississippi, her dad would take her out of school and take her fishing with him. I have seen her nail a catfish by the head to a post and then skin the catfish. When she cooks catfish in her own special way, you have never had a better meal."

All-Pro Catfish

From Jerry and "Wink" Kramer
Former lineman at the University of Idaho
and five-time All-Pro with the Green Bay Packers

Note from Wink: Mine is a pretty basic catfish recipe — nothing fancy, no exotic spices — but I never met anyone who didn't love it. Give me a big ole plate of catfish with sides of hushpuppies, dill pickles, baked or white beans, coleslaw and iced tea, and I won't have room for that banana pudding for hours! Oh, my goodness, I think I just gained 5 pounds thinking about it!

INGREDIENTS:

6 to 8 (4 to 6 ounces each) catfish filets

2 cups milk

1 cup all-purpose flour

1 cup plain white cornmeal (yellow cornmeal can be substituted)

2 teaspoons salt

1 teaspoon ground black pepper

Peanut oil

(If you enjoy spicy flavors, you can also add a little garlic powder, hot sauce or ground red pepper)

DIRECTIONS:

• Use an oil with a high-smoke point; I always use peanut oil. If you have refrigerated your filets, let them sit at room temperature for about 10 minutes before beginning to cook. Remove excess moisture from fish before dredging in dry ingredients. Dredging is easier if you use one hand for dredging and the other hand for frying. A large deep fryer or deep cast-iron skillet is perfect for frying fish. It is important that the oil be hot before adding your room-temperature filets. Take care not to overcrowd the skillet or fryer, and always bring your oil back up to hot temperature before adding next batch. Maintaining the hot temperature of your oil will ensure that you get beautiful golden brown filets that are crispy on the outside while still tender, moist and flaky on the inside. Keep fried filets warm between batches by placing them, uncovered, on a wire rack in a shallow pan that has been lined with paper towels, and set the oven to 225 degrees. If you live in the Midwest or Northeast, this recipe will also work great with walleye filets.

REKINDLING FRIENDSHIPS IN IDAHO

Idaho State, located in Pocatello, plays its games in Holt Arena, an indoor facility that was the "first covered football stadium on campus in the country," according to ISU officials. Outside, even when weather conditions are not the best, like in late fall, there is hearty and celebratory tailgating taking place. All you have to do is ask Mari Tush and Deb Tompson.

When asked what is special about tailgating at Idaho State, they explained in detail.

"A lot of people don't see each other during the summer, so rekindling friendships during football season is great. A special bond forms with fans, even during a losing season. The scenes surrounding Holt Arena and the fall are terrific.

"It is a kid-friendly atmosphere. Beanbag toss, throwing footballs and other playing games can be seen in the RV area. The ISU Marching Band comes through the tailgate area prior to the game.

"There is one group of tailgaters who have named themselves the Eastside Tailgaters. Terrific tailgate — a game and a food choice (Griz cabobs, Eagle wings and such) are selected. People dress up and decorate their RV spots. Some park their vehicles the night before the game. Typically, folks come three to four hours before game time. Tailgating after games often lasts deep into the evening hours.

"Interestingly, Idaho State law does not allow alcohol on campus, but we can drink responsibly by using Solo Cups. We police ourselves."

A homecoming bonfire is a big tradition at Idaho State. Photo by Bethany Baker.

Buffalo Blue Potatoes

From Donna Hays, Idaho State University Executive Director, Bengal Athletic Boosters & Sport Clubs

INGREDIENTS:

5 cups unpeeled sliced potatoes (1/4-inch); if potatoes are big, slice them lengthwise first

1 red bell pepper sliced into rings

1 medium onion thinly sliced

1/2 cup butter melted

1 to 2 tablespoons Franks RedHot sauce

1/2 teaspoon garlic powder

1/2 cup grated Parmesan cheese

1/2 cup blue cheese crumbles

DIRECTIONS:

• Melt butter in a pan, and add hot sauce and garlic powder. Bring grill to high heat. In a 9x12 grill-proof pan, layer half of the potatoes, peppers and onions. Drizzle half of butter mixture over first layer. Spread blue cheese and 1/4 cup parmesan over layer. Layer remaining potatoes, peppers and onion. Drizzle remainder of butter mixture and top with 1/4 cup parmesan cheese. Cover with foil, lower heat to medium. Place pan on heat and cook indirect for 60 minutes on until potatoes are tender. Remove foil for last 15 minutes to crisp up the top.

Idaho Tailgate Potatoes

From Donna Hays, Idaho State University Executive Director, Bengal Athletic Boosters & Sport Clubs

INGREDIENTS:

3 potatoes, skins on, washed and cut in half, or wedges if you prefer

1/4 cup butter, melted

1/2 cup grated Parmesan cheese

1 tablespoon garlic powder

1 to 2 teaspoons Montreal steak seasoning (to your liking)

DIRECTIONS:

• Preheat gas grill to medium high to high, or stage charcoal to side of kettle and cook indirectly. Melt butter and pour into a 9-inch by 9-inch foil pan. Ensure butter is evenly spread across the bottom of the pan. Sprinkle Parmesan cheese over the butter — be generous! Sprinkle the garlic powder and any other seasonings over the cheese — to the taste you prefer. Lay the potatoes "cut side down" on top of the butter, cheese and garlic powder. Cover with foil. Grill for 45 minutes, while rotating every 10 minutes or so to prevent burning. Allow to cool slightly before serving. Serve with sour cream. Serves four people.

THOUGHTS ON FLOYD & HAYDEN

One of the most appreciated traditions at Iowa is the annual battle with Minnesota in which the winner gains possession of a trophy known as "Floyd of Rosedale." It is a bronze likeness of a pig. It dates back to 1935 when the governors of the two states bet a pig on the outcome of the game.

The original Floyd was a real pig, which led to the bronze statue, which today goes to the winner of the game. Through the 2013 season, Minnesota held a 61-44-2 advantage on the strength of dominating the series in the 1930s and '40s.

When you think of Iowa, you think of Floyd of Rosedale, Nile Kinnick — the 1939 Heisman Trophy winner who lost his life on a training mission during World War II — and head coach Hayden Fry, the colorful Texan who won 143 games for the Hawkeyes in 20 seasons. He took his teams to 13 bowl games, including three trips to Pasadena's Rose Bowl, and won three Big Ten championships.

Nobody had more friends in coaching than Hayden, who coached at North Texas State and Southern Methodist before taking over in Iowa City. His success got him elected to the College Football Hall of Fame in 2003. When Hayden was at SMU, Lee Iacocca, chairman of Ford Motor Company, came into the locker room after SMU had nearly beaten Michigan and announced that Ford would be coming out with a new car, which they would call the "Mustang." Hayden would have been happier to have won the game.

Hayden is a devout aficionado of chili. For Hayden, the hotter the chili the better — spice not heat. Someone once asked him what was the difference between three-alarm chili and four-alarm chili. Hayden, a connoisseur of one-liners, said, "Four-alarm chili is when you put the armadillo in live."

2 Alarm Chili

From Hayden & Shirley Fry
Former head coach at Iowa,
North Texas State and SMU

Note: Coach Fry's friends are aware that he married a terrific cook. He was wise in regard to marrying Shirley. For the record, Shirley says, "Hayden has never cooked anything in his life. He will go hungry first and then find a restaurant."

DIRECTIONS:

• Our chili starts with the Wick Fowler's 2 Alarm Chili Kit, which is not available where we live in Mesquite, Nevada, so I get it online. It is basically a package of seasoning packets (salt optional). We then add ground beef or cut stew meat, tomato sauce and water. I also add pinto beans or sometimes black beans. Then top it with shredded cheese. The kit comes in hot, medium or mild. We have found that chili is great for football weekends. You can get it going early and enjoy before, during or after the games.

Brian Maudsley/Shutterstock

LEXINGTON IS A FULFILLING PLACE

Most college football fans would rather see their favorite team play at home, but when it comes to road games, you would be hard pressed to find a more enjoyable and stimulating atmosphere, a more fulfilling social environment, than Lexington, Kentucky.

The Wildcats, original members of the Southeastern Conference, are better known for their basketball success, but Kentucky has produced some outstanding football players over the years.

Lexington! What a place to visit. When you are in horse country, you find nothing but beautiful farms and white fences, rolling bluegrass pastures with little hoss colts frolicking about. There are classy barns and furrowed tracks, pounding hoofs at post time, and a joyful occasion if you have wagered with a sage eye.

Kentucky is bourbon country, and the distilleries host tours that offer a sample of the limestone-influenced product that makes Kentucky famous and inviting to visitors every year. Ask for a bourbon at a Kentucky tailgate and you will get the finest bourbon made in the Bluegrass State.

Tailgating is big at Kentucky's Commonwealth Stadium. You get the traditional fare of burgers and hot dogs, but you also get burgoo, a traditional stew that always calls for a second helping. Then there are all those bourbon options. Bourbon and burgoo in a bluegrass setting. Kentuckians will tell you they have the finest tailgating atmosphere you will find anywhere.

Keeneland, just outside Lexington, is one of the prettiest horse tracks in the country. There's plenty of bourbon available when you go to the track, but you would be missing something if you didn't order a bowl of burgoo.

Traditionally, when certain SEC teams play Kentucky in Lexington, it is the last Saturday of the fall meeting at Keeneland. There is no better road trip than to Lexington in the fall when the horses are running at Keeneland.

It would be difficult to imagine anybody — including those steadfastly opposed to pari-mutuel betting — coming to the Keeneland Race Course in Lexington and not experiencing a surge in emotions. Gentle excitement permeates, and the mood is forever festive.

Bluegrass, thoroughbreds and autumn leaves in the fall in a pastoral setting — life is good and in order. Kentuckians would have you believe that their bluegrass is the finest of grasses, owing to its limestone influence, the same limestone that makes Kentucky's bourbon unparalleled.

The grounds are kempt and the grass clipped neatly. The landscaping reflects a becoming tidiness in an atmosphere that has a "come hither" appeal to all classes. It can be a rich man/poor man environment, with a lot of variety in between. Choose the clubhouse, and you are required to wear a tie — no jeans allowed — a nice tradition with no quick release in sight. Raise a toast to Keeneland's old-fashioned policy. If you prefer the grandstand and general admission, you likely will mix with the haves as well as the have-nots.

Find a rail position at the paddock where the sleek thoroughbreds parade by, and your anticipation heightens, as Bucky Sallee, of nearby Georgetown, in his green-and-gold jacket and black top hat, steps on the racetrack to call the horses to post. "When the horses leave the paddock, Sallee greets them, with a rift of 'Boots and Saddles,'" Jim Williams, former track public relations director once wrote, "and as post time approaches, he plays a few bars of 'Assembly.'" Those sounds warm the horse aficionados the way college alumni are warmed by the fight song of their alma mater.

Whenever you go to Keeneland, you'll find burgoo, the traditional spicy stew along with Kentucky sweet cornbread. An introduction to Fran Taylor, executive director of the Keeneland Foundation, might bring about possession of her handsome book, *Keeneland Entertains*, a treatise on "traditional bluegrass hospitality and favorite recipes." With Fran's book, you come away a winner even when you failed to connect at the betting window.

Keeneland Burgoo

From Ed Boutilier
Executive chef at Keeneland Race Course
in Lexington, Kentucky

Author's note: I have decided to include this recipe from Keeneland executive chef Ed Boutilier because in the fall, football and burgoo go well together. Don't forget the cornbread muffins!

INGREDIENTS:

1 cup celery, diced

1 cup carrots, diced

1 cup onion, diced

3 pounds stew meat, cubed

1 teaspoon ground thyme

1 teaspoon ground sage

1 teaspoon granulated garlic

1 teaspoon ground oregano

1 12-ounce can diced tomatoes in juice

3 pounds frozen mixed vegetables (corn, lima beans, green beans)

17-ounce can tomato puree

17-ounce can tomato sauce

1 pound frozen okra, sliced

1 tablespoon beef base

1 teaspoon Worcestershire sauce

1 teaspoon lemon juice

1 teaspoon Tabasco

1 cup sherry wine

1 cup red wine

3 pounds potatoes, diced

DIRECTIONS:

• Brown stew meat with herbs and garlic. Add remaining ingredients and cover with water. Bring to a boil and then reduce to a simmer for a minimum of two hours, or until ingredients have been tenderized but do not dissolve. The potatoes should be "fork tender" but hold their shape. Adjust seasoning to taste, and thicken with cornstarch if needed. Serves 10 to 12 people.

Peanut Butter Brownies

From Hal and June Mumme
Former head coach at Kentucky

INGREDIENTS:

8 squares of unsweetened baking chocolate

3 sticks (or 1 1/2 cups) butter

4 cups granulated sugar

6 eggs

1 tablespoon vanilla

2 cups flour

1 10-ounce bag peanut butter chips

DIRECTIONS:

• Preheat oven to 350 degrees. Spray 13-inch by 9-inch baking pan with baking spray, or grease the pan. Microwave chocolate and butter in large microwavable bowl on high for 3 minutes or until chocolate is melted, stirring half at 1 1/2 minutes. With a hand-held mixer, add sugar and vanilla, and then mix. Add eggs two at a time. Add flour and mix well. Stir in one bag of peanut butter chips. Bake for 45 to 50 minutes or until a toothpick comes out with fudgy crumbs. Do not overbake.

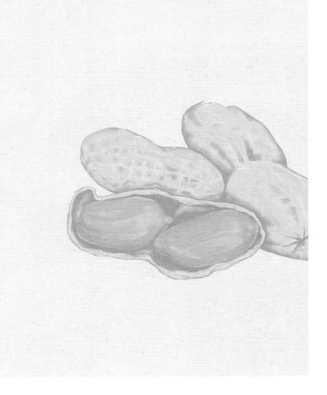

TIGAH TAILGATING

Jambalaya. Crawfish pie. File' gumbo. These aren't just words to a song, which you likely know about if you have any affection for country music and the singing of the late Hank Williams.

"Those," says Bud Johnson, speaking of jambalaya, crawfish pie and file' gumbo, "are just a few of the regional dishes you will find at an LSU tailgate party, items you are unlikely to encounter anywhere else on a football Saturday in the Southeastern Conference."

Johnson — a former LSU Sports Information director, Tiger tailgating aficionado/addict and historian — knows the tailgating scene in Baton Rouge better than anybody. Come along for a good ride into Cajun country and game day at LSU.

"If the Tigers are playing Florida, you will definitely see a gator being grilled at someone's tailgate party," says Bud. "And if Arkansas is in town, there is not just pork roast to sample. You can actually watch someone prepare a pig for the pregame feast.

"'Tigah Tailgating' is unlike any other in these United States," Bud continued. "It is a blend of Carnival, a Louisiana Cajun festival, a music celebration and a seafood fete. The people responsible for this happening have been to the Mardi Gras. Many times. They have been thoroughly taught how to party. They have attended Louisiana festivals in every corner of the state. They love to cook and to compare recipes."

Hold on, because Bud is just getting warmed up.

"LSU fans have never lost a tailgate party," he continued. "There is good food, good music, adult beverages — and people ready to pass a good time. Families have been tailgating in the same location on the LSU campus for generations. They arrive early and stay late. Louisiana, naturally, is well represented, but so too are fans from nearby states. The party sprawls in every direc-

LSU fans prepare a pig prior to a game against Arkansas. Photo courtesy of Bud Johnson.

Tailgate Jambalaya

From George Boudreaux
LSU Superfan

Note from George: Everyone has a different recipe for "their Jambalaya." We have found that the Zatarain's Jambalaya Mix is the easiest and quickest way to make it. We usually use four to eight 40-ounce boxes for our tailgate, and we jazz it up, using the following ingredients and method for each 40-ounce box.

INGREDIENTS:

40 ounces Zatarain's Jambalaya Mix

1 1/4 pounds boneless, skinless chicken cut into serving pieces

1 1/4 pounds sausage, cut into serving pieces

1 cup bellpepper, chopped

1 cup celery, chopped

1 cup onion, chopped

11 1/2 cups chicken broth

1/4 cup vegetable oil

DIRECTIONS:

• Pre-cook the chicken and sausage. In a large cooking container, roaster oven or iron Cajun kettle, add the pre-cooked chicken and sausage, onion, celery and bell pepper (the Holy Trinity of Cajun Cooking), chicken broth, oil and contents of the seasoning packet. Bring the mixture to a rolling boil. Add the contents of the rice package, stir thoroughly and return to a boil. Stir, cover and reduce heat to low. Let simmer for 15 minutes. A low bubbling action should be visible. Check the texture of the rice to determine that it is almost done. Remove from heat. Cover tightly and let stand for 5 minutes. Before serving, stir gently to fluff and mix. Garnish with green onions, if desired. Geaux Tigers!

tion. Everyone has a favorite location. Here are just a few places to visit on your next trip to LSU:

"Go to the grounds in front of Pleasant Hall, and you will find some families from Jackson, Mississippi, who partied in this location for 30 years.

"Go to the Parade Grounds across from the LSU Student Union, and under an oak tree you may be welcomed by Tiger fans from the Florida Panhandle.

"Adjacent to the Bernie Moore Track Stadium you are likely to encounter fun-loving groups from the River Parishes, or the Bayou Country of Houma and Thibodaux. They will invite you to sample their fare and compare it to anything else you will taste on campus. If you are wearing the visitor's colors, be prepared for a feast. They want to impress you with their good food in hopes of converting you to their side before game time.

"For elaborate parties on Friday night, Touchdown Village is the place to go. You will meet LSU fans from Lafayette, Lake Charles, New Orleans, St. Tammany, Monroe, Shreveport, Mississippi and Texas. The folks in the big motor homes spare no expense in their preparations to entertain their guests. If you don't have an invitation, just yell 'Geaux Tigers' a few times. You will discover their password.

"Food and drink are in ample supply everywhere. Most tailgate sites have their own music, giant TV screens and a theme. Costumes are prevalent. Some groups have their own program, beginning with the "Star-Spangled Banner." Others award prizes for the best costumes and best recipes. If you haven't tried tailgating in Tigah Country, you have missed a one-of-a-kind experience.

"Many tailgaters at LSU favor locations near Tiger Stadium — the Indian Mounds, the Journalism Building, the Pete Maravich Assembly Center and Mike the Tiger's Habitat. They prefer the proximity to Victory Hill. The LSU team walks down Victory Hill on their way to the stadium at an advertised time. No one wants to miss that. Another major punctuation of the day for the tailgaters is the arrival of the Golden Band from Tigerland — also marching down Victory Hill. They get the crowd fired up by playing two different fight songs. When it seems that everyone in earshot is ready to play in the game, the band marches into the stadium. The times of these events are published in the newspaper and on websites. Many families line the street an hour before the scheduled time for a good view of Les Miles and his boys — and the Tiger Band.

"Touchdown Village is not the dominant story of Tigah Tailgating, but for memorable Louisiana cooking in a central location, it's hard to beat. Touchdown Village is located at the corner of Highland Road and Nicholson Extension on the LSU campus. More than 600 motor homes park there for Tiger home football games. Some have arrived as early as Thursday. Most depart by noon Sunday. For some, the tailgate party, which sometimes lasts for the better part of two days, rivals the game.

"One of the most colorful characters in Touchdown Village and one of its noteworthy chefs is George Boudreaux of Covington, Louisiana. He takes his brand of hospitality to home games, to road games and to Omaha for the College World Series. He prepares shrimp, crab or jambalaya for his guests wherever he goes and often feeds from 150 to 300 guests on a football weekend in Baton Rouge.

"'We cook not only for our guests, but for anyone who might stop by our motor home,' George says. 'I can't ever remember running out of food. You sure can meet a lot of people — and have a good time, too.' Shrimp, crawfish, marinated oysters, fried catfish and even stuffed flounder can be found on the menu at nearby motor homes in Touchdown Village. A visitor can be selective.

"'We entertain LSU fans and also those from the opposing schools,' George continued. 'People who follow Kentucky or West Virginia don't usually eat Louisiana seafood at a tailgate party. They never forget our tail-

gate party. They invite us to come see them when LSU plays on their campus. It is not uncommon to find an LSU celebrity such as Athletics Director Joe Alleva or baseball coach Paul Mainieri at one of the Boudreaux's tailgate parties on a Friday night before a home game.'

"Boudreaux has traveled to most of the SEC schools in his colorfully decorated motor home, which is as unforgettable as his cooking. His seafood servings have become favorites at many places in the SEC. A trip to Auburn is one of his favorite memories. George and his wife, Debbie, brought 350 pounds of fresh shrimp to their tailgate party on the Plains. 'The Auburn fans had

(Top and above) Cooking small alligators is popular at LSU when Florida comes to Baton Rouge. Photos courtesy of Miles Williams.

You will always find crawfish etouffee at LSU tailgate parties. Photo courtesy of Bud Johnson.

Crawfish Etouffee

From George Boudreaux
LSU Superfan

INGREDIENTS:

2 cups butter

1 cup onion, finely chopped

1 cup celery, finely chopped

2 tablespoons minced garlic

Salt (to taste)

Pepper (to taste)

2 cups green onions, finely chopped

6 pounds blanched crawfish tails

3 tablespoons all-purpose flour

6 cups chicken stock

1 cup chopped parsley

DIRECTIONS:

• Melt butter in a large skillet or Dutch oven, and then saute onion and celery until tender, about 10 to 15 minutes. Add minced garlic, green onions and crawfish tails, and simmer 5 to 10 minutes. Blend flour into the mixture and add chicken stock, stirring constantly until thoroughly mixed. Continue cooking over medium heat for 15 to 20 minutes, stirring occasionally. When sauce is thickened, fold in parsley. Season with salt and pepper to taste. Serve over hot rice. Serves about 20 people.

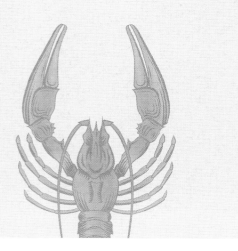

such a good time at our party,' Boudreaux says, 'that they wanted us to come back for their next home game.'

"Boudreaux is famous in Louisiana as the pharmacist who created Boudreaux's Butt Paste, a cream originally designed for the treatment of diaper rash. Now, parents and professional athletes sing its praises. He has since sold the company but remains as a promotional consultant for his creation."

Perhaps, you could say after all that is that Boudreaux is famous throughout the Pelican State for relieving pain — whether it is on your backside or from hunger!

THEY DO THINGS DIFFERENT IN BATON ROUGE

"It's Saturday night in Tiger Stadium!' What glorious words those are to hear as the crowd roars in approval just before kickoff on fall Saturday evenings on the campus of LSU in one of the great college football settings there is," says longtime LSU tailgater Miles Williams. "I personally attended my first game when I was 8 years old in the fall of 1969. I've been hooked ever since. Through victory and defeat, good seasons and bad, I have always been grateful for the wonderful experience that is LSU football — there is no game-day experience quite like it."

I'll let Miles tell the rest of the Baton Rouge tailgating story.

"Our traditions are a little different than others," Miles continued. "Like our great state, the LSU fan base is unique. We play football at night, and as loyal Tiger fans, we play hard all day getting ready 'to make a difference' in Death Valley when the sun goes down. We take great pride in our reputation as one of the loudest, most rabid fan bases there is. The setting can be very intimidating to the visiting team, and we believe that we really do influence the outcome of the game. In true Les Miles fashion, our coach once said 'Tiger Stadium

LSU fans prepare a batch of jambalaya. Photo courtesy of Bud Johnson.

is where opponent's dreams come to die.' If you are a Tigah fan, you gotta love it.

"My earliest remembrances of tailgating involved going with family friends, as my parents were not in position to bring me themselves. We had one very gracious family, the Percys, who set aside two tickets per game for my family to share. I have six brothers, so each of us was able to attend two or three games a year. They shared an RV with another family, and I have the greatest memories of throwing the football for hours before games, piling into the games just before dark in a group of 20 or so, and then throwing the football for two hours after the games in the dark until the traffic cleared out. And as you might guess, almost every time, the end of the all-day event involved them waking me up in the back of the RV because they were dropping me back at home at 1 a.m. If we won, I couldn't wait to get up the next morning to read every part of the sports page. If we lost, I couldn't bear to read anything until Thursday or Friday before the next game.

"Over the years our tailgating experience has 'matured' into a three-day logistical/spiritual/social event. It begins by getting the RV (ours is a 45-foot Mountain Aire) out of storage after lunch on Friday. This is generally a two-man job that includes getting diesel and filling up the water tanks. In the meantime the Sam's Club run is underway to get all the accompaniments to the planned menu for the weekend. And let's not forget bottled water, soft drinks, ice and adult beverages — especially purple and gold Bud Light to set the mood.

"We then gather at the house to load everything up — barbeque pits, ice chests, prepped foods, snacks, drinks and all the extras that we've gotten together to execute the menu that we decided on earlier in the week. After loading, we take the RV out to campus five miles away, usually getting there an hour or so before dark. At that point a few folks will gather while coming home from work to help with the preliminary set up. What that really means is that we run out the RV slides, put down the outdoor carpets, get out a few chairs and have cocktail hour in the shadow of Tiger Stadium. ESPN is on the TV and music is playing in the background from all of our RV neighbors who mostly roll in from out of town, places like Lafayette, Shreveport, Houma, Biloxi and Houston. Next thing you know we are in the middle of the low-key pre-party that only the diehards really appreciate. There's not a bunch of whooping and hollering — just a bunch of dedicated LSU fans relaxing, visiting and talking football in anticipation of a Saturday of tailgating

Les' Favorite Tuna

From Les and Kathy Miles
Head coach at LSU

INGREDIENTS:

Fancy Albacore Solid White Tuna
Hellmann's Real Mayonnaise
Chopped onions
Chopped Kosher Dill Pickles

DIRECTIONS:

- Mix all together and serve with crackers.

Even though the weather is usually hot on the LSU campus, the chili is even hotter. Photo courtesy of Bud Johnson.

and college football — south Louisiana style. After a few hours we shut it down for the night and head home to catch the news and high school football scores, and the end of the Friday night college game on ESPN.

"Our spot is really special. It is located where right field used to be on LSU's old baseball field, the original Alex Box Stadium. From where we are you can look east across Nicholson Drive and see the mammoth west side of Tiger Stadium. Less than a mile to the west is the Mississippi River.

"Our menu, prepared by men who are expert and versatile, usually has a theme depending on opponent and weather. You see pots, burners, barbecue pits, oyster shucking table and utensils to prepare for breakfast some days. Then there is barbecue, seafood trifecta, gumbo, wild-game day, jambalaya and Gator balls. All of this for family, friends and anyone that walks by, but especially visiting fans, as we share with our neighbors.

"Excitement builds as kickoff approaches. Then, hand out tickets, head to stadium. This is what we came for. After the game, in victory or defeat, we tailgate, eat leftovers, and talk about the game and other games.

"Then it's over, but guess what? We get to do it all over again next Saturday."

A fan stirs a batch of gator picadillo. Photo courtesy of KathyMillerTime.com

This is George Boudreaux's pregame setup in Touchdown Village. Photo courtesy of George Boudreaux.

A MIAMI TAILGATING FLASHBACK

John Underwood, whose cogent verbiage at *Sports Illustrated* segued into several books, grew up in Miami — a real Conch, who couldn't leave the water.

When he joined *SI*, writers and editors all lived a relatively short train ride from the office in Manhattan. John lived in Connecticut but longed for the balmy temperatures and the azure waters of his native city. He lobbied successfully for an arrangement, the first writer at the magazine to pull this off, where he could live in Miami and travel on assignment. What is the difference in embarking out of LaGuardia as opposed to Miami International, anyway?

This enabled John to sail, fish and enjoy the sun when there was down time. It also meant that he could follow his favorite college team, the Miami Hurricanes.

Miami plays its games today at Sun Life Stadium in Miami Gardens, but in Underwood's time, the Hurricanes played in the old Orange Bowl. The Orange Bowl was built in 1937 and was surrounded by a cozy neighborhood. People would drive in for Hurricane games and

Tabbouleh

From Donna Shalala
President at the University of Miami

INGREDIENTS:

1 cup of finely cracked wheat
Juice of 5 or 6 lemons (about 1 cup)
2 cups of chopped fresh mint leaves
1 1/2 cups of seeded, chopped tomato
3 bunches of scallions, trimmed and sliced
1 tablespoon of extra virgin olive oil
Salt
Freshly ground pepper

DIRECTIONS:

• Soak the wheat in the lemon juice overnight. Using your hands, squeeze as much liquid as possible from the soaked wheat and place it in a serving bowl. Add the parsley, mint, tomato and scallions. Drizzle on the oil and toss. Season to taste with salt and pepper. It makes 4 to 6 servings. Note that it is important to dry the parsley and mint, and to drain the tomatoes well. You can replace some of the lemon juice with water if desired.

Shutterstock

Irresistible Brie

From John and Donna Underwood
Author and Miami native

INGREDIENTS:

1 pound wheel brie cheese, rind removed

1 cup chopped pecans

2 cups brown sugar

2 tablespoons vodka

DIRECTIONS:

- Preheat oven to 300 degrees. Place brie on an oven-proof serving dish. Cover top of the brie with pecans. Pat brown sugar over the top, and drizzle with vodka. Heat for 8 to 10 minutes or until brie melts. Serve with unsalted crackers.

find parking places in the neighborhoods. They would pay $10 to park in a yard where they set up their tailgate.

"Tailgating in somebody's back yard became a tradition," Underwood says with a laugh. "It was very collegial, and like everywhere else, the tailgating tradition became almost as important as the games themselves."

If you have ever flown into Miami over the Atlantic, you may have noticed what look like fishing shacks sitting atop several poles in the ocean. They are fishing shacks built in the old days as retreats. Some were used for gambling and other illicit activities. They are beginning to disappear. By law, once a house on stilts — a community of which brought about the name "Stiltsville" — collapses, it can't be rebuilt or replaced. "Some of my favorite tailgate parties," says Underwood, "were in Stiltsville." You could always catch a fish and take it to the next Hurricanes neighborhood tailgate party.

You may remember some of Underwood's classic books: *Bear*, about you-know-who at Alabama, and *The Science of Hitting with Ted Williams*. Thirty years ago, John wrote *The Death of an American Game*, suggesting that money and greed were capable of destroying college football. We are now beginning to appreciate what he was writing about way back then.

Shutterstock

Blondie Recipe

From John and Ingrid Harbaugh
Miami of Ohio alum, head coach of
the Baltimore Ravens

INGREDIENTS:

2 cups brown sugar

1/2 cup Crisco shortening

2 eggs

1 cup chocolate chips

1 teaspoon vanilla

2 cups flour

1 teaspoon baking powder

1/2 teaspoon salt

1/4 teaspoon baking soda

DIRECTIONS:

• Preheat oven to 350 degrees. Cream together shortening, sugar, eggs and vanilla in electric mixer or by hand. Add remaining ingredients and pour into a greased 13-inch by 9-inch pan. Bake for 25 minutes or so, but it is better to under bake a little more than over bake. Best eaten the same day! Great to make the morning of a tailgating event. Enjoy!

IT'S ABOUT GOOD FOOD & GOOD PEOPLE

By Gaspare Calandrino, the Ultimate UM Tailgater

What makes a good tailgate? Easy! Good food and good people. Tailgating at your college is like returning home to friends and family. Most of us see our tailgate family more than we see blood relatives. We've seen births, deaths, weddings, divorces and everything else a normal family experiences.

There is nothing quite like strolling the campus or the your old haunts in the college town you attended. The crisp air and beautiful colors of falling leaves of a Midwest college bring back many great memories. The University of Michigan is no different. It's always enjoyable to walk through the Diag, past the Burton Tower,

Angel Hall, Engineers Arch, past the Union where John F. Kennedy announced the Peace Corps and through the stately beauty of the Law Quad. You can visit the local restaurants and pubs on South University Street and buy the latest in Wolverine swag for the game. With UM nestled in the small town of Ann Arbor, the downtown is easily accessible with a couple of good legs.

While many Michigan fans tailgate at the golf course, some are also in prioritized pass lots. We have tailgated in the Grey Lot near Yost Ice Arena, the track and Wilpon Baseball Complex for over 30 years. We host anywhere from 40 to over 100 people, including guests from the opposing school. We have hosted bowl representatives, college and professional athletes, media members, astronauts, the NHL's Stanley Cup and live bands. We also sport our own "tailgate logo" we've embroidered on jackets, shirts and hats.

My typical tailgate week starts on Thursday. I buy food, beverages and anything that needs refilling. Friday I ice down the coolers, and purchase buns and perishables. I fill my SUV with eight 6-foot tables, a genera-

Don Sweeney, left, and Gaspare Calandrino with a ham outside Yost Ice Arena on the Michigan campus.

GRIESE SPOON CHEESEBURGERS

From Brian Griese
Former Michigan quarterback &
MVP of the 1998 Rose Bowl

INGREDIENTS:

1 1/2 pounds ground beef (serves 6)

1/4 cup Worcestershire sauce

1 egg

1/2 cup bread crumbs

2 tablespoons garlic powder

Salt

Pepper

6 slices cheddar cheese

6 hamburger buns

DIRECTIONS:

• Mix all ingredients together in a large bowl and then form 6 patties. Grill the burgers over medium-high heat for 3 minutes, and then flip them and grill for 4 to 6 more minutes. Add cheese and then cover for 1 minute, remove and eat!

Note from Brian: You can season the patties with Tony's Creole Seasoning before grilling to add some zip. You can also top them with lettuce, sweet onions, dill pickles and mustard.

tor, three to five coolers, six to eight 24-gallon plastic containers filled with food, cups, plates, alcohol, cooking utensils, serving platters, knives, tent canopies and charcoal, and I strap the grill onto a trailer hitch. I use a checklist to remember what to pack. Everything has a specific place in the SUV in order to get it all to fit. Others bring chairs, TV, satellite dish, heaters, and more food and drink.

Game-day Saturday I get up at 3 a.m. and drive to Ann Arbor for the 6 a.m. parking lot opening. I have help unloading and setting up the site. Everyone has their specific job. Those unfortunate to not have a ticket are usually found guarding the cooler and grill while watching the game on a big-screen TV with satellite dish. Many volunteer to give up their ticket to help out with this duty.

We consider the football game as halftime of the tailgate. The tailgate continues two to four hours after the game while we celebrate a UM victory as the traffic subsides. Sunday I unload the SUV, clean washable plates and utensils, empty and clean food and beverage coolers, dry tents if needed, refill the generator with gas, and start the process over for the next game.

Chih Lee sets up his Chinese buffet for a tailgate party.

Karl Kroshinsky, Tom Keller and Jim Tachar carve a tailgating turkey.

Wolverine Chili

From Lloyd and Laurie Carr
Former head coach at Michigan

INGREDIENTS:

2 pounds ground beef

2 cups sliced onions

1 cup diced celery

Dash of garlic powder

2 large cans stewed tomatoes

2 1/2 tablespoons chili powder

1/2 cup cold water

2 teaspoons salt

1 tablespoon sugar

1 tablespoon Worchestershire sauce

1 large can kidney beans

1 large can chili hot beans

Dash of Tabasco sauce

DIRECTIONS:

• Brown ground beef, add onions, celery and garlic. When the onions are wilted, add tomatoes, chili powder that has been mixed with water, salt, Tabasco, sugar and Worchestershire sauce. Simmer for 45 minutes. Add drained beans and cook for 20 minutes.

Our food consists of regular stuff like burgers, brats, hot dogs, steak, Cajun salmon, shrimp, chips, dips and plenty of sweets. We have also had a ham, deep-fried turkey, lobster, Italian beef, Philly cheese steaks, chili, stews and peameal bacon. We have had almost every creature that appeared on Noah's Ark on the grill at some point through the years. Most of our grilled fare is cut into bite-sized pieces and served on a platter to be eaten on a "stick" — a fork given to each attendee.

For beverages we have a full bar with blender, coffee and hot chocolate maker, water, sports drinks, soft drinks and plenty of cold beer, and our famous Jell-O and pudding shots in all flavors, including some non-alcohol shots for the kids.

We sometimes have themes like a Hawaiian tailgate complete with flowered shirts, grass skirts and umbrella drinks, a Chinese buffet tailgate with catered food from one of our own tailgater's restaurant, and "band games" where we hire a live band.

Tailgaters start heading to 112,000-seat Michigan Stadium in time to see the Marching Band take the field 20 minutes before kickoff and to see the team run onto the field though the tunnel to touch the "M Club Supports You" banner at midfield. The singing of the "Victors" is also looked forward to after another Michigan victory.

Then we head back for the second half of the tailgate. After all, it is better to sit celebrating with another burger and a cold beverage watching the later games than it is to sit in traffic while the equivalent of three times Ann Arbor's normal population makes its way to the highways and home.

And then we do it all over again the next week! Go Blue!

THE PEOPLE MAKE THE GROVE

By John Currence, owner and chef at City Grocery

I came to Oxford from New Orleans in 1992. I knew of The Grove, but had never experienced it. It would be a decade before I first attended, as running restaurants — combined with football weekend crowds — conspire to keep a man busy. In those years, I saw the happy faces, I heard the stories, but indulging in it eluded me.

To say my first impression, as I strolled into the fray, was "overwhelming" would be a disservice to the word. The Grove is a hundred times that, and we just don't have a word that approaches the magnitude of it, short of "suffocatingly impressive." The scene is a 14-acre seething mass of red, white and blue nylon popup tents, seersucker, chino, bourbon and coke, pimento cheese, charcoal lighter fluid and smoke, Chanel No. 5 and Axe Body Wash. Coat and tie is more common here than in mass at St. John's Catholic Church, just a stone's throw away. And every inch of the green space The Grove occupies is laid claim to by one soul or another, some for generations. It is a joyous gathering, but is one as exclusive as it is ebullient.

Red and blue are the colors of record. Rarely do you see opposing fans weaving through the pathways of The Grove, and even less frequently do you see them sharing a drink with local fans. The Grove, quite simply, is a church of college football. It is a religion for one. It is where mention of men like Charlie Flowers, Archie Manning and Johnny Vaught bring both silence and bellowing cheers to a room. It is where ladies are still treated as such. It is where you love Ole Miss or leave it.

By all accounts, 50,000 — you often hear it is much more than that — Ole Miss faithful will gather under the oaks in The Grove each Saturday the Rebels play in Oxford. They travel from all corners of the country. Their dedication to their team is not uncommon, but their ritual is. Set up for tents and tables happens at a predetermined time each week and happens like a somewhat civilized version of the 1840s gold rush. A rope drops and people appear from every crevasse like cockroaches, and the grounds go from dead empty to covered in a matter of minutes. They dress for the occasion. Whether it be what they wear or set the table with, propriety rules the day. Silver service, linen and chandeliers are not at all uncommon. Each week, several hours before kickoff, the team gathers for a walk through The Grove. Thousands line a walkway eight or 10 deep to high-five their favorite players and build their boys up. At game time, they leave their valuables, coolers and flat-screen TVs and head for the stadium with little fear of purloining. It's a beautiful thing that this kind of scene can still exist.

It looks like St. Charles Avenue on Mardi Gras night when it is all over. But in perfect rhythm, a cleaning crew sweeps in, and before the dew is burned off on Sunday morning, it is spotless.

I have tried to find my entry point on those Saturdays for years, but I am not an alum and fear I will forever be relegated to carpetbagger status. I can find a glass of bourbon or a cold beer from time to time, but I will

THE MANNINGS KNOW GOOD COOKING

With a longtime residency in New Orleans, dating back to Archie Manning's rookie year with the Saints in 1971, the Mannings know about good cooking — and not just from the many elite restaurants in the French Quarter.

Olivia, Archie's wife, came from a Southern cooking background, growing up in Mississippi. Whenever a Manning shows up in Oxford, Mississippi, he or she is a regular at City Grocery, the best-known restaurant in Oxford. Chef John Currence has a national reputation, and food aficionados from Memphis often drive down to dinner.

"The Mannings love to eat at our restaurants, and we love feeding them," Currence proudly says.

Led by the matriarch of the Manning family, we are also including recipes from the spouses of the Manning boys. Bon appetite!

never lay claim to Saturday real estate because it is not my birthright or scholastic right. It is welcoming and it is warm. It is convivial and it is civilized. It is curious and confounding. It is a place for those who love Ole Miss and Oxford. It is steadfast in its exclusivity. And these are all things I love.

So I will continue to paddle through the crowd, knowing I will find a friendly face and a three-finger pour of liquid courage here and there. I will celebrate wins and suffer similar pain in loss. I will wear the colors and purport myself accordingly. And while I am at peace with knowing I will never own a slice of the legacy, I will always be a little lost in the crowd.

I am inspired by a dedication to this place and have grown to love it like my own. The Grove is, as it turns out, not the oaks and tents and coolers and pompons and the seven-layer dips that make it the place it is. It's the people in it. They are people with an indelible passion for a past glory. They are people with an unconditional love for a perennial underdog. They are people who truly believe great things are possible. And, most importantly, they are my people — whether they like it or not.

DR. KHAYAT REFLECTS ON THE GROVE

Robert Khayat was a three-year letterman at the University of Mississippi and later played three years of pro football with the Washington Redskins, making it to the Pro Bowl as a kicker. He was an accomplished student-athlete who later became chancellor of Ole Miss. Dr. Khayat lives in Oxford today and is a frequent visitor to The Grove, which he expresses his affection for in the following essay:

The Grove at Ole Miss
When the trees reach high their branches
To the whispering southern breeze

This verse from the Ole Miss "Alma Mater" rings familiar to all those who have visited The Grove at Ole Miss...Fourteen acres of gently rolling green space resting in the shade of oak, maple, dogwood and sycamore of varying ages.

Shrimp Appetizer

From Archie and Olivia Manning
Parents of great quarterbacks,
Ole Miss alums

INGREDIENTS:

6 pounds raw shrimp in shells
2 bay leaves
1 teaspoon celery seed
1/4 cup salt
1 teaspoon cayenne pepper
2 cups oil
1/2 cup catsup
3 tablespoons lemon juice
1/4 cup apple cider vinegar
1 tablespoon Worcestershire sauce
1 5-ounce jar fresh horseradish
1 5-ounce jar hot Creole mustard
1 cup thinly sliced yellow onion
Salt
Pepper

DIRECTIONS:

• Make this a day ahead. In a large pot, place shrimp and cover with water. Add bay leaves, celery seed, cayenne pepper and salt. Bring to a boil and cook five minutes until shrimp are pink. Drain and peel. Combine remaining ingredients. Add shrimp. Cover and refrigerate. Serve on toothpicks or on crackers.

For 166 years, students, faculty, staff, alumni and visitors have experienced the loving embrace of this hallowed ground. As one enters the historic Ole Miss campus, his initial greeting is from The Grove and the message is clear: "Welcome — I am here to serve you."

Best known to most as America's premier game-day picnic site, The Grove is a versatile sanctuary that accommodates young lovers, annually welcomes thousands of parents, relatives and friends for commencement, provides an amphitheater for concerts and a playground for weekend Frisbee, football and softball. Young parents strolling children or tossing a ball — weddings and receptions — and summer dance and cheerleader camps affirm the utility of the generous, beautiful space.

(continued on page 107)

Jake Gibbs' "Damn Yankee" Ribeye

INGREDIENTS:

1 12- to 14-pound slab of ribeye
Olive oil
Salt
Pepper
1/2 cup Worcestershire sauce
1 1/2 teaspoons garlic powder
Aluminum foil

DIRECTIONS:

• Take the ribeye and rub it down with olive oil. Add a teaspoon of salt and pepper. Place in roasting pan with 12 ounces of water to keep it moist. Put in oven at 450 degrees, meat uncovered, for 30 minutes. After 30 minutes, add 1/2 cup of Worcestershire sauce on top of the ribeye. Spread 1 1/2 teaspoons of garlic power evenly across the top of the meat. Place back in the oven, but lower the temperature to 325 degrees, and cook for an hour. Then turn the temperature down to 250 degrees and cook for 1 1/2 hours. At this point, also put a cover over the meat; if you don't have a large pan with a cover, then use aluminum foil. If you like it rare, don't cook quite as long.

Note: Every 30 minutes, collect the juices on the bottom of the pan and put on the top of the meat to keep it moist.

JAKE GIBBS: A VERSATILE ATHLETE

Jake Gibbs was one of the most accomplished in a long line of Ole Miss quarterbacks. In addition to making All-America and leading the Rebels to an SEC championship in both football and baseball, Jake was quarterback of the Ole Miss team that won the national football title in 1960.

Jake then signed a big-bonus contract with the New York Yankees, playing 10 years in baseball's Big Leagues. He later returned to coach football and baseball at his alma mater but spent much of his post-campus career managing and coaching for the Yankees. He longed to return home in the offseason — to Oxford where the living is easy, laidback and peaceful.

In fact, he turned down opportunities to remain with the Yankees because of Oxford's allure, which prompted the late owner of the Yankees, George Steinbrenner, to remark, "We really like Jake and wanted to keep him active in our organization, but we just can't get him out of Mississippi."

Jake, a versatile athlete, is quite adept when it comes to his backyard grill, his specialty being ribeye steak.

Shutterstock

Pound Cake

From Cooper & Ellen Manning

INGREDIENTS:

2 sticks butter

3 cups sugar

6 eggs

3 cups flour

1 cup whipping cream

1 teaspoon vanilla

DIRECTIONS:

• In a large bowl, cream butter and add sugar gradually. Beat in eggs one at a time. Add flour alternately with cream, blending well. Add vanilla. Pour into greased and floured tube pan. Place in cold oven. Turn to 325 degrees and bake 1 hour and 15 minutes, or until a toothpick inserted in center comes out clean. Cool in pan 30 minutes before turning out. Do not be concerned that it shrinks after it comes out of the oven.

Jalapeno Crescent Pinwheels

From Hugh and Jill Freeze
Head coach at Ole Miss

INGREDIENTS:

2 8-ounce boxes of cream cheese, softened

3 cans crescent sheets

1 can diced jalapeno, drained

DIRECTIONS:

• Mix cream cheese and jalapeno. Roll out crescent sheets and spread with cream cheese mixture. Roll up long ways and press seam together. Slice into 1-inch pinwheels. Place on cookie sheet and bake at 350 degrees for 8 to 11 minutes. Makes about 40 to 45 pinwheels.

Fudge Brownies

From Eli and Abby Manning
Former Ole Miss quarterback

INGREDIENTS:

2 1-ounce squares of semi-sweet chocolate

1/2 cup butter

1/2 cup flour

1 cup sugar

1/2 cup finely chopped nuts

Frosting for brownies

1 1-ounce square unsweetened chocolate

1 tablespoon butter

2 cups powdered sugar

2 teaspoons vanilla

2 or 3 tablespoons boiling water

DIRECTIONS:

Brownies:

• Preheat oven to 350 degrees. In a small saucepan, melt chocolate and butter. In a large bowl, sift flour and sugar. To flour mixture, add nuts, eggs, chocolate and butter. Mix well. Pour into 8-inch by 8-inch greased pan and bake 20 to 25 minutes.

Frosting:

• In a saucepan, melt chocolate and butter. Stir in sugar and vanilla. Add water. Beat vigorously 3 to 5 minutes. Frost brownies after they have cooled, and then cut in squares. Should be very moist. Makes 16.

Shutterstock

It has been said that Ole Miss is "mood and spirit" and, to a great extent, The Grove inspired those words.

For the academic community, the tone of the campus is set by The Grove. Faculty and students recognize and draw from the sanctity and beauty of the landscape which wash away the tension and pace of the outer world.

For commencement audiences, The Grove extends its arms and embraces the celebrants by providing a stage worthy of the milestone in the lives of the graduates and their families. As the pre-processional music floats across the land and through the trees, the joy of the occasion implies a victory song.

The spectacle of 2,500 participants converging on the scene, clad in academic regalia, excites the audience of 10,000 family members, friends and observers. A sense of communal achievement shines through the symbolism and formality of the program....unexpressed but deeply felt awareness of the family journey begun in the nursery, through kindergarten and 12 grades of "formal" education. Conferring degrees, presenting diplomas and recognizing the special awards recipients complete the "exercise" in the midst of cameras flashing, handshakes and hugs. Truly a moment to remember.

These graduates and thousands of others will participate time after time, year after year in pregame picnics on beautiful autumn Saturdays. Friendships are renewed and the finest southern cuisine consumed to the melo-

dies of the Pride of the South Ole Miss Marching Band as thousands gather in colorful tents resting comfortably in the safety and sanctity of The Grove.

The revelers begin to arrive before daylight to claim a small area for their tents, tables and chairs, and to "spread" the picnic fare. Regardless of the time the game is to begin, the party is underway early and lasts late into the evening.

Ostensibly, all have come to witness a football game. In reality, the picnic in The Grove is as much a part of the game as the blocking, tackling, running, passing and kicking. Our old friend we call The Grove is the magnet that brings friends together — young and old — from across the nation to enjoy a day being fed by the unique relationships between the people and the land.

Regardless of one's interest in football or one's school affiliation, life is incomplete until you enjoy game day in The Grove at Ole Miss.

But sanctity and designation as hallowed ground require more than picnics, fun and games. Places our society identifies as holy must be home to the serious, somber events of our lives as well.

The Dogwood Garden within The Grove is such a place. When tragedy struck our campus in 1987, five young women were killed in a pedestrian-automobile accident that stunned our community. Absent war or natural disaster, multiple deaths of students are rare and we have no model for dealing with the pain and reality

BBQ Wings & German Sweet Potato Salad

From John Currence
Chef/Owner at City Grocery Restaurant
Group in Oxford, Mississippi

INGREDIENTS:

Buffalo BBQ Sauce:

2 tablespoons bacon fat

1 tablespoon grape seed oil

2 teaspoons minced garlic

1/2 cup red onion, diced small

2 cups KC Masterpiece BBQ Sauce (or your favorite)

1 cup pork or veal stock

3 cups apple cider vinegar

1 teaspoon Liquid Smoke

2 teaspoons red pepper flakes

2 teaspoons black pepper

1/2 cup coffee

1 pinch cinnamon

German Sweet Potato Salad:

1/2 gallon sweet potatoes, diced and boiled*

1 cup Big Bad Bacon Bits

2 cups minced yellow onion

1/2 cup apple cider vinegar

1/2 cup sherry vinegar

1 1/2 cups grainy mustard

3 tablespoons brown sugar

1 cup boiled egg, chopped

1/2 cup parsley, chopped

1 cup scallions, chopped

Salt

Black pepper

DIRECTIONS:

Buffalo BBQ Sauce:

• Saute onion and garlic in bacon fat and oil until transparent. Stir in remaining ingredients and simmer over low heat until reduced by one-third. Season with salt and black pepper to taste.

Wings:

• Fry wings in a manner that is your favorite. Remove from oil and drain on a brown paper bag. Place wings in a stainless bowl and toss with enough of the BBQ sauce to coat. Serve warm.

German Sweet Potato Salad:

• Whisk together vinegars, mustard and sugar, and set aside. Combine rest of the ingredients in a stainless bowl and pour dressing over the top. Season to taste with salt and black pepper.

*Start peeled diced sweet potatoes in salted room temperature water and bring them slowly up to a boil. Let them cook ONLY until you can pierce them easily with a fork, but they hold their shape nicely. Remove them from the water immediately, place in a single layer on a cookie sheet and place sheet in fridge to cool.

---

of the moment. Our loss of vital, young members of the community was, of course, marked by profound sadness and deep regret. That painful day has not been forgotten.

Human beings are resilient and almost always find ways to live with the unimaginable horror of pre-mature death. As a permanent reminder of promise, youth and beauty, a group of dogwood trees were planted in The Grove as a memorial to the lives of those wonderful women. The trees are gently nurtured by our landscape staff and provide the spiritual beauty of youth as the white cross-shaped blossoms appear each spring. Hallowed ground.

Following a visit to the Grand Canyon, Mr. Percy wrote:

"I almost died at the sign of it. It is God's most personal creation; you feel He has just walked off and is expected back any moment."

I suspect the gentleman would have had a similar experience had he witnessed a sunrise across The Grove at Ole Miss.

— *Robert C. Khayat, Chancellor, 1995-2009*

Rebel Yell Salad

From former Ole Miss Chancellor Robert Khayat, who also played football at Mississippi

INGREDIENTS:

1/3 cup balsamic vinegar

1 tablespoon hot & sweet mustard

1/4 cup fresh parsley, chopped

1/2 teaspoon salt

1/4 teaspoon freshly ground pepper

1/2 teaspoon Creole seasoning

1/4 cup extra virgin olive oil

2 ears fresh corn, cooked, kernels off cob (about 1 1/2 cups)

1/2 pound fresh black-eyed peas, seasoned and cooked with ham or bacon

1 medium red bell pepper, chopped

1 medium Vidalia or red onion, chopped

3 stalks celery, chopped

DIRECTIONS:

• Blend vinegar, mustard, parsley, salt, pepper and Creole seasoning. Whisk in oil and set aside. Combine corn, peas, bell pepper, onion and celery. Toss dressing with vegetables and refrigerate until ready to serve, but not longer than 12 hours.

Hotty Toddy Peppers

From Robert and Patti Fabris Former Ole Miss letterman

INGREDIENTS:

12 jalapeno peppers

1 package of ground Jimmy Dean's regular sausage

1 large cream cheese

Creole seasoning

Cheddar cheese, shredded

DIRECTIONS:

• Wash the peppers and slice in half lengthwise. Seed and hull the peppers, and then place on a foil-lined cookie sheet. Brown the sausage and drain. Place sausage back into pan and add cream cheese. Blend together over low heat. Season to taste. Let mixture cool slightly and fill pepper halves. Top with shredded cheese and bake at 350 degrees for approximately 15 minutes or until cheese melts and peppers begin to soften. You can make these the day before. Add cooking time if the peppers have been refrigerated. You can also use Italian sausage and top with mozzarella cheese. This recipe is easy to cater to your individual tastes. These peppers disappear quickly each time we make them for The Grove!

The Grove on the Ole Miss campus.

Shout Hallelujah Potato Salad

From John T. Edge and Blair Hobbs
Southern Foodways Alliance at
the University of Mississippi

INGREDIENTS:

5 pounds petite yellow-fleshed potatoes (such as Yukon Golds)
4 hard-cooked eggs, peeled
1 4-ounce jar diced pimentos, drained
4 large drops of Tabasco
2 teaspoons celery salt
2 tablespoons seasoned rice wine vinegar
2 tablespoons fresh lemon juice
1 cup sweet salad cube pickles
1 tablespoon extra-virgin olive oil
1 cup plus 2 tablespoons mayonnaise
1/4 cup prepared yellow mustard
1 or 2 seeded and minced jalapeño peppers
1/2 cup of red onion, chopped
1/2 cup of green bell pepper, chopped
4 stalks of celery, chopped
1/4 cup flat-leaf parsley, chopped
Salt
Ground black pepper
2 teaspoons smoked hot paprika

DIRECTIONS:

• Cook the whole, unpeeled potatoes in a large pot of boiling salted water until they are easily pierced with the tip of a sharp knife, or about 20 minutes. Drain and peel, with your fingers, under cool running water (as if peeling hard-cooked eggs). Transfer to a large chilled bowl. Add the eggs and chop into large, bite-sized chunks. Plop on the pimentos, hot sauce, celery salt, vinegar, lemon juice, pickles, oil, mayonnaise, mustard, jalapeños, onion, bell pepper, celery and parsley. Don't stir; dive in with your hands and mix well, mashing some of the potatoes to bond the intact golden chunks. Season with salt and pepper. Transfer to a serving bowl or platter and shape into a pretty mound with a spoon or spatula. Dust the top with paprika. Cover and refrigerate until chilled. Serve cold.

"WE WOULDN'T TRADE ANYTHING"

"SEC folks know that tailgating in the beautiful and historic Ole Miss Grove (and all over the campus) is the premiere tailgating experience in America," says Warner Alford, an Ole Miss football letterman and former longtime athletic director at Mississippi.

"For us old Reb players, however, it is like when you go home to Mama's and see all the kith and kin. Our buddies now bring two younger generations of their families with them, as do we. Between the excitement of the bands playing, players walking through the Arch of Champions, the aroma of barbecue wafting through the air, campus cuties in their cocktail attire completed by cowboy boots, seeing so many old classmates and friends who are drawn here from all over the country, and swapping tales of past victories (and agonies of defeat) — it is a complete menu of emotions, for which we wouldn't trade anything."

Prairie Fire Dip

From Warner and Kay Alford
Former Ole Miss athletic director

INGREDIENTS:

3 cups chili
3 cups fresh hot tamales (or canned equivalent) mashed
2 1/2 cups shredded cheddar cheese
Onion juice (to taste)
Garlic juice (to taste)

DIRECTIONS:

• Stir, heat and then serve with chips.

THE VIEW FROM THE VERANDA

Frank Jones, an assistant coach at Mississippi State, was imbued with sensitive real estate instincts. Connections, too. His father-in-law was Wallace Butts, the great coach at the University of Georgia. While he was coaching in Starkville, Frank bought a farm on the edge of town in the 1960s that would one day become prime real estate as the university enlarged and expanded.

Years later, his son, Frank Jr., who grew up cheering for the Georgia Bulldogs and later played at Richmond, would become a Mississippi State aficionado. He still cheers for the Bulldogs, but it is for the Mississippi State Bulldogs. He has developed the property that his dad bought while coaching in Starkville. He owns and operates The Veranda Restaurant, the most popular joint in town. You will find him on game day preparing for diners *and* tailgaters.

Tailgating in Starkville usually involves shrimp. Photo courtesy of Randy Journeay.

Grits Casserole

From Frank Jones and Jay Yates
Co-Owners of The Veranda Restaurant
In Starkville

INGREDIENTS:

1/2 gallon prepared grits (stone ground is best; just don't use instant)

1 stick butter, diced

3 cups sharp cheddar cheese, shredded

1 pound package Jimmy Dean Sage Sausage, cooked, drained and crumbled

1 cup thin-cut green onions

1 can whole kernel corn, drained

6 eggs

Salt

Black pepper

DIRECTIONS:

• Cook the grits. While they are still hot, place into a mixing bowl and add all other ingredients except the eggs. Whisk vigorously to melt cheese and butter. Now your grits have cooled a bit. Break the eggs into a separate bowl to ensure there are no shells. Whisk the eggs into the grits while still warm. Pour the mix into greased casserole dish. Salt and pepper to taste. Bake at 350 degrees until the top is browned, or about 25 minutes.

"Tailgating in Starkville," Frank Jr. says, "has evolved exponentially in last few years. When we converted the tangle of roads adjacent to the stadium known as 'Malfunction Junction' and made it into what is today — 'The Junction' — it became the turning point. Our restaurant, The Veranda, has become a popular pregame hangout. Some consider this their tailgate club.

"For me, game day is exhausting, but rewarding," Frank continued. "I arrive at 6 a.m., restock from the insanity the day before and prepare for a 19-hour nonstop rollercoaster day. It is a challenge, but so much fun! I prepare a big carb-heavy family meal for the staff to fill up for what, to us, is the 'Longest Day.' At The Veranda, we prepare a lot of specials — high-end dishes that fit the festive atmosphere, from cowboy ribeyes to kobe burgers to lobster, to name a few.

"Catfish is very popular in Mississippi," says Frank. "We partner with Simmons Catfish, a family owned, 100 percent Mississippi farm-raised company. They have a 'Delacata' center cut filet with the skin side trimmed off. It has an amazing taste and takes well to expert chef-driven preparations. We change it every game day and our Bulldog fans love it!

"At The Junction, Bulldog alumni have their own large tailgates set up and are very gracious about hosting anyone who passes by, especially our rivals. I am biased, of course, but my restaurant seems to be very popular with that crowd. We've developed relationships with many visitors by giving that personal touch and uncompromising food quality that our guests appreciate. Many folks park at The V and walk to the game. You can see and hear the stadium from our front door. Starkville is a small town, so one can go to various spots quickly and easily, such as the Cotton District adjacent to campus, downtown and, of course, The Veranda."

Randy Journeay

Chipotle Pepper Glaze

From Frank Jones and Jay Yates
Co-Owners of The Veranda Restaurant
In Starkville

Note from Jay: I came up with this recipe long before we opened The Veranda and before chipotle peppers were everywhere. Similar to barbecue sauce, it's sweet, spicy and has some unique ingredients that go with many different meats and seafood. We use it on ribs to finish on the grill, as a pulled pork sandwich condiment, to glaze whole roasted chickens, on fried chicken wings, to glaze sausage on the grill, and to glaze bacon-wrapped jumbo shrimp.

INGREDIENTS:

1 7-ounce can chipotle peppers in adobo

1/2 cup Dijon mustard

1 bunch cilantro with some stem

1 1/4 cups cider vinegar

1 1/4 cups local honey

1/4 cup light brown sugar

1/3 cup good barbecue sauce, like Cattleman's

DIRECTIONS:

• Place chipotle pepper with adobo, brown sugar, cilantro and mustard into a food processor (you can try it in a blender, and it can be done, but it isn't easy). Process until a pretty fine paste forms. Scrape into a bowl, add the rest of the ingredients and whisk. This is a surefire unique sauce that your tailgate neighbors will be jealous of. If you really want to get crazy, glaze your steaks with it, or put a spoon of it in your Bloody Mary. Boom!

PERSPECTIVES FROM OLD MIZZOU

Charles Davis, a native Georgian who taught at Missouri, is a diehard sports fan. Football, basketball, baseball — whatever the competition, he's up for it. He is now the dean of the UGA Henry Grady School of Journalism.

"Having spent our formative years tailgating in the SEC, my wife, Julie, and I landed in Columbia, Missouri, during the dark days preceding the arrival of coach Gary Pinkel and his staff, when 35,000 fans braved the elements — and the football," says Charles. "We dove right in, navigating the strange new world (to us) of the Big 12, and began a wonderful tradition of tailgating with a group of friends on elementary school playgrounds.

"We settled in a neighborhood adjacent to campus, so our tailgating was rather unorthodox: we gathered in one another's backyards, sharing food and drinks before and after games, since we all lived within walking distance of Faurot Field," he continued. "It was tailgating without tailgates, and I was a bit adrift at first, missing the ambiance of a parking lot filled with the pageantry of game day. The company was so engaging, and the living rooms often so warm, that as the years went by, I forgot what we missed in forgoing the traditional tailgate for our neighborhood soirees.

"Several years ago, we began having one 'real' tailgate each season on campus — coolers and tents and all. It was then that I realized that it was not the accoutrements that mattered, but the friendships formed in those backyards over all those years. I had not missed the true essence of tailgating after all!

"Missouri tailgaters are a proud, hearty lot, not easily swayed by the elements, which of course can play a major role even in the relatively benign days of autumn," says Charles. "The lots nearest to the stadium fill early, with the diehards lining the areas to the west and to the south of Faurot Stadium. Do not miss the giant black-and-gold RVs, as they contain the best tailgating atmosphere of all. The Tiger Walk is always a highlight, and takes you right through the best tailgating areas.

Cherry Chocolate Squares

From Gary Pinkel
Head coach at Missouri

INGREDIENTS:

3/4 cup plus 1 tablespoon butter

1/4 cup sugar

1/3 cup cocoa

1 egg

1 1/4 cups graham cracker crumbs

1/2 cup coconut

1/3 cup walnuts (optional)

1 tablespoon water

2 tablespoons maraschino cherry juice

1 teaspoon almond extract

2 cups confectionary sugar

1/2 cup cherries, chopped

1/3 cup chocolate chips

DIRECTIONS:

• For the first layer, combine 1/2 cup of the butter, 1/4 cup sugar and 1/3 cup cocoa in a heavy saucepan over medium heat. When melted, stir in 1 fork-beaten egg, then cook until slightly thickened and remove from heat. Stir in 1 1/4 cups graham cracker crumbs, 1/2 cup coconut, 1/3 cup walnuts and 1 tablespoon water. Press firmly into an ungreased 9-inch by 9-inch pan.

• For the second layer, beat together 1/4 cup of the butter, 2 tablespoons maraschino cherry juice, 1 teaspoon almond extract and 2 cups confectionary sugar. With paper towel, blot 1/2 cup chopped cherries and then stir them into the mixture. Drop dabs here and there on the first layer, then spread. Let stand 10 minutes and then use your hand to pat it down smoothly.

• For the third layer, melt 1 tablespoon of the butter in a small saucepan. Add 1/3 cup chocolate chips and stir until melted. Pour over the second layer with a teaspoon to smooth it out. Chill and serve.

3 Greek Recipes

From Craig and Mary Kuligowski
Missouri defensive line coach

Mary Kuligowski says: I graduated with a BA in finance in 1990 from the University of Toledo, where I met my husband. Craig and I were married in 1991. After Peyton and Madeline were born, I got into baking and started my own cake business. My Greek recipes I learned from my mother. Most were unwritten, measured by handfuls and what looked right to her. I had to put them to paper so that I could reproduce them for myself. I did a pretty good job and they soon became requested at tailgates. Dawn Ford, Mary Beth Steckel and Mary Kay Jones and I have been tailgating since 1991. Our kids have grown up together and we each appreciate each others' talents in bringing a good tailgate together each game-day Saturday. Dolmades, Baklava and Galatoboureko are three of my favorite recipes. Enjoy!

DOLMADES INGREDIENTS:

6 pounds ground beef
3 jars grape leaves
3 cups rice
6 medium onions, chopped
2 bunches parsley, chopped
1 cup dill, chopped
1 handful mint, chopped
1 cup olive oil
1 cup tomato puree
1 large can chicken broth
1/2 cup lemon juice
1 handful salt
1 tablespoon pepper

DIRECTIONS:

• Mix by hand. Roll mixture into individual grape leaves, kind of like a burrito. Stack rolled dolma on top of each other in large casserole dish. Layer torn leaves on top as a seal of sorts. Add chicken broth, lemon juice and olive oil into casserole. Add seasonings with herbs to taste. Add boiling water if necessary to have enough liquid to just see to top. Cook at 350 degrees, covered, for 1 hour.

BAKLAVA INGREDIENTS:

1 1/2 pounds walnuts, chopped in food
    processor
1 pound phyllo dough
2 or 3 sticks butter, melted

DIRECTIONS:

• Brush a 9-inch by 13-inch pan with butter. Lay one sheet of phyllo. Repeat until you have 8 to 10 sheets down. Sprinkle on a light layer of chopped walnuts. Top with sheet of dough. Brush with butter. Repeat using dough and nuts until 8 to 10 sheets are left. Complete top as bottom using remaining sheets of phyllo. Score pieces into rows of diamond shapes. Bake at 350 degrees until dark golden brown. Top with cooled syrup to fill between each row and sides. Put cut pieces into baking cups to serve.

SYRUP:

2 cups sugar
1 cup water
1 teaspoon lemon juice
1 teaspoon cinnamon

DIRECTIONS:

• Boil together until syrup is sticky on back of spoon, and then let cool before topping the Baklava.

GALATOBOUREKO INGREDIENTS:

6 cups milk

6 eggs

1 cup sugar

1 cup semolina (usually found in bulk aisle)

1/2 pound phyllo dough

Butter, melted

DIRECTIONS:

• Combine semolina with milk in pot. Cook at medium heat while stirring constantly so it does not stick to the bottom. Combine sugar and eggs in bowl. Add to mixture just before it reaches a boil. Cook until it separates from side of pot. Brush bottom of a 9-inch by 13-inch pan with melted butter. Lay one sheet of phyllo, and repeat until you have 10 sheets down. Spread custard mixture on top. Top with sheet of phyllo. Brush with butter and repeat with 10 sheets of phyllo. Score into squares. Bake at 350 degrees until golden brown on top. Top with cooled syrup (use the syrup recipe for Baklava).

"Tailgating begins bright and early at Mizzou. The real pros arrive Friday night, of course, but there is a steady stream from all across the state early Saturday morning. By 10 a.m., even with a night game, the lots are teeming and the grills lit. Bratwurst is the coin of the realm at the Midwest's contribution to the SEC, and the smell of thousands of sausages hitting the spit simultaneously on a crisp fall day crystallizes all that is Mizzou to me. That, and oceans of Budweiser products — after all, this is Anheuser Busch's backyard.

"If the win is truly epic, the party always ends up at Harpo's, a downtown watering hole. In the days before retractable goalposts, the crowd carried the goalposts all the way downtown and then a hacksaw was produced, and souvenirs were dispensed. I will never forget following the goalposts through town on the evening of Oct. 19, 2010, when Mizzou knocked off Oklahoma.

"No trip to Mizzou is complete without a stroll from Faurot Field to the historic Mizzou Quadrangle, the spiritual home of the University of Missouri. The majestic columns frame the original academic buildings on a lovely green. Make sure to check out Thomas Jefferson's original tombstone, which was placed on the Quad to honor Mr. Jefferson's role in securing the Louisiana Purchase and setting the course for the first public university west of the Mississippi. The campus culminates at the School of Journalism, my home for 14 years and the world's first school of journalism. It is a heady experience, and visiting fans will be met with warmth and friendship. Mizzou may be a newcomer to the SEC, but it already is well known as one of the nicest fan bases anywhere."

* * *

Professor Jim Sterling is the Missouri Chair of Community Newspaper Management at the University of Missouri. A Tiger tailgater with good taste and energetic, but reserved, enthusiasm, he brings color and insight to his view of Mizzou tailgating.

"Starting with the first game in 1891, Mizzou traditions on the gridiron grew along with the stately columns, Jefferson's tombstone, the Gothic tower at the student union and other historical icons," says Jim. "Games have been played at Memorial Stadium since 1927 and it has been known as Faurot Field, after the iconic coach who invented the split-T formation, since the 1970s. Arguably, homecoming was started at the University of Missouri. So you would think we'd be master tailgaters.

"Truth is, we are playing a little catch-up in Columbia, but we are coming on fast," he continued. "For many years we just ate fried chicken or sandwiches out of our trunks and guzzled a beer or 20. Games used to start at 1:30 p.m. and television hadn't yet set our game times from 11 a.m. to 9 p.m., sometimes even on Thursdays.

"Now with a lighted field and varying start times, plus seeing what our new playmates in the SEC were doing, has led us to more elaborate tailgating. And while we don't have shady spots like The Grove at Ole Miss, we do have acres and acres of paved parking all around the stadium.

"It has been my good fortune in the last quarter century to park just outside the west gates of the stadium," says Jim. "For many years the only smell floating in the autumn breezes was that of the Boone County Ham grilling in the concession stands. For some reason, never fully explained to the purists among us, it is long gone.

"Today the breezes carry the smell of a thousand grills smoking a variety of meats all over the lots around the stadium. Barbecued pork is a favorite, doused with tasty secret sauces in the Missouri tradition. But there is also the run of hot dogs, steaks, hamburgers, brats, pork steaks, chili and sometimes, fried fish.

"One of the best setups I've seen is Greg Martinette's 50-gallon-drum cooker, set on end with a smoke stack out the top. He loads it up in his monster black pickup in Kansas City and it looks like a wood-fired Toyota roaring down I-70. I can't disclose his secret recipe, but his pork shoulder and ribs are the best I've ever had anywhere. And I eat barbecue from North Carolina to Texas.

"Another favorite spot is where Jack Smith, a former Chicago ad man, sets out his grilled chicken legs, clam dip and bloody bulls. And if we are really lucky, his wife Donna will bake some of her sweet specialties. Ummm good.

"I've tailgated for years, but have dropped off recently, deciding it might be fun to go see what everyone else is doing. I was doing summer sausage and cheese with crackers and sometimes pimento cheese sandwiches as if this was The Masters. My tailgating partners, Tom and Chris Sowers, would do Chicago Dogs, sometimes smoked salmon and sometimes Ozarks barbecue.

"But the best thing isn't the food or the drink. It is seeing old friends coming home to Old Mizzou."

Gooey Butter Cake

From Steve Ethun
Mizzou grad, director of communications at Augusta National Golf Club

No gathering at the expansive tailgating scene that surrounds Memorial Stadium at the University of Missouri is complete without a few pans of Gooey Butter Cake, a St. Louis delicacy. Its versatility of being anything from a breakfast to a dessert makes it perfect for any kickoff time throughout the season, and its long connection to the state of Missouri provides instant credibility and likeability to whomever arrives with this amazingly simple bite-sized delight.

INGREDIENTS:

1 box yellow cake mix
3 large eggs (2 beaten)
1 stick butter or margarine, melted
8 ounces cream cheese, softened
2 cups powdered sugar

DIRECTIONS:

• Preheat oven to 325 degrees. Combine cake mix, 1 egg and melted margarine or butter. Press into a greased 9-inch by 13-inch pan with your fingers. Blend together cream cheese, 2 beaten eggs and powdered sugar until smooth, and then spread over the first batter. Bake for 40 to 45 minutes, or until edges are brown. Dust with powdered sugar on top after the cake has cooled. Cut into bite-sized pieces for easy snacking.

A GREAT TRADITION AT NAVY

By Brad Chatlos, former Navy linebacker

Tailgating at Navy is centered around more than just football. It's a celebration of patriotism, leadership and service. Every Navy fan, friend or family member understands that the Navy players belong to something greater than a football team and that they would give their lives to protect those in the stands!

The Navy football players arrive by bus at the stadium, dressed in uniform and ready to deliver as fans line both sides of the sidewalk to cheer on the ultimate student-athletes and future officers.

The Midshipmen march over from campus (two miles away) through downtown Annapolis while fans line the streets cheering on the Mids, showering them with candy

and thanking them for their service. As they enter the stadium, the announcer introduces the 30 "companies" and company commanders (the 4,000-plus Midshipmen all live in Bancroft Hall and are split up into 30 groups called companies). The entire brigade of Midshipmen does a unified chant/cheer to kick off the game.

When the teams run onto the field or at kickoff, planes or helicopters streak over the stadium from Navy and Marine Corps aviation units. The crewmembers are usually academy grads, and they make it back to the stadium by the second half and are honored and introduced on the field.

After the game, win or lose, the entire football team respectfully pays tribute to the opposing team as it sings the opponent's alma mater. The Navy team then turns to the stands to face their fellow Midshipman, and the entire stadium sings "Blue & Gold," while closing with BEAT ARMY!

On the tailgating front, tents and infrastructure are set up Friday, and as soon as the gates open, fans head to their tailgate spots. There are hundreds of long-standing tailgates. Due to overcrowding and demand, the Academy moved to pre-purchased parking passes with assigned parking locations. A number of larger areas for

Debbie Latta and friends tailgating in Annapolis.

Pecan Cheese Torte

From Roger and Marianne Staubach
Former Navy quarterback, 1963 Heisman
Trophy winner, member College and Pro
Football Halls of Fame

INGREDIENTS:

3 cups grated sharp cheddar cheese

1 cup finely chopped purple onion

1 1/2 cups chopped pecans

1/2 teaspoon pepper

1/4 cup chopped parsley

Mayonnaise to moisten

8 ounces jalapeno pepper jelly

DIRECTIONS:

• Combine cheese, onion, pecans, parsley and pepper. Add mayo 1 teaspoon at a time until it holds together. Press into a 7-inch spring form pan. Chill well. Remove spring form and spread with jelly. Serve with crackers or melba toast. Best when made ahead.

Glazed Strawberry Pie

From Roger and Marianne Staubach
Former Navy quarterback, 1963 Heisman
Trophy winner, member College and Pro
Football Halls of Fame

INGREDIENTS:

1 3-ounce package cream cheese, softened

1 9-inch pie shell, baked

1 quart drained hulled strawberries

1 1/2 cups strawberry juice

1 cup sugar

3 tablespoons cornstarch

1/2 pint heavy cream, whipped

DIRECTIONS:

• Spread cream cheese over bottom of baked pie shell. Cover with half of the strawberries. Mash remaining strawberries and strain until juice is extracted. Add water if necessary to make 1 1/2 cups of juice. Pour juice in a small saucepan and bring to a boil, and then stir in sugar and cornstarch. Cook over low heat, stirring constantly until mixture comes to a boil, and boil for 1 minute. Pour mixture over the strawberries in the pie shell. Cool for 2 hours. Before serving, top with whipped cream.

Note from Marianne: If desired, the juice can be cooked slowly for 10 minutes, stirring occasionally, rather than boiled. Let it cool before pouring over the strawberries.

Shutterstock

big tailgates with groups like alumni year-classes set up and welcome friends and guests. Navy tailgating is very hospitable.

When it comes to food, Annapolis is Crabtown USA. We start with Bloody Marys, various delicious recipes for crab cakes and crab dip — and anything else with crab or Old Bay in it. Midshipmen come from all 50 states and territories. You'll see everything in tailgate food: fried chicken, sausages, pulled pork BBQ, tamales, Polynesian dishes, fried turkey and pig roasts. You name it, we eat it!

The United States Naval Academy yard as a whole should never be missed and is a "must see" if you come to Annapolis. There are dozens of attractions and memorials to see, but one in particular is Tecumseh. The Mids decorate Tecumseh. The figurehead called Tecumseh has, for many years, played a prominent part in the traditions of the United States Naval Academy. The original wooden image was sent to the Naval Academy in 1866 after being salvaged from the wreck of the old ship *Delaware*, which had been sunk at Norfolk during the Civil War to prevent her from falling into Confederate hands. The builders of the *Delaware* intended the figurehead to portray Tamanend, the great chief of the Delaware, a lover of peace and friend of William Penn. For the midshipmen of the period, there was nothing in the name of

Tamanend to strike the imagination. The effigy was also known by various other names, including Powhatan and King Phillip. Finally Tecumseh, a great and heroic warrior, struck the fancy of the Midshipmen.

For 40 years, the wooden figurehead kept its stern vigil in the Yard at Annapolis until the winds, sun and rain began to take their toll. In 1906, a facelift with the aid of cement, putty and paint temporarily removed the signs of age. When the ravages of the weather again threatened, the Class of 1891 raised a fund to immortalize the old fellow in bronze. The delicate task was accomplished at the U.S. Naval Gun Factory.

In the spring of 1930, a bronze statue, mounted on a pedestal of Vermont marble adorned with the Naval Academy seal, was erected on its present site from which the grim old warrior gazes eternally toward the main entrance of Bancroft Hall, the Midshipman dormitory. Tecumseh has become not only the "God of 2.0" — the passing grade point average at the academy — but also the idol to whom loyal Midshipmen give prayers and sacrificial offerings of pennies. Midshipmen offer a left-handed salute in tribute to Tecumseh, and they toss pennies his way for good luck in exams and athletic contests.

Tecumseh and tailgating, just a couple of things to experience when you visit the Navy Academy on game day.

HAVE A BALL IN LINCOLN!

The Cornhuskers of Nebraska, now members of the Big Ten Conference, are not quite as dominant as they once were on the football field — if you recall the heady times of Bob Devaney and Tom Osborne — but tailgating and enjoying pregame festivities in Lincoln is as compelling as ever.

If you consider that Nebraska home games have been sellouts since 1962 — over a half-century — you know that enthusiasm for Cornhusker football is at the highest level of any college football community in the country. That has to be a record that no school will surpass any time soon. And the streak goes on. The passion for Cornhusker tailgating and football is reflected in the commitment of Kurt Kechely.

"Our tailgate team," says Kurt, one of Nebraska's best-known tailgaters, "includes Ron Preston, Tod Masin, Bill Misko and Jim Novotny. Our tailgate takes place at the same location for every home game. We've been at it for the last 15 years. We have only had to move our tailgate once since it started. We use our tailgate as an opportunity to invite clients and friends to share in our experience and enthusiastically support Husker football.

"Our group discusses the menu and starts prepping the week before," Kurt continued. "We each have our specific duties and work extensively throughout the actual event. Our group also travels in a motor home to away games. Set up and tear down typically take 30 minutes. We usually start five hours prior to kickoff, unless it's an evening game, then it could go all day. Each season, our games can be scheduled to start at 11 a.m., 2 p.m. or 6 p.m. The weather in Nebraska can be warm or cold, depending on the month.

"On an 'average' game, we will host about 100 people and 'big' games we host up to 200. Our tailgate is so popular that Nebraska staff and administrators will drop by. We have even hosted Mötley Crüe drummer Tommy Lee, who was filming at the University of Nebraska for his reality series 'Tommy Lee Goes to College.' Our tailgate was featured in one of his episodes. We also welcome guests from the opposing team with open arms, as we pride ourselves on universal hospitality.

"Typical tailgate items include a Go-Galley Grill, enclosed trailer, tables, chairs, music system, patio heaters, fans (if needed), numerous coolers and our tents. Beverages served include Husker Bloody Marys — a must at all games — coffee, water, soda, beer and regular bar (various cocktails and mixes). A Husker rule is that all alcoholic beverages must be in cups rather than cans or bottles.

"Morning tailgates consist of breakfast pizza, breakfast burritos, doughnuts, cinnamon rolls, breakfast breads (usually made by our spouses) and our specialty, which is Egg McMasins (named after team member Tod Masin). Egg McMasins are made with a grilled sausage patty, scrambled eggs, American cheese and his special hollandaise sauce that is sandwiched between a toasted English muffin.

"All other tailgates consist of soups, chili, chips, dips and various desserts. We always grill burgers, brats and hot dogs. On top of that, we prepare many Nebraska specialties by using hometown Nebraska-made sausage, bologna and brats. We will also smoke wild turkey breast, pork butt and chicken wings, and grill aged Nebraska prime beef such as ribeyes, New York strip and prime rib. We also like to take our garden-fresh jalapenos and stuff them with cream cheese to be put on the grill for some good stuffed poppers.

"One of our biggest hits is when we serve meat we've obtained through hunting, such as pheasant and quail. We take a half strip of bacon and wrap it around a quarter-sized chunk of breast meat with a slice of jalapeno and slice of water chestnut, skewered together with a toothpick, and grill it. The other big hit is when team member Jim Novotny brings 'Rocky Mountain oysters' to be fried. When Jim's cattle have calves and they are castrated in the summer, Jim saves the 'oysters' so they can be seasoned, breaded and fried at the tailgates.

"That's why we always say, 'Nebraska Tailgating! Come have a ball!'"

Stuffed Game-Day Green Peppers

From Tom and Nancy Osborne
Former Nebraska head coach and
athletic director

INGREDIENTS:

1 medium onion, chopped
1 pound lean ground beef
2 cups bread crumbs, crumbled
2 hard-cooked eggs, chopped
1 cup diced celery
1/4 cup Romano cheese
1 large tomato, peeled and diced
1 teaspoon sugar
3/4 cup water
6 large green peppers

DIRECTIONS:

• Saute onion in olive oil until transparent. Add beef and brown. Add remaining ingredients, except green pepper. Salt and pepper to taste. Mix well. Remove tops of green peppers. Stuff the peppers with mixture and set them in a deep pan with a little water in the bottom. Bake 1 hour at 375 degrees and then cool.

OSBORNE APPLAUDS TAILGATERS

"Nebraskans," says former Cornhusker head coach and Athletic Director Tom Osborne, "have a reputation for being prodigious tailgaters with elaborate spreads. And they pride themselves on hospitality and kindness to opponents.

"Most opposing fans send letters, indicating how much they appreciate the way they and their teams are treated," he continued. "Often, opposing coaches express similar sentiments."

Hip, hip, hooray for Nebraska. It would be good if more fans of more teams would take note of this overt expression of hospitality and start a similar trend on their own campus. Instead of booing the visiting team when it takes the field for pregame warm-ups, how about a round of applause? After all, they are our guests!

Kurt Kechely's tailgating team before a Nebraska home game.

Mini Ham Puffs

From Anne Hackbart,
assistant to Tom Osborne

INGREDIENTS:

5 ounces ham
1 small onion
1 cup shredded Swiss cheese
2 eggs
1/4 teaspoon pepper
3 teaspoons Dijon mustard
1 8-ounce package crescent rolls

DIRECTIONS:

• Preheat oven to 350 degrees. Chop ham and onion finely, put in bowl. Add cheese, egg, pepper and mustard, and then stir. Unroll crescent rolls and press into large rectangle, pinching together all perforations. Cut into 24 squares. Spray mini-muffin pan with Pam, put a piece of crescent roll into each muffin tin and press in with tart maker. Scoop in ham filling. Bake for 15 minutes or until lightly browned.

Chicken Wing Dip

From Trev and Angie Alberts
All-America linebacker at Nebraska

INGREDIENTS:

1 rotisserie chicken, meat chopped into bite-sized pieces
1 jar Frank's Wing Sauce
1 block cream cheese
1 jar Naturally Fresh Bleu Cheese Dressing
1 bag Mexican blend shredded cheese
Fritos Scoops

DIRECTIONS:

• Preheat oven to 350 degrees. Grease a two-quart casserole pan. Mix chicken and wing sauce, and pour into the pan. Whip cream cheese and dressing, and then layer over chicken and wing sauce. Top with shredded cheese. Bake for 25 minutes at 350 degrees. Serve with Fritos Scoops.

NEBRASKA'S SPECIAL HOT DOGS

At Memorial Stadium, there is nothing like a Fairbury hot dog when you are ready for a snack. Or a full meal. Cornhusker fans think that there is no treat at a Nebraska game to compare with a Fairbury dog.

You can get 'em at the concession stands throughout the stadium, but if you are lucky, the "derviener slinger" will send one your way. Normally at football (and basketball) games across the country, the cheerleaders appear a few times a game with a CO_2 gun blasting T-shirts, soft-cloth dolls and mascot images into the crowd. At Nebraska, they shoot a hot dog your way — a Fairbury chicken and beef hot dog that Nebraskans will tell you is the best hot dog you will ever taste.

Tom Roode, a graduate of Nebraska, worked in the family business for years, making and selling Fairbury hot dogs, which were sold at Nebraska games. Eventually, he was asked to pay a rights fee to sell his hot dogs, but felt that it would not work for him from a business standpoint. There was a brief absence of Fairbury hotdogs at Memorial Stadium, but the fans were so disappointed that they complained and clamored until the Fairbury hot dog again appeared at Nebraska home games. You could say there was a rude reaction by Cornhusker fans, until Tom Roode returned to the concession lineup.

Kurt Kechely

IT'S ALL ABOUT FRIENDSHIP

"The email goes out on Tuesdays," says Stephen Archbell, a University of North Carolina tailgater from the Outer Banks. "It travels across North Carolina, making stops in Kitty Hawk, Columbia, Fayetteville, Reidsville, Pinehurst, Hickory, Lake Norman and Chapel Hill. Beyond our state, it heads north to Boston and west to Los Angeles.

"'What's on the menu?' is the question," Stephen continued. "It could be breakfast or lunch, depending on game time. As replies flow in, a plan is set, and the second biggest news of our week — behind anticipation of a Tar Heel victory — will be what we are eating. Breakfast may offer goose sausage from Dare County or pork sausage from Dortches, a Peach Bellini or a Bloody Mary, sensible low-fat yogurt or Aunt Francis' sinful rum cake. The choice is ours.

"Lunch can range from a fresh Outer Banks seafood fry to a perfect Piedmont beef tenderloin; from the elegance of smoked salmon to the down-home comfort of burgers, brats and dogs; from the annual Eastern North Carolina vs. Western North Carolina barbecue competition to a unique wild-game festival featuring venison and bear. The choice is ours.

Stephen Archbell and his friends have tailgating down to an art.

"And, of course, there are the old standbys, holding their honored place on the table — no true Southern tailgate is proper without them: sausage balls, pimento cheese, deviled eggs, fried chicken, biscuits and brownies, all of which is permissible for either breakfast or lunch. Again, the choice is ours.

"The preparation will be demanding. Packing the cars alone will take hours, but that's OK. The week will end with a football Saturday. We are dreaming of the Heels at home. And, already, we are going to Carolina in our mind!

"We each have a role in our group and take pride in our cherished positions. The hardcore founding tailgaters will arrive on 'the Hill' Friday evening for pregame

Tar Heel Pork Barbecue Sandwiches

From Marie Dooley, wife of Bill Dooley
Former head coach at North Carolina, Virginia Tech & Wake Forest

When Bill Dooley became the head coach at the University of North Carolina in 1967, he traveled across the state and spoke at Rams Club meetings from Manteo to Murphy. He learned very quickly that Tar Heels love their barbecue. He does, too!

Whether your taste is sliced (Western North Carolina) or chopped (Eastern North Carolina), barbecue is a great addition to your tailgate party. You can eat it in a bowl and pour your favorite sauce over it, or put it on a fresh roll with cole slaw on top.

Bill married an Eastern North Carolina girl, so I favor chopped barbecue and the vinegar-based sauce. To prepare the sauce, mix 2 quarts of cider vinegar, 1 1/2 ounces of crushed red peppers and salt to taste.

To prepare a Boston butt roast on a grill, marinate overnight in the vinegar-based sauce. Slow cook the meat on a grill for 5 to 7 hours, or until the meat separates from the bone.

I prefer to slow cook the pork roast overnight. Brown a 4 to 5 pound Boston butt roast. Line sliced onions in the bottom of a slow cooker and place meat on top. Add 1/3 cup of cider vinegar and 2 tablespoons of molasses, cover and cook on low until the meat is falling apart. This takes about 10 hours. Transport the slow cooker in a small cooler. Just before serving and while the pork is still warm, "pull" the meat by using one fork to steady and the other to pull shreds of pork off the roast. Place the barbecue on a soft white roll, add vinegar sauce and top with cole slaw.

Nothing could be finer!

Barbecue is big at North Carolina games. Photo courtesy of Kevin Best.

strategy and cocktails. Our communication chief, who sends out the menu email, doubles as bar back, making sure that the bar is fully stocked by Saturday morning. The early risers are at the gates of Eringhaus parking lot first, securing prime real estate for the group. With each arrival, excitement builds. Greetings and hugs welcome old friends and new friends alike, for our group is ever evolving. Although food is a huge part of this tradition, fellowship is even more important. These gatherings, at least six times a year, have strengthened our bonds, grounding us with what's really important in life: staying connected with friends.

"Under the leadership of our stager, the setup is done in a flash with no complaints — a team effort. Grills are lifted and rolled into place, tents assembled and an-

chored, tables arranged with both sides accessible, chairs circled in groups, the bar open and ready for business.

"Our space has grown more elaborate each year, now having nearly all the comforts of home. Carolina blue abounds. You can see us from a mile away with our 50-foot UNC flag spiraling upward. Our DJ has a booming speaker and a tailgate playlist that draws crowds from across the parking lot. You may find us doing the Cupid Shuffle or trying to Wobble — if our dance coach can convince us to arise from our chairs. The grills are lit, and soon, an enticing aroma fills the atmosphere. Everyone's hungry, but no one's in a hurry. Cold drinks are sipped, brownies are nibbled. Perhaps the Florentines said it best, "festina lente," hurry up slowly. That, friends, is the essence of tailgating. It's a football Saturday morning in

Kevin Best

Chapel Hill. The conversation is relaxed and easy. And right now, nothing could be finer than to be in Carolina!

"Every great show has a finale, that spectacular moment of closure that recaptures the theme and reminds the audience why they came. Our tailgate is no different. Once our official timekeeper gives the signal, clean up begins. No one in this group wants to miss kickoff. The finale crew aligns cups to spell 'UNC' on a recently cleared table. Shots of Southern Comfort with a splash of fresh lime fill each cup. A loud whistle calls for quiet. 'Gather round' everyone yells.

"We are often joined by fellow fans we've never met. Each season we welcome good-natured fans from opposing teams. Always, our legacies join us, our children, the next generation, future Tar Heel fans loved and men-tored with care, young tailgaters in training. Together, we lift our cups, remembering why we're here. Toasts are made, hopes raised for victory. United, we join to sing the grand words of the Carolina fight song. 'I'm a Tar Heel born. I'm a Tar Heel bred. And when I die I'm a Tar Heel dead …'

"Then we head to Kenan Stadium, ready to cheer like crazy for our student-athletes on the field. It is not just any Saturday. It's tailgate Saturday. Rah, rah Car'lina-lina! Rah, rah Car'lina-lina! Rah' rah Car'lina!'"

4 PERSPECTIVES ON NOTRE DAME TAILGATING

"Notre Dame is a national university with alumni and friends from every state," says Jeff Kohler, class of '79. "ND tailgaters run the gamut of foods from regional (Cajun jambalaya) to very upscale (sliced beef tenderloin) to Grandma's secret recipes (chili and soups when the weather turns colder) to every Midwest staple like grilled brats, hot dogs and burgers.

"There is another option, and this is not very exotic, but it is a tradition. I have found a consistently popular item that would score as the most common offering: homemade fried chicken from Martin's Supermarket. I validated this by sending a blind survey to 11 of my pals who host their own tailgates. In second and third place were Martin's chicken tenders and wings.

"Martin's is a family-owned regional grocery chain. Their store is within blocks of the ND campus and is an absolute circus starting on Thursday and continuing through Saturday. Especially on game-day morning, you will see hundreds of people picking up their buckets of chicken and trays of tenders and wings. Among the very many ND tailgater food offerings, chicken is most com-

mon. And the preparer of choice is Martin's Delicatessen for Martin's famous Deli Fried Chicken.

"Everybody knows that it just doesn't get any better than Martin's chicken. Over the years, Martin's chicken has been the star of everything from a weekday lunch for one to events hosting thousands. Either traditional by the bucket or by trays — featuring variations like tenders, wings and boneless wings — there are more ways than ever to enjoy that famous taste."

* * *

For Tom O'Donnell and his crew, location is paramount for their tailgate.

"For almost 25 years," he says, "it has been in the same location, about 200 yards south of the stadium. We began with a few friends, tables and a single grill. Now we have several industrial-sized grills, smokers, tents with gutters and downspouts, television, generators, outdoor rugs, dozens of tables, comfortable chairs, a fully stocked bar, a golf cart and a truck and trailer to transport it all. We use the golf cart to provide mobility for any guest who may require a little help getting to the game.

"The area covered by our tailgate is approximately 600 square yards. Our staff of 10 includes a chef with two assistants and three bartenders. The team that hosts the dining area is an extended family. Without their dedication and enthusiasm, all of this would be impossible. They arrive at 6 a.m. to secure our location as the parking area opens. The next several hours are devoted to setting up the equipment and cooking the food.

Tom O'Donnell and his crew get fired up prior to a Notre Dame game.

"Depending on the weather, they will continue to service our guests until 10 p.m. Before the game they will serve an average of 400 guests. The menu includes all the tailgate traditional necessities including brats, hot dogs, hamburgers, barbecue ribs and chicken. Additionally, the chef's specialty offerings include pulled pork, pizza, stews and soups. During the postgame celebration, the chef serves complete dinners including steaks, chops, ham and turkey with all the sides and trimmings. He will serve from 100 to 200 dinners depending on the weather.

"Each week we are graced by random entertainment, which can include bagpipers, poms and drum line, fiddlers and various choral groups, all contributing to our guests' game-day experience.

"Our ND tailgate has an open architecture. We welcome everyone, even extending invitations to our opponent's fans who might pass by.

"This tailgate event is entirely sponsored by six generous and gregarious Notre Dame families who welcome all to join us in our celebration of the Notre Dame Spirit. They extend a kind word, a warm greeting and a handshake to all. We try to create a cordial social environment based on friendship and camaraderie.

"We see ourselves as ND's front door on football Saturdays, where first-time visitors to the university will form lasting impressions. We hope that our hospitality will contribute to making that impression a rousing 'Welcome to Notre Dame.'"

* * *

Another passionate Irish tailgater is Michael Leo Desrosiers, class of '81, who sounds like he might be the head of the campus public relations office.

"The campus is very traditional and beautiful," he says. "It's a walking campus with limited roads or access to vehicles. Everyone walks from place to place. While tailgating is an event that stands alone, most 'Domers' and their families spend time walking around campus in addition to tailgating. The Notre Dame family and the local community are very friendly and welcoming to visitors from everywhere — even our rivals.

"It still gives an alumnus a thrill to visit the RV lot near the Joyce Athletic and Convocation Center (JACC), a popular place to wander by to see the elaborate tailgate spreads. You never tire of visiting the Library's Touchdown Jesus entrance to watch the Irish Guard lead the band into Notre Dame Stadium. Many people wander through the campus to buy food from students selling brats, burger, dogs and steak sandwiches at concession

Paul's Favorite Corn Pudding

From Paul and Angela Hornung
1956 Heisman Trophy winner
at Notre Dame

INGREDIENTS:

1 15-ounce can white corn
5 tablespoons sugar
4 eggs
4 tablespoons melted butter
8 tablespoons flour
1 tablespoon salt
3 cups milk

DIRECTIONS:

- Drain corn in bowl and then add flour, salt, sugar and butter. Set aside. Beat the eggs very well until frothy, add milk and then stir into other ingredients. Pour into baking dish and bake at 350 degrees for 40 minutes. Please note that you must stir from the bottom three times during baking.

stands near dorms to raise money. And almost everyone visits the Grotto — a replica of the Grotto in Lourdes, France."

* * *

"For the past dozen or so years we have attended almost all of the Notre Dame home football games," says Joan Dautromont Gluck, class of '74. "We began that tradition when our daughter Meredith was a freshman at Notre Dame.

"Our tailgate consists of two to three families," Joan continued. "We park in the stadium lot next to my roommate from ND, Annie, and her husband, Steve. The third car belongs to two more of our classmates, Dan and Peg. Three parking spots and SUVs provide plenty of space to set up tables, grills and coolers. Annie and Steve travel from Chicago and, in addition to the normal tailgate equipment, they provide the grill and a flag pole that flies three flags, the last being hot pink and easily recognizable in the parking lot for our friends to find us. Dan and Peg have tents that are stored in the garage of

Pizza Dip & Chutney Cheese Ball

From Bill and Sandy Lewis
Former assistant coach at Notre Dame,
and head coach at Georgia Tech
and Wyoming

INGREDIENTS:

Pizza Dip:

1 8-ounce package cream cheese

1 14-ounce jar pizza sauce

1/3 cup chopped onions

1 1/2 cups grated mozzarella cheese

1 6-ounce can black olives, drained and chopped

2 ounces pepperoni, finely chopped

Chutney Cheese Ball:

2 8-ounce packages cream cheese

1/2 cup chutney

1/2 cup Monterey Jack cheese

1/2 cup colby cheese

1/4 cup scallions

1 clove garlic, minced

Salt

Pepper

DIRECTIONS:

Pizza Dip:

• Press cream cheese into the bottom of a 9-inch pie pan. Spread pizza sauce over the top of cream cheese. Layer onions, mozzarella cheese, olives and pepperoni in order listed. Bake for 25 minutes. Serve with chips.

Chutney Cheese Ball:

• Combine all ingredients and chill. Then roll in chopped pecans. Serve with crackers. This is a hearty one because of the chutney and seems to be well liked by men!

their just-off-campus condo. These are our saving grace in the extreme heat of the early season games, but, more importantly in South Bend, they save us from the rain.

"We fly to South Bend from Philadelphia on one of the first flights out the Friday before game day. We rent a large SUV at the South Bend airport, and that becomes the beginning of tailgate central for us. We have stayed in the same hotel for over a decade, and the manager has been kind enough to store our tailgate paraphernalia in the hotel storage room during football season (during offseason, it moves to a family friend's basement!).

"The ride from the airport to the hotel provides me the opportunity to order some of our hot food for early Saturday morning pickup: Chick-fil-A chicken nugget trays and special hot Italian hoagies. Gotta love the folks in the Midwest. Our hoagies come from a local Italian restaurant. Their baker comes in each day at 6 a.m. to bake the fresh bread for the restaurant. That baker makes our sandwiches for us on that fresh bread and has them cut and ready for us to pick up by 8:15 a.m., long before the actual restaurant opening at 11 a.m.

"Friday night after campus activities finds us in Meijer's, a local grocer, doing the balance of our tailgate shopping: chips, dips, crackers, cheeses, salami, nuts, garnishes for our cocktails, beer, wine, water, sodas, mixes and liquors. Homemade baked goods travel on the plane with us, usually one or two types of cookies, dessert bars or brownies. Then, it's back to the hotel to cut the garnishes and make the skewers for the Bloody Marys!

"Game day comes very early with a 5:30 a.m. wake-up call. Barry and I throw clothes on and load the car with the coolers, tables, chairs and tub of tailgate essentials. Our spots at the stadium lot are not reserved, so we try to coordinate with our friends to be there by 8:30 (kickoff is 3:30 unless it is a night game). We try to secure the same spots as close as we can each game. First ones to arrive hold two places until we all arrive. Once we are all in place, time allows for a trip across campus for one more coffee and a walk to the Grotto.

"Our tailgates are attended by at least 100 people on game day, and at least twice that for the biggest rivalry games and the night games. We welcome our classmates, friends, and their friends and families. We welcome the fans of the opposition. That is the Notre Dame tradition." ('Welcome to Notre Dame. Enjoy the game!').

"Our tailgating has been an amazing way for us to stay connected to the university, our classmates, our friends and our children's friends, and to meet new folks to widen our circle."

WELCOME TO THE HORSESHOE

Tailgating scenes at the famous Horseshoe — officially named Ohio Stadium — are as big as the legend of Woody Hayes, the irascible Buckeye coach. While I have never asked anyone in officialdom at Ohio State, it is unlikely that Woody ever tailgated, although his rage on the sideline at various junctions in his coaching life would suggest that he must have had one too many at a Buckeye tailgate party before kickoff. One thing we know is that Woody, being the passionate Buckeye that he was, would likely have proclaimed, if he had been asked, that nobody is better at tailgating than Buckeye fans.

What Woody did in his illustrious career as head coach of the Buckeyes was to give Ohio State fans plenty to celebrate before the game and after the final whistle. He won 13 Big Ten championships and took eight teams to the Rose Bowl. Woody was bigger than life.

His sometimes volatile temper emanated from a deep and abiding competitive spirit. He abhorred losing, and created a confidence among the Ohio State fan base that the Buckeyes were likely to prevail. He encouraged his players to underscore academics as much as blocking and tackling. When the Buckeyes traveled out of town for a game, he found historical sites for his players to visit. A sound mind was as important to Woody as a well-trained body for the competitive game of football.

When I visited Columbus in the fall of 2013 as Ohio State hosted Penn State, I walked along the Olentangy River from the Jack Nicklaus Museum to the stadium, and I watched as the scarlet-and-gray-themed tents and accessories dominated the scene. The Olentangy, a Delaware Indian name meaning "river of the red face paint," is a reminder that in another day, Native American boys played on the banks of the river. There was no Big Ten Conference, there was no Rose Bowl, but the spirit of competition in the form of wrestling, running and jumping was a staple of life back then — who could snare the most birds, and who could spear the biggest fish? It was a forerunner of tailgating today. You bring the bounty home and cook it for the family. A good time was enjoyed by all back then just like it is today when crowds one-tenth the size of Columbus gather to sing the praises of the Buckeyes on game day.

* * *

It would be difficult to imagine anybody other than Dr. Derrill Habitzel, Ohio State class of 1944, winning the Tailgating Longevity Award. If anyone can top "Hab's" record, we invite them to speak up immediately or forever hold their peace.

Hab, a retired dentist, has not missed a Ohio State home game since 1936, except during World War II. You will find him outside the big Horseshoe every Saturday, tailgating with his family and friends.

At age 95, he began the 2013 tailgating season just like always: get there early, enjoy the tailgating scene and move inside Ohio Stadium to see the Buckeyes win another game. "There is nothing like it," Hab says of tailgating and the game-day experience.

Dr. Derrill Habitzel, center, with family before a game in Columbus. The 95-year-old has not missed an OSU home game since 1936, except during World War II.

Hab roomed with Les Horvath, the Buckeyes' Heisman Trophy-winning quarterback/halfback in 1944, when they were in OSU's dental school. Hab was a friend of Woody Hayes and started tailgating at Ohio State games when he was a student.

"We didn't really call it 'tailgating' back then, but we partied before and after the games," says Hab. "We began on Friday night and kept the party going right on through the games, which were all day games back then. Today, you never know when kickoff will be, but I still enjoy the games.

"My family carries on in the same tradition," he continued. "For 23 years we stayed in Room 120 at a motel near the campus. We had to make other arrangements when they tore it down. We have always enjoyed the friendships that developed because of Buckeye football. We had four kids at Ohio State at the same time, which meant that our circle of friends expanded. Everybody was welcome at our tailgate. We always had a parking place near the stadium, still do, and that is very important. I'd probably lose interest if we didn't have that parking spot.

"We always drove down to Columbus on Friday afternoons and did some grocery shopping. We bought a lot of sandwiches, potato salad and cold cuts, and, of course, burgers and hot dogs for the grill.

OSU Football Sandwiches

From Dr. Michael Hablitzel, OSU alum

INGREDIENTS:

1/2 cup softened butter
1/4 cup minced onion
1/4 cup sweet mustard
1 tablespoon poppyseed
1 pound Bavarian ham, thinly sliced
1/2 pound Swiss cheese
8 rolls or buns

DIRECTIONS:

• Mix together the softened butter, onion, mustard and poppyseed. Spread the mixture on both the tops and bottoms of the buns. Layer the ham and cheese. Wrap each sandwich in foil and bake in oven. You can also freeze them until needed, then bake when ready.

Neal Lauron photo

Buckeye Dip

From Dr. Michael Hablitzel
Ohio State alum

INGREDIENTS:

16 ounces cream cheese

12 ounces hot wing sauce

2 boneless chicken breasts, cooked and shredded

2 cups shredded cheddar cheese or 1 cup crumbled blue cheese

Fritos Scoops or tortilla chips

DIRECTIONS:

• Preheat oven to 400 degrees. Melt the cream cheese and mix in the hot wing sauce. Then mix in the cooked and shredded chicken breasts. Pour everything into baking dish. Bake for 10 minutes at 400 degrees. Remove from oven and sprinkle with shredded cheddar cheese or crumbled blue cheese. Return to oven and bake for 10 minutes. Then get ready to scoop it up!

Clam Dip

From John and Helen Cooper
Former head coach at Ohio State,
Arizona State and Tulsa

INGREDIENTS:

1 8-ounce can minced clams

2 3-ounce packages cream cheese

1 teaspoon Worcestershire sauce

1 teaspoon finely grated onion

1/2 teaspoon Grey Poupon mustard

4 tablespoons reserved clam juice

DIRECTIONS:

• Use an electric hand mixer to blend all ingredients. Refrigerate at least 1 hour. If too thick to spread on crackers, add a small amount of clam juice and mix.

"In our early days, we followed the team on the road. It was always great fun to go to the Rose Bowl, and that happened a lot of times when Woody was coaching. I have enjoyed a lot of great times involving Ohio State football. I have always enjoyed the band, for example. I saw the first script performance by the band in 1936. I once got to lead the band when they were passing through town and stayed overnight. That was some experience, because we always watched the band rehearse before the games."

So here's a toast to Dr. Hab, the "longest standing" tailgater in college football today!

* * *

You may discover from the vast television coverage of the college game that the enthusiasm and commitment to college football knows no bounds — which means that in every section of the country, there is the view that nowhere is the game so appreciated than at the fan's own alma mater. The SEC may have won seven national titles in the last 10 years, but Buckeye fans won't concede that the game is more important than the brand played in Ohio Stadium, the horseshoe-shaped facility built in 1922. The parking lots pregame resemble what you see in Athens or Tuscaloosa or Clemson or Austin or Norman or Ann Arbor: food spreads as varied as anywhere in college football; kids tossing a football; libations in abundance; and a monitoring of other games across the country on a generator-powered television in the parking lot.

Earl Bruce, the coach who succeeded Woody Hayes, once told me about visiting a fraternity at Ohio State in late January. There was elevated toasting, singing and celebration, which caused the bemused coach to ask what had brought about the excitement. "Coach," he was told, "there's only 312 days left 'til the Michigan game."

Food outside Ohio Stadium can range from sub sandwiches to various kinds of grilled meat. Photos by Neal Lauron.

GRIFFIN SAYS TAILGATING LIFTS TEAM

Players and coaches, understandably, don't have the opportunity to tailgate. Administrators also fall in this category. They, however, gain appreciation vicariously. Just listen to Archie Griffin, the two-time Heisman Trophy winner from Ohio State, who is president and CEO of the Ohio State University Alumni Association.

"When I was a freshman, I remember riding in on the team bus and seeing all the tailgaters, cooking and enjoying themselves, and I realized how much the game meant to them," says Griffin. "It got me fired up, and I have never forgotten that scene. When the game started, you didn't want to let those people down.

"I have always admired those folks who are out there, grilling and enjoying their pregame meal," he continued. "Buckeye tailgaters are amazing. They come in the day before and put up their tents and get into the mood starting early on Saturday morning. They play the fight songs and celebrate school tradi-

tions in the most passionate manner. How can you not appreciate all that if you are a coach or a player?

"There have been times in the past when I have had the occasion to walk through the Ohio State tailgates. It gives you such a lift. You can feel the energy as the fans tailgate and demonstrate their school spirit. It is part of the Ohio State tradition to tailgate with the same commitment you have for the team when the game starts.

"When the team plays on the road, we try to find a place where we can hold a 'Buckeye Bash' for our alumni who travel with us. If we can find a place on campus where we can put up a tent, that is what we prefer. If that is not possible, we find a motel or a catering facility where we can do something special for our fans and alumni who travel to support the team.

"The Buckeye tailgate tradition is very important to those who follow the Buckeyes, and that includes those of us who work for Ohio State."

You could almost hear Archie singing the school fight song. This is a man who was described by his iconic coach Woody Hayes as "a better young man than he is a football player, and he's the best football player I have ever seen."

It is easy to understand how Buckeye fans follow their leader.

Buckeye Candy

From Liz Brinson, a Columbus native

INGREDIENTS:

1 stick margarine or butter

1 1-pound box powdered sugar

1 1/2 cups peanut butter

1 teaspoon vanilla

1 12-ounce package chocolate chips

1/2 stick paraffin

DIRECTIONS:

• Mix butter or margarine, powered sugar, peanut butter and vanilla. Form into small balls and refrigerate overnight. Melt chocolate chips and paraffin. Stick the peanut butter balls with a toothpick and then dip in the chocolate/paraffin mixture 3/4 of the way in and then place on a sheet of parchment paper to dry. Repeat until all balls are finished. Allow the candy to harden for about an hour. They can also be refrigerated to preserve for longer periods of time.

Another former Buckeye coach, John Cooper, once said, "They love their football here without question. In fact, if you didn't play here, you didn't play football."

* * *

Kaye Kessler, longtime sports editor of the *Columbus Citizen-Journal*, had good timing in his journalism career. He was there when both Woody Hayes and Jack Nicklaus were in their primes. Kaye had these thoughts about latent involvement with tailgating.

"I have learned more about tailgating worldwide than I actually knew about tailgating at the OSU stadium, which was born a horseshoe in the same 1923 year I drew my first breath. Amazingly, I covered OSU football 45 years and witnessed tailgating all 45 years but never experienced it as I wove my way through the madness getting to the press box. I've witnessed this exercise at every Big Ten campus, at colleges throughout the country, at bowl games from Pasadena to Miami, New Orleans, Arizona and San Diego, but never was I stunned with the scene as much as at OSU where I did take time to mingle with masses when I went back for the OSU-Wisconsin game last fall.

"Visiting an Ohio State tailgate today makes me wonder why I spent all that time in the press box during pregame. I would have had more fun with the tailgaters!"

Neal Lauron photo

RED RIVER SHOWDOWN

Since 1900, Oklahoma and Texas have been competing in an annual football game in the Cotton Bowl in Dallas. The two schools began competition before they had their respective nicknames. The idea was to enhance the attraction of the Texas State Fair. Nothing has changed over the years except the name, which in 2014 was changed to the AT&T Red River Showdown.

Texas and Oklahoma feuded — with lawmen from each state gathering and governors squabbling — about a bridge over the Red River, dating back to 1931, which suggests the two schools have been at odds historically over something or another for over eight decades.

The game was intense and a heated rivalry from the days Texas was a member of the Southwest Conference and Oklahoma played in the Big Eight. When the two teams became members of the same conference, the Big 12 in 1994, the game took on new meaning. The game suddenly had not only conference championship implications, but national as well. Playing in the South Division of the league means that the winner often has the advantage on the road to the conference title.

"I grew up following the game, which has always been a big-time rivalry," says Carl Mayhall, an Oklahoma graduate from Ada, Oklahoma, but now living in Dallas. "But when the two leagues merged, the game's intensity went up a level or two. It was always something; now it's something else."

Carl and his wife, Kathy, are consummate sports fans — from auto racing to golf to NFL games to college football. They reserve their greatest passion for their alma mater, Boomer Sooners nonpareil.

While civility rules in their household — daughter Stephanie is a Texas graduate as is son-in-law Shannon McQuiag, and 10-year-old grandson Alex Smith is a bud-

Shutterstock

Sooner Coffee Cake

From Bob and Carol Stoops
Head coach at
the University of Oklahoma,
former All-Big Ten defensive back at Iowa

INGREDIENTS:

Coffee cake:
1 gluten-free yellow cake mix
1 small instant vanilla pudding
4 eggs
1/2 cup oil
1 cup sour cream

Topping:
1/4 cup sugar
1/4 cup cinnamon
1/2 cup nuts

DIRECTIONS:

• Mix everything together, except the topping ingredients. Put in greased jellyroll pan. Sprinkle topping mixture on top. Bake at 325 degrees for no more than 20 minutes.

• Note from Carol: You can also use a bundt pan. This serves about 10 people.

Polish Sausage Soup

From Barry and Becky Switzer
Former head coach at Oklahoma

INGREDIENTS:

3 large leeks, chopped
4 green bell peppers, chopped
4 red bell peppers, chopped
4 zucchinis, chopped
4 yellow squash, chopped
2 cans whole peeled plum tomatoes
3 packages Polish kielbasa sausage, cut up
Red pepper
Paprika
Brown rice
Olive oil
Salt

DIRECTIONS:

• In a very large covered pot, cook the chopped leeks on low heat with at least 1 cup of olive oil. Chop peppers and add to the pot, then chop zucchinis and add to the pot, and then chop the squash and add to the pot. Add the canned tomatoes and then the sausage, salt (to taste), red pepper and paprika. Mix with brown rice and serve.

---

ding Longhorn fan — the weekend of the Texas State Fair makes the Mayhalls nervous and intense. "My brother Paul gets so uptight, he won't come to the game anymore," says Carl. His mother, Vedo, whose husband was a friend of Bud Wilkinson, showed up for the Red River Shootout until she was 90 years old. She started in 1945. Now that she can't travel anymore from her home in Ada, she watches the game on television with the same enthusiasm she had all those years when she attended the game in the Cotton Bowl.

"I can't imagine emotions getting any higher for a game," says Carl. "The cross-border rivalry is bitter, lasts all year and carries over into other Big 12 sports competitions — even in the daily lives of citizens in both states.

With a 50/50 split of the tickets at the Cotton Bowl, where they have played the game since 1932, the game is a not-to-be-missed college football spectacle.

"The tailgate begins with a meeting of family and friends at the 70-foot tall 'Big Tex' statue," Carl continued. "Thousands of beers are consumed by fans and fairgoers all around the stadium. One of the unique features of the game is that at halftime you can go out and enjoy one of the rides on the midway and grab another beer and a Fletcher's corndog. You can't go to this game without enjoying beer and a Fletcher's corndog.

"When the game is over, the victor celebrates into the night while the loser reaches for another beer, screaming, 'Wait 'til next year!'"

Barry and Becky Switzer's polish sausage soup. Photo courtesy of the Switzers.

Rye Bread Dip

From Jay and Rita Wilkinson
Son of Bud Wilkinson

INGREDIENTS:

3 cups Hellmann's mayonnaise

3 cups sour cream

2 teaspoons dill weed

2 to 3 tablespoons minced onion

2 to 3 packages dried smoked beef

1 large boule rye bread

DIRECTIONS:

• Combine all ingredients except the bread. Hollow out the bread to make a bowl. Cut remaining bread into strips. Fill bread bowl with dip, and place on a large platter. Surround bread bowl with bread strips. Open a cold one and enjoy!

WALT GARRISON STILL GOING STRONG

Boone Pickens is perhaps the best-known Oklahoma State graduate who is committed to Cowboy football, but you could say that the most colorful OSU graduate would be Walt Garrison, who shows up in Stillwater occasionally.

Nobody has ever fit the name of their school better than Garrison does. You don't expect a wolverine to appear in the team's lineup literally at Michigan or tigers at Auburn to dress out, but the day Walt showed up on campus in Stillwater, he was a walking, talking, living, breathing cowboy. Today at his ranch in Argyle, Texas, 40 miles from Dallas, he has a ring on his property where he still ropes for fun, and sometimes competes. "No different than a fellow who loves golf heading to the golf course to do what he likes to do," says Walt. "I just like to rope. Been doin' it all my life, and I still love to rope."

Walt is also an expert carver who often resorts to referring to his hobby as a "whittler." He has a "whittling" room and hangs out there throughout the year, producing wood carvings that he will sometimes donate to charity for auctions, and they go for big bucks.

When his pro football career ended, Walt's varied interests kept him busy and involved with many business liaisons. He has a food company, Walt Garrison Foods. On his website, you are advised that, "Walt Garrison Foods are all about barbecue . . . pure and simple. Look for Walt's line of salsas, rubs, and sauces at your local grocery store."

Walt, the advocate of "just a pinch between your cheek and gum," has been a cowboy all his life. He grew up Western to the core in nearby Lewisville, signed and played collegiately with Oklahoma State's Cowboys, and — wouldn't you know it — became a Dallas Cowboys running back.

Mesa Vista Ham Loaf

From Boone Pickens
Oklahoma State donor and alum

INGREDIENTS:

2 pounds ground ham

1 1/2 pounds ground pork

2 eggs

1 cup dried bread crumbs

1 cup evaporated milk

1/8 teaspoon salt

1/8 teaspoon ground black pepper

1 cup brown sugar

1 tablespoon mustard powder

1/4 cup cider vinegar

DIRECTIONS:

• Preheat oven to 350 degrees. In a large bowl, combine the ham, pork, eggs, bread crumbs, evaporated milk, salt and ground black pepper. Mix all together well and form into a loaf. Place loaf into a lightly greased 9-inch by 13-inch baking dish. Bake at 350 degrees for 90 minutes. While the loaf is baking, combine the brown sugar, mustard powder and vinegar. Mix well and pour over the loaf in the final 15 minutes of baking.

He suspects that if he had been drafted by some distant NFL team with a faraway address, he still would have ended up right where he is today — on his tree-lined ranch. He likes the way life has treated him, and he gets up every day with "roping" on his mind. Just go down to the coral and rope a steer.

Football and roping have been Walt's life. Even when he was a high-paid running back for the Cowboys, he roped on the side. He kept telling management that roping was safe. Tom Landry, the first coach of the Cowboys, showed up at a rodeo to see for himself and came away relieved that a steer wasn't likely to sideline his durable running back. In the end, however, there was a rodeo accident and Walt's career was over. "Didn't really cause any problems, I was done anyway," he says with a drawl. Done after nine years with "America's Team" but what a time it was! Dallas made it to the playoffs six years straight from 1966 to 1971, although a championship seemed to elude them, bringing frustration to a franchise bent on winning titles. Then in 1971, there was that breakthrough. Walt Garrison and the others — including Roger Staubach, Mike Ditka, Dan Reeves and Bob Hayes — were champions. That would be the highlight of Walt's career.

It would be accurate to say that Walt lives alone, but you could also counter that when you visit his "whittling" room, where he spends countless hours carving images with humorous sayings etched into the woodwork. "Slim and Nun" would be a carving of a tall, skinny fellow with a Catholic nun standing beside him. "Stool Samples" would be a flat base with three stools side by side. "Chain Smoker" is a Western-looking hombre with a pipe and a long chain. He carves a lot of walking canes. "Looks like I'm gonna be needin' one pretty soon," he cracked. There is a big pot-bellied stove in the middle of the whittling room. "That's so I can burn my mistakes," Walt said, a reminder that this colorful character is naturally a very funny man.

Walt Garrison's Famous BBQ Sauce

From Walt Garrison
Former Oklahoma State running back

These are the ingredients I use for my barbeque sauce. Try it, you'll like it!

INGREDIENTS:

20 ounces salt
2 ounces black pepper
1 1/2 ounces red pepper
1 1/4 ounces garlic powder
1 ounce onion powder
1/2 ounce paprika
1 1/2 ounces chili powder

THOUGHTS FROM BOONE PICKENS

If you wind your way through the tailgate scene at Oklahoma State games in Stillwater, you are not likely to see Boone Pickens, the billionaire supporter of the Cowboys. Then again, don't be surprised if you look up and see him.

Boone Pickens is Oklahoma's highest-profile fan, who sets the bar high when it comes to contribution to alma mater. When he attends Cowboy basketball games, he interacts with students, explaining that older people are often afraid of change. "Young people are not, which is why I enjoy spending time with them. I like young people."

Boone, as his staff refers to him, is a generous man and sets a fine example within his company. When his company enjoys a good year, Pickens is generous with bonuses. When he hands out bonus checks, he reminds his employees that bonuses for the next year, will again, be based on performance. Then he will add, "Be generous."

In his office, there is a pillow with this poignant message: "Be the person your dog thinks you are."

Shutterstock

After a conversation with Walt, you quickly realize that this is one former player who found a way to use the money he made in the NFL in a fulfilling and productive manner — to buy the property and build the home he always wanted. He used his sports celebrity to connect in business and his down-home personality to make friends who appreciate his genuineness.

Lately, his food business has been flourishing. Walt Garrison Foods makes barbecue sauce, hot salsa, black-eyed pea salsa and sauce for marinating steaks. His company also makes the best of rubs and about anything you would need for an outdoor cookout. "You ain't had salsa until you've had my salsa," he said as he shared a recipe for his favorite rub. It is not uncommon for him to promote two of his products in the same breath.

During his time in Stillwater, Walt helped lead the Cowboys to their first victory over rival Oklahoma in 20 years. What does he remember most about the game?

"If you were a Cowboy football player, you couldn't pay for a beer in town for a week," he says. "The week after that game was one continuous tailgate party — the best tailgate party I have ever seen."

Chicken Tortilla Casserole

From Gary and Sandra Darnell
Former Oklahoma State linebacker,
head coach at Western Michigan and Tennessee
Tech, and assistant coach at nine schools

INGREDIENTS:

1/2 cup chopped onion

1/2 cup chicken broth

1/4 cup celery, chopped

3 cups cooked and shredded chicken

10 to 12 corn tortillas, each cut into 12 wedges

1 4-ounce can green chiles, chopped

1 10 3/4-ounce can cream of chicken soup

1 teaspoon pepper

1 cup grated cheddar cheese

1 cup grated Monterey Jack cheese

1 cup salsa (mild, medium or hot)

DIRECTIONS:

• Combine onion, chicken broth and celery in a small saucepan and bring to a boil. Reduce heat, cover and simmer for 3 or 4 minutes or until vegetables are tender. Transfer to a large mixing bowl. Add chicken, tortilla wedges, chiles, cream of chicken soup and pepper, and mix well. Stir in 1/2 cup cheddar cheese and 1/2 cup Monterey Jack cheese. Spread in a lightly greased 9-inch by 13-inch pan. Top with salsa and remaining cheese. Bake at 350 degrees for 30 minutes. Let stand 5 minutes before serving or transporting to the game!

EVERYTHING IS JUST DUCKY IN EUGENE

If you live in the state of Oregon, you know about the heated rivalry between the University of Oregon in Eugene and Oregon State University in Corvallis. "It is almost bloody," said the rotund Dee Andros, the one-time head coach of the Beavers. "They don't call it the 'Civil War' for nothing."

There are some interesting incongruities about the Oregon-Oregon State Civil War, however. Mitch Parker, the play-by-play voice of the Beavers, is an Oregon alumnus. The field at Oregon's Autzen Stadium is named for Rich Brooks, who played football at Oregon State, coached at his alma mater and became the Ducks' head coach. Autzen Stadium is named for Thomas Autzen, who was an alumnus of Oregon State.

Sounds to me like Oregonians are more civil than their reputation when it comes to the instate football rivalry. For example, I don't think you would find a player at Texas or Texas A&M, or at Auburn or Alabama, becoming the head coach at the other school — and to have the field named for you!

There are at least two reasons why Duck fans are fond of Rich Brooks. First, he won the Pacific Coast Conference championship in 1994, which brought about a Rose Bowl invitation for the Ducks. The other? He posted a 14-3-1 record against his alma mater, Oregon State, during his time as the Oregon head coach.

If you enter in conversation with an Oregon fan, you learn right away there is enduring respect in Eugene for Brooks, who often returns to campus for Duck home games — like Carrie Blythe, the daughter of one of Brooks' good friends, Chris Blythe. Carrie works for the Duck Store on the Oregon campus. "That's where you get the best Duck stuff for whatever you need," says Carrie. Spend time with Carrie and then head to the game, "looking Ducking good."

"The one thing that is special about tailgating at Oregon is how the whole town comes alive for game days," Carrie says. "Local businesses, the staff and almost all cars are decorated with green and yellow, supporting the beloved Oregon Ducks. The atmosphere at Autzen

Oregon's Carrie Blythe and her friends are big fans of tailgating.

Cheese Enchiladas

From Rich and Karen Brooks
Former head coach at Oregon and Kentucky

INGREDIENTS:

For the enchiladas:

8 small flour tortillas

4 cups shredded pepper jack cheese

8 tablespoons green onions, sliced

For the sauce:

1/4 cup butter

1/4 cup flour

2 cups chicken broth

1 cup sour cream

1 can diced green chilies

DIRECTIONS:

• Fill the tortillas with cheese and onions. Roll and then cut in half, and place it in a greased baking dish.

• To make the white sauce, melt butter and add the flour, then stir. Stir in the broth to make a thick sauce. Remove from heat and add sour cream and chilies.

• Pour the sauce over the tortillas and bake at 350 degrees for 20 minutes or until it bubbles.

Stadium is electric on game days and truly makes it a special place to tailgate.

"Before every home game, the Moshofsky Center, the indoor practice facility, turns into a large tailgate party, where fans can gather, enjoying food and drinks while listening to the live radio broadcast and participating in the activities that are offered," she continued. "Then, usually about two hours before kickoff, the team and coaching staff does a walk through as they make their way to the locker room, which is something fans always get excited about. Other traditions that you wouldn't want to miss if you were to tailgate at Oregon would be to just walk around the various tailgaters located in the Autzen parking lot. Personally, my friends and I have a tradition to shotgun a beer at every tailgate, so you wouldn't want to miss that either. The gates to the parking lot at Autzen open four hours prior to kickoff, so usually fans are lined up to go in then. My family and I usually get to the stadium at least three hours before kickoff. Many fans bring their motorhomes and stay overnight before the game. Most fans enjoy a postgame party, but if it's a blowout, which has been the case in recent years, the parking lot gets pretty empty.

"Our tailgates don't take place on campus since our stadium is across the river, which separates the campus from the stadium. Duck fans enjoy 'the walk' across the footbridge, which leads you from campus, over the Willamette River, to the stadium. 'Animal House' was filmed here back in late 1970s, so some of the old buildings are still here. Oregon is also known as Track Town USA, which includes the famous landmark Pre's Rock, which is dedicated to the famous runner, Steve Prefontaine. It is located where his fatal car accident happened. A lot of runners often leave their shoes and other items in his honor."

Tailgating allows old friends to catch up and have a good time. Photos by Carrie Blythe.

QUITE A SCENE IN STATE COLLEGE

State College is one of those small communities where learning and football are staples of endearing pride by the local inhabitants — the latest population figures show State College home to nearly 42,000 people. State College is small-town America at its best.

Nestled into the Allegheny Mountains, State College is in the heart of Pennsylvania. If you placed a bull's-eye in the center of the geographically square state, you would likely place it near State College, which is 191 miles west of Philadelphia and 135 miles east of Pittsburgh.

State College is anchored in a rural setting, and when Beaver Stadium is filled to capacity with 106,572 fans, it would rank as the fourth-largest city in the state after Philadelphia, Pittsburgh and Allentown.

Penn State, recovering from NCAA sanctions, is making a comeback. On game day in the fall, nobody is more enthusiastic about the home team than Nittany Lion fans who are undisputed national champions when it comes to RV participation.

West of the stadium there are acres and acres of spaces for RV units, which come prepared to tailgate and enjoy game day. Becky McWhorter, wife of a one-time Penn State assistant Mac McWhorter, has observed tailgating wherever her husband has coached, including Georgia, Clemson, Georgia Tech and Texas.

"Penn State has absolutely the best parking for tailgating that we have seen anywhere in the country," Becky says. "About six weeks prior to the first home game, every stitch of grass is lined like a parking lot with concrete markers, so they are able to get at least 25 percent more folks in their lots. According to the athletic director's office, there are three big RV lots, and an RV is parked every 48 seconds.

"Sites to visit are the Nittany Lion statue at Rec Hall, the secret gazebo behind the engineering building and anywhere on College Avenue — nothing has changed much in the last 30 years, so you can always revisit your old hangouts," Becky continued.

"Penn Staters are tough — they are accustomed to tailgating in adverse conditions, so they are not fazed by any kind of weather. Lots open at 7 a.m. for games that begin at noon, and at 8 a.m. for any game that starts after noon. Folks are lined up well in advance of that.

"You can wander into any tailgate and folks will welcome you — there's a great sense of camaraderie — and you don't have to bring food or drink. You are still welcome.

"Penn Staters enjoy their pirogues, Italian wedding soups, sausages, brats and most of all, their adult drinks — you'll find a stocked bar worthy of a business establishment at each tailgate."

* * *

One of the best-known Penn State graduates is Todd Blackledge, who quarterbacked the Nittany Lions to their first national championship in the Sugar Bowl in 1981.

Todd, now an analyst for ESPN, is one of the best-known food advocates around and has written a book on the restaurants in college cities called *Taste of the Town*. Todd seems to find the best place for food in every town he visits, and eating establishments are eager to host him when they know he is coming to campus to work a game.

Todd often visited us during the time that he was a CBS analyst. After he moved over to ESPN, his assignment did not include SEC games, or at least not very often. There were times when he would bring along one of his kids. Then he traveled one year in a motor home with his wife, Cherie, homeschooling their four boys: Harrison, Quinn, Eli and Owen. They joined us for dinner one night and fit right in with our friends.

Penn State fans outside the stadium before a "white-out" game.

Kiboki Steak With Marinade

Todd and Cherie Blackledge
ESPN and Penn State alum

INGREDIENTS:

1/2 cup soy sauce

1/2 cup teriyaki sauce

2 tablespoons sugar

1/4 cup green onions, sliced

1 tablespoon garlic, crushed

2 teaspoons fresh ginger, ground

3 tablespoons olive oil

3 tablespoons sesame seeds

4 to 5 pounds flank steak, double tenderized

DIRECTIONS:

• Combine ingredients and stir well. Slice meat into 1-inch-thick strips and place in a container to marinate. Pour the liquid over meat and marinate for 6 to 8 hours, turning and flipping to ensure all meat gets covered with the sauce. Grill for 2 to 3 minutes per side. Serve immediately and watch it fly off the platter!

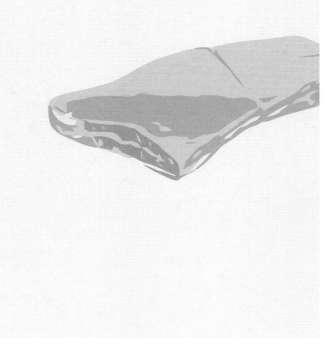

Shutterstock

Todd enjoys college football and is a wonderful ambassador for the game. With a quarterback's prospective, he has an excellent grasp of the game as it plays out. What he applied to basic talent and communication skills, is due diligence and hard work. He is always well prepared with a smooth and unruffled delivery.

We have had many conversations about life and sports on our back porch. If you make friends in this business of college football, you will always be the beneficiary of a lot of fulfilling and enlightening conversations.

In his book *Taste of the Town*, Todd wrote about the places he frequented when he played for the Nittany Lions during the peak of the Joe Paterno era — places like Ye Olde College Diner, The Waffle Shop and Herwig's Austrian Bistro. But there was a certain creamery that he could not resist writing about. "It's a rarity," he wrote in his book, "to have a major dairy farm operation right on a college campus, and that's what makes the Berkey Creamery such a special part of the Penn State experience. I just love the fresh homemade ice cream, which is offered in tons of fun flavors. Anyone who goes to a Penn State football game, or anyone just visiting campus for any reason, has to stop by the Berkey Creamery to get ice cream. In my basement at home in Ohio — and I am talking about right now — I have insulated bags to transport the ice cream I buy at the Berkey Creamery. Whenever I visit Penn State, I buy at least two half-gallons of ice cream and put it on dry ice and bring it home."

Todd also wrote about the honor of being the starting quarterback on the first official national championship team at Penn State, riding the blue school buses from the locker room to Beaver Stadium and sitting by Joe Paterno during his varsity years. That seat, next to Paterno, was always reserved for the starting quarterback.

"It was not a long trip," Todd wrote, "but we would slowly wind our way past thousands of cheering blue-and-white-clad tailgaters. It was always amazing to see what went on all around Beaver Stadium in the hours before a game."

Tailgate Ham Sandwiches

From Bill & Colleen O'Brien
Former head coach at Penn State, Head coach of the NFL's Houston Texans

INGREDIENTS:

1 package of party-size rolls, 24 total

8 medium-think slices of boiled ham (about 1.5 pounds)

12 slices of Swiss cheese

1 stick of butter

1 tablespoon of yellow mustard

1 to 2 teaspoons of Worcestershire sauce

1 tablespoon poppy seeds

DIRECTIONS:

• Melt butter in a sauce pan or microwave. Add Worcestershire sauce, mustard and poppy seeds, and blend. Place the bottom half of the rolls in a 9-inch by 13-inch pan. Brush half of the butter mixture on the bottoms of the rolls. Place the ham on the rolls. Layer the cheese slices over the ham. Put the dinner roll tops back on. Brush the tops of the rolls with the remaining half of the butter mixture. Cover with foil and bake in a 375 degree oven for 15 minutes or until the cheese is melted. You can also refrigerate them unbaked overnight and cook for a bit longer. Enjoy!

"IT ISN'T ALL ABOUT FOOTBALL"

"Tailgating at Purdue is highly festive, wonderfully social, decidedly creative and thoroughly enjoyable," says Jim Meyer, a longtime Purdue tailgater and alum.

In truth, notwithstanding the celebrated exploits of iconic past Purdue quarterbacks like Drew Brees, Bob Griese, Gary Danielson and Len Dawson, the more notable highlights of recent Purdue football Saturdays are much more likely to be of the tailgate than of the game itself.

"A typical Purdue tailgate commences early and is located in the parking areas north of Ross-Ade Stadium at the northwest end of campus," says Jim. "Our favorite spot for some excellent food and libation is found on the adjacent golf course that turns into a primetime mecca. Our son Andrew's fraternity, the Delta Delta chapter of Sigma Chi, has an excellent tailgate hosted all game long in this sought-after locale, and it offers fare that rivals any you will find anywhere. Attended by current, past and future Boilermakers — from octogenarians to frat stars to beautiful coeds to pre-schoolers, all dressed in Old Gold and Black — it often lures people away from the nearby stadium scene. Succumbing to the temptation of spending the day at this tailgate instead of one's 40-yard line seat is not uncommon in recent years as Purdue's win totals have steadily declined and the tailgating has steadily improved.

"The food and drink are in abundance, of course," Jim continued. "Food items include favorites like fried chicken, sandwiches, chips and dip, deserts, etc. but also includes Midwestern delights like grilled bratwurst,

Shutterstock

THRIVING AT PURDUE

In his role as manager of the Purdue Trademark Licensing Office, Jim Vruggink patrols the Boilermaker parking lots pregame to make sure there are no violators of licensing policies. This also allows for a monitoring of the tailgate scene. Jim has learned who the most versatile and passionate tailgaters are, including Jeff McKean.

"Jeff and his friends, mostly from Indianapolis, rank among the best," Jim says. "They are always cordial and generous with food, snacks and beverages — and above all, supportive of Purdue football through thick and thin. Unfortunately, we've had a lot of 'thin' lately, but the McKean tailgate still thrives famously.

"In general, we have a great setup for tailgating at Purdue with several lots plus an adjacent university-owned golf course. Another prime location is a hilltop grove of trees that overlooks an amphitheater, part of the athletic complex and spacious intramural fields that are all available for tailgaters.

"Tailgating is usually at its best and most robust for the Notre Dame game, which usually happens in September in alternating years," Jim continued. "Those classic fall days when we host Notre Dame become unforgettable. The weather is perfect, and the day-long buildup for an 8 p.m. game under the lights is like one gigantic party, with the Goodyear blimp floating overhead in the bright blue sky, and roar (amid load music) of thousands of people having a great time."

This is a scene that is played out on campuses all over the country, not just Purdue, reminding us again that college football is the greatest of games.

Bob Griese's Cuban Sandwich

From Bob and Shay Griese
All-American quarterback at Purdue, member of the College and Pro Football Halls of Fame

INGREDIENTS:

1 sweet onion, finely chopped
Green relish (or pickles)
1 loaf Cuban bread
Yellow mustard
Mayonnaise
Spiced pork, sliced
Ham, sliced
Swiss cheese, thinly sliced
Butter or vegetable oil

DIRECTIONS:

• In a bowl, mix onion with an equal amount of green relish, and then set aside. Slice the bread lengthwise and remove the soft part, leaving a trough. Slather one side with yellow mustard and the other side with mayonnaise. Layer the sliced pork and ham until the sandwich is about 1/2-inch thick. Sprinkle the onion and relish mixture along the length of the bread and then cover with Swiss cheese. Cut the sandwich in half, butter — or spray lightly with vegetable oil — and place in a panini press (or a cookie sheet, or a shallow frying pan). After heating, cut the sandwich into 2-inch diagonal pieces and serve.

Note from Bob: This Cuban travels well when wrapped in foil. If you don't have a panini press as we didn't years ago, take a cookie sheet, put the sandwich on the sheet and place a brick on top of that to give it weight to press the sandwich flat. Cook over low heat until the cheese is melted and the bread is toasted. If you use a shallow frying pan, you will need to flip the sandwich to toast the other side.

hamburgers, liverwurst and onions, summer sausage, fresh cheese and crackers with all the condiments. Drinks range from spicy Bloody Marys to sweet mimosas to chilled bottles of Pinot Grigio to cold beer of all varieties, and the most determined Purdue tailgater might actually start his day with a true 'Boilermaker,' although it's hardly recommended for the faint of heart or weak of stomach.

"In addition to the wonderful aroma of the grilled bratwurst and the taste of a good Bloody, the senses are also tingled by the sounds of Purdue on game day. After listening to a pregame concert by the Purdue Orchestra

DANIELSON STILL PREPARED

Gary Danielson, one of the many quarterbacks who got their collegiate schooling at Purdue and then became starters in the NFL, is one of the most enthusiastic sports announcers there is in the business.

The *Sporting News*, a few years back, rated him the best announcer, including the play-by-play guys. "He is so well-prepared, he can anticipate what is going to happen before it takes place," is how one expert put it.

Sometimes when I am in South Florida in the spring, I try to visit with Gary and talk football. There is no offseason for Gary. He "studies up" on the game and the SEC year-round. He tries to make sure he doesn't miss anything, including off-the-field developments. Spend time with him, and you'll understand how the *Sporting News* came to its cogent assessment.

When Gary stops by to visit with us in the fall, he often comes out back and watches the tenderloin as it cooks. He asks questions. "Why do you do that?" he might ask when water is poured on the meat as it turns. The reply, "To keep the meat moist," makes him nod approvingly. You know he is making mental notes for consideration the next time he fires up his own grill in Bonita Springs, Florida. A well-respected and highly regarded color announcer is always inquisitive — even away from the game.

Shrimp In Beer With Red Onions Appetizer

From Bob and Shay Griese
All-American quarterback at Purdue, member of the College and Pro Football Halls of Fame

INGREDIENTS:

3 bottles regular beer
Old Bay Seafood Seasoning
Fresh or frozen shrimp, cooked and peeled
Mayonnaise
Juice from 1/2 lemon
Red onion, finely chopped
Green onions, finely chopped
Lettuce leaves

DIRECTIONS:

• In a medium stockpot, combine beer and seasoning, and bring to a boil. Add cooked and peeled shrimp, and bring back to a boil for 5 to 10 minutes. Drain and let cool, and then remove the shrimp tails. Pour into a mixing bowl and add more seasoning, mayonnaise to lightly cover and lemon juice. Add the red onion and mix, and then refrigerate. Cut the end off the other half of the lemon and place in the center of a platter. Using large lettuce leaves, make a bed for the shrimp on the platter. Stick toothpicks into the lemon that folks can use to poke the shrimp. Arrange the chilled shrimp on the platter and then sprinkle with green onions.

on nearby Slater Hill, one can hear the renowned Purdue Marching Band winding its way through the carefully parked (by Purdue engineers) RVs, SUVs and tents, with 'Hail Purdue' as the undisputed crowd favorite. Another sound that new Purdue tailgaters won't likely forget hearing the distinctive train whistle of the Purdue Boilermaker Special, a replica train locomotive driven around campus prior to football games for 75 years by the Purdue Reamer Club. The verbal highlight for many is the famous 'I am an American' soliloquy performed right before kickoff.

"I must say that no tailgater has been more loyal than my wife Kim's 82-year-old mother and Purdue alum Skipper Christen. Although she can't drive herself for the 4 1/2-hour trip from Toledo, Ohio, can't walk without assistance and no longer is escorted by her beloved departed fellow alumnus and husband Fred Christen, she finds a way to make it to almost every Purdue football game and never misses an "I am an American." She can always be found with fellow John Purdue Club members at their seats in the Shively Suites no matter what the score of

White Bean Chili

From Drew Brees
Former All-Big Ten quarterback at Purdue, quarterback for the New Orleans Saints

INGREDIENTS:

2 tablespoons olive oil

1 large onion, chopped

1 4-ounce can chopped green chiles

2 teaspoons garlic powder

2 teaspoons salt

2 teaspoons ground cumin

2 teaspoons ground oregano

2 teaspoons ground coriander

1/4 teaspoon cayenne pepper

3 15-ounce cans Great Northern white beans, drained

2 5.2-ounce cans chicken, drained

2 15-ounce cans chicken broth

DIRECTIONS:

• In a large pot, heat oil over medium heat. Add the onion and sauté until brown. Add the next seven ingredients and stir until mixed well. Stir in remaining ingredients and return to a boil. Reduce heat and simmer 20 minutes or until heated throughout.

Jeff McKean's tailgate party always draws a crowd.

the game. Hope springs eternal in the heart of a true Purdue fan, and she is clearly at the top of that list.

"The food, drink, sights and sounds of a Purdue tailgate are terrific, but the best part for Kim and me is clearly the chance to spend time with our son Andrew, our beloved mother-in-law/mom Skipper, and our faithful friends who brave the cold, the wet, the early and often the lopsided defeat to enjoy a remarkable time at a great university. See, it isn't all about football everywhere."

THOUGHTS ON GRIESE

Bob Griese, the quarterback who helped lead the Miami Dolphins to an undefeated season in 1972, the only NFL team with such distinction, never tailgated much, as you would expect.

That was, however, the year he had planned to go to a postgame tailgate party. But a not-so-funny thing happened. He broke his ankle, not only missing the tailgate party, but much of the season. He returned to action during the second half of the playoff game against the Pittsburgh Steelers, and then on to the Super Bowl championship and a perfect record.

Griese is one of 15 Purdue quarterbacks who became NFL players, including Drew Brees, Scott Campbell, Gary Danielson, Len Dawson Bob DeMoss, Jim Everett, Mark Herrmann, Kyle Orton, Curtis Painter, Mike Phipps and Dale Samuels.

Bob's wife, Shay, has authored a nice cookbook, which she titled, *Griese Spoon*.

IT ALL STARTED WITH RUTGERS

College football had its beginning when Rutgers defeated Princeton 6-4 on Nov. 6, 1869, in New Brunswick. It was more like a baseball score, and the game hardly resembled what we see today when college teams face off on fall Saturdays.

The first game was played under rugby rules derived from the London Football Association. The game was an instant hit, although history tells us that originally the two teams were scheduled to play a three-game series. The first one played at Rutgers we know about, the one that made history. The second game took place at Princeton, which the Tigers won, an indication that we would always take note that there was a home-field advantage in this classic sport, which long ago captured the fancy of Americans. The rubber match was never played. Following the second game, the faculties weighed in and decreed that the game was "interfering with student studies." That, some cynics would say, was the last time academics exercised control of football.

In that first season, the Scarlet Knights shared the national title with Princeton, but has not particularly distinguished itself when it comes to championships. Rutgers has won three Middle Atlantic Conference titles and one Big East championship since 1969.

Kate Burkholder Copp, a 2008 graduate of Rutgers who has spent time at Duke and Georgia, says that while tailgating is popular at Rutgers, "it is very different from that of the Southern schools. Casual clothing is standard — jeans, t-shirts and player jerseys." She adds, "Everybody, men and women, wear red — always.

"You see a lot of activity before Rutgers kickoffs," says Kate. "Touch football, Frisbee and cornhole games are popular, as they are on all campuses. You see the block 'R' everywhere. The most popular foods are burgers and hot dogs on the grill, and everybody knows the Rutgers cheer, 'Upstream, Red Team.'"

R-U, rah, rah,
Woo-Raa, Whoo-Raa;
Rutgers Rah,
Up-Stream Red Team;
Red Team Up-Stream
Rah, Rah,
Rutgers Rah!

Fans gather to greet the Rutgers squad when the team buses deliver the Scarlet Knights to the stadium. Players enter the stadium via the Scarlet Walk, passing by the "First Game" statue that commemorates that first game between Rutgers and Princeton. They touch it for good luck before entering the stadium.

"Yankee" Dip

From Tom Stephens, RU Faculty Athletics Representative

Note from Tom: "The name 'Yankee Dip' came from some friends in England who love this recipe and call it Yankee because we are Americans — or 'Yanks' or 'Yankees' to them. The name has nothing to do with the North of the United States. Any Southerner, which I am, can tell you about pimento cheese sandwiches at all picnics and covered-dish suppers. Actually, this recipe originally comes from a friend in Pennsylvania, who took a simple pimento cheese recipe and added onion. It is always a hit at tailgates, parties or at home in front of the TV watching your favorite team.

INGREDIENTS:

10 ounces extra sharp cheddar cheese, grated

1 small-medium strong-flavored onion, grated

1 small jar chopped pimentos, drained

Mayonnaise to moisten, about 6 ounces

DIRECTIONS:

• Place all ingredients in mixing bowl. Add mayonnaise slowly, checking for thickness. Mixture should not be runny, but more like the texture of fresh guacamole. Stir thoroughly and chill. Serve with Ritz Crackers or similar crackers, hard pretzels or pita wedges. Serves 4 to 6 people as a snack or appetizer.

"THERE REALLY IS A SLIPPERY ROCK"

"**A**lthough Slippery Rock University tailgating probably occurred prior to 1937, Oct. 9, 1937, changed everything — forever," says Dr. Robert J. Watson, former vice president for Student Affairs at Slippery Rock. "The name Slippery Rock University and its predecessors — Slippery Rock State College, Slippery Rock State Teachers College and Slippery Rock State Normal School — conjure up different ideas in peoples' minds, but one question has always stood out: is it real?

"Those near and dear to the university with an unusual name know it's real from the allegiance and green and white pride coursing in their veins, but others not associated have wondered about its legitimacy for years," Bob continued. "All of that doubt was put to rest by William Gary Cunningham, a Boston sportswriter, as he created, almost singlehandedly, the coming-out celebration for little old Slippery Rock State Teachers College, founded in 1889. And, on that fateful fall day, as head coach N. Kerr Thompson and assistant coach A.P. Vincent led their little-known Slippery Rock football team onto the Fenway Park field to do battle with the hometown favorite, Boston University, the nation and beyond found out 'there really is a Slippery Rock.'

"Perhaps not ranking up there with the largest Slippery Rock tailgate, one thing is for sure, the Fenway Park game became the catalyst for thousands of Slippery Rock tailgates and their fans for decades to come. It was this single game that ushered Slippery Rock onto the big dance floor and caused so many across the nation to want to know more about the darling from western Pennsylvania. From that day forward, Slippery Rock scores began to be announced at stadiums all over the nation, from Michigan to Texas and from Florida to New England. Football fans wanted to know how Slippery Rock was making out against their opponent that day.

"With the interest in the game scores came the increased tailgate conversations — everywhere. Maybe the Slippery Rock tailgates were not as big as many larger schools, but the talk about Slippery Rock was big. Home and away game tailgates where SRU was competing were not the only tailgates where 'The Rock' was being discussed. Instead of a mere dozen or so tailgate parties a year, Slippery Rock discussions have claimed hundreds more.

Sausage Balls

From George & Laura Mihalik
Head coach at Slippery Rock

INGREDIENTS:

2 rolls of Bob Evans Hot Sausage

2 cups grated sharp cheddar cheese

2 cups flour

Chopped onion

DIRECTIONS:

• Mix together and form into balls. Bake on a wire rack at 350 degrees for about 45 minutes.

Shutterstock

"First in the mid-1950s and then in the early 1960s, a newer magazine targeting those who followed athletics, *Sports Illustrated*, wrote about the little western Pennsylvania town, their college, their football team and their tailgate parties. A writer even traveled to campus to take in a weekend, a football game and, of course, a tailgate! Slippery Rock continued to be noticed by many. Some say it was the undefeated and championship football teams beginning in 1907 that led Slippery Rock State Normal School to fame. Others talk about the great teams of Coach Thompson in the teens, 1920s, 1930s and 1940s as the impetus for fame. Some point to the three state championship teams led by Coach DiSpirito in the 1970s. Many tailgate conversations focus on the current coach, Dr. George Mihalik, whose name is written, along with Coach Thompson, on the stadium forever. Dr./Coach Mihalik has been there from the 1970s, and coached many great teams and players, and has certainly been the topic of many tailgate conversations.

"Nevertheless, as the warmth of summer draws to a close and a chill in the air begins to be noticed, the hardwoods of the Northeast begin to adorn their fall colors of orange, gold and red. These and other signs signal the arrival of football season and tailgating. Whether it's out of a large motor home or a subcompact, the tailgates will form wherever Slippery Rock plays and beyond.

"Slippery Rock fans have their specialties for tailgating, oftentimes homemade," Bob continued. "Whether it's burgers made from premium Angus beef from one of the small butcher shops in the area, great smoked meats from Willies in nearby Harrisville, or venison from the surrounding farms or woodlots, one will smell the grilled flavor in the air. Some may suggest that one sandwich or dish reigns over another, but Slippery Rock tailgate foods are like the fans who prepare them — diverse and plentiful! Yes, it's true that there are bigger tailgates all over the nation like at the Big House in Michigan, but our fan tailgates are no less passionate.

"Slippery Rock has been the brunt of jokes for decades from colleges and universities all over the nation. And, like the 1937 Fenway Park fans found out, Slippery Rock University is real. Our fans carry a sense of pride with them no matter where they go, and no matter where they tailgate. Slippery Rock fans believe that the Slippery Rock name attracts attention and creates jealousy — that's right, jealousy. That's why we refer to all the other colleges and universities as Slippery Rock wannabes! Go Rock!"

ALL ABOARD THE SOUTH CAROLINA TAILGATE!

When it comes to South Carolina history, every Gamecock knows about George Rogers, who won the Heisman Trophy in 1980. Likely they know that there have been some hot names in the coaching profession to wear garnet and black, including Dan Reeves, a former player who took the Denver Broncos and the Atlanta Falcons to the Super Bowl as head coach. They remember the late Paul Dietzel, who won a national championship at LSU; Lou Holtz, who won one title at Notre Dame; Joe Morrison, who distinguished himself with the New York Giants before winning 39 games in Columbia; and, of course, the current head coach, Steve Spurrier, who won a Heisman Trophy while playing at the University of Florida and a national championship while coaching in Gainesville.

They can tell you about Sterling Sharpe, who was an All-Pro receiver with the Green Bay Packers and whose jersey was retired at South Carolina. And, Hootie Johnson, who played for the Gamecocks and became chairman of the Augusta National Golf Club.

But what about Ed Robinson? That question might cause even the most astute Gamecock fan to scratch his or her head before attempting an answer.

Robinson's impact on Gamecock lore and legend, however, will live as long as the Cockaboose leases on a quarter-mile spur of railroad track are renewed. Right now, there are 75 years remaining on the leases. It was Robinson who came up with the idea of what has become one of the neatest game-day features to college football tailgating. It was his concept that led to the Cockaboose Railroad.

The spur, owned by CSX Railroad, is near Williams-Brice Stadium, less than a football field away. After securing a lease with the railroad, Robinson and a partner, Carl F. Howard, bought 22 cabooses and moved them onto the spur. The cabooses were pretty much shells of

Peach Pie

From Dan Reeves
Former South Carolina quarterback, and former head coach for the Dallas Cowboys, Denver Broncos, New York Giants & Atlanta Falcons

INGREDIENTS:

1 large can peaches, drained and cut in medium-sized pieces

1 large package cream cheese

1 can Eagle Brand condensed milk

1 large container of Cool Whip

Juice from 2 lemons

2 large or 3 small Graham Cracker piecrusts

DIRECTIONS:

• In a large mixing bowl, cream the softened cream cheese and condensed milk. Add juice of lemon and Cool Whip. Add peaches (other kinds of canned fruit may also be used). You can save a few pieces of fruit to garnish the top of the pies. Divide the filling between the piecrust and refrigerate until ready to serve.

South Carolina fans depart the Cockaboose Railroad. Photo courtesy of KathyMillerTime.com.

HAWKINS STICKS TO HIS STORY

Alex Hawkins played at the University of South Carolina and then became one of the most popular players of the doting Baltimore fans, the Johnny Unitas Colts.

Playing cards and drinking beer all night became routine for him, even after he retired after 10 years in the National Football League.

"Hawk" wrote two very fine books, *That's my Story and I'm Sticking to it* and *Then Came Brain Damage*. He wrote them without a ghostwriter, and the books were well written. Interestingly, the title of the first book is a well-traveled story among football players across the landscape. He told it on himself.

One morning, Hawk related, he came in about the time his first wife, Libby, was preparing breakfast for the kids before they headed out to school. "OK, Hawk, where were you this time?" Libby inquired.

"Well," Hawk began. "I played cards until well past midnight, and when I got home, I realized I didn't have my house key. I didn't want to wake you up. I looked for the hide-a-key and couldn't remember where we put it. So I just slept in the hammock out back."

"Hawk," Libby intoned, "we took that hammock down two years ago."

Undaunted, Hawk replied, "That's my story and I'm sticking to it."

Shutterstock

what they once were, which meant that after buying a caboose for $45,000, you then had to pay to spruce it up. "That," says Bob Davis, who came into an ownership position with one of the original purchasers, "can be whatever one wants to spend." Some have spent lavishly — $100,000 and more. All are becoming and bring about curious onlookers on game day.

There is a sitting room and a kitchenette downstairs, with the top of the caboose becoming a deck where people can relax and enjoy the sights and sounds of the nearby stadium. "We can actually see the big video board at the stadium," says Dr. Hank Jolly, Davis' partner in Cockaboose No. 10. Some Cockaboose owners put grills and flat-screen TVs on their roof.

While Gamecock game day is the focal point of the owners, the Cockabooses have been used for concerts and high school playoff games at the stadium, church socials, bachelor parties, bridal showers and wedding re-

Steve Spurrier's Favorite Beef Barbecue Sandwiches

From Steve and Jeri Spurrier
Head coach at South Carolina,
and former head coach at Duke and Florida;
two-time All-America quarterback
at Florida

INGREDIENTS:

3 ounces Liquid Smoke

Minced garlic, to taste

Pepper, to taste

Onion salt or garlic salt, to taste

Meat tenderizer

Worcestershire sauce, to taste

1 6-pound boneless sirloin steak

Barbecue Sauce:

1 14-ounce bottle catsup

1 12-ounce bottle chili sauce

1/2 teaspoon prepared mustard

1 1/2 cups packed brown sugar

2 tablespoons pepper

1 1/2 cups wine vinegar

1 cup lemon juice

1/2 cup thick steak sauce

Tabasco Sauce, to taste

1/4 tablespoon soy sauce

2 tablespoons vegetable oil

1 can beer

Minced garlic, to taste

DIRECTIONS:

• Combine the Liquid Smoke, garlic, pepper, onion/garlic salt, meat tenderizer and Worcestershire sauce in a large container. Add the steak. Marinate in the refrigerator for 24 to 48 hours. Place the steak in a roasting pan. Pour the remaining marinade over the steak. Bake, covered, at 275 degrees for 5 hours. Let cool in the refrigerator. Slice just before serving to avoid dryness. Serve on sandwich rolls with horseradish, lettuce, tomato and mayonnaise or with the barbecue sauce below.

Barbecue Sauce:

• Combine the catsup, chili sauce, mustard, brown sugar, pepper, vinegar, lemon juice, steak sauce, Tabasco Sauce, soy sauce, oil, beer and garlic in a large bowl and mix well. Pour into six 1-pint jars. Store in the refrigerator or freezer until ready to use.

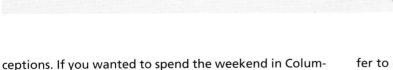

ceptions. If you wanted to spend the weekend in Columbia and stay at your Cockaboose, you could.

Bob and his wife, Sally, invited Hank and his wife, Michelle, of Gaffney, to become co-owners in 2000. The Jollys are dentists and longtime season ticket buyers. The two couples have a core group of about 20 friends who tailgate with them at every Gamecock home game. "Most of the Cockaboose owners," says Bob Davis, "pre-

fer to cater, but most us of have grills for cooking burgers and hot dogs."

"The big thing," says Hank Jolly, "is that we socialize and enjoy ourselves. It is a very festive atmosphere. It's a lot like a family reunion in the fall. We get to see our friends every home game."

When Ed Robinson and Carl Howard put the 22 empty cabooses up for sale in 1991, they sold out in three days. All the cabooses look the same on the outside, but when

A COMPETITIVE NICE GUY

When Dan Reeves was playing all the high school sports in Americus, Georgia, he earned a reputation for excelling at everything he did. However, the two in-state schools — the University of Georgia and Georgia Tech — did not offer him a scholarship following his senior year in high school in 1960. Some of that had to do with his missing several games with a broken collarbone.

Weems Baskin, the track coach who doubled as a football recruiter at South Carolina, felt Dan was a "diamond in the rough," so he offered him a scholarship when no other major school showed much interest. Dan committed to Baskin and the Gamecocks.

An interesting development soon would take place. Dan was invited to play in the 1961 summer all-star game where his excellent performance brought him MVP honors. Immediately he got the big rush from Georgia, Georgia Tech and other Southern schools.

It wasn't, however, a dilemma for Dan. He talked it over with his father and they agreed: "We gave Coach Baskin our word that we would go to South Carolina and we should keep our word."

Loyalty is something of a trademark with Dan Reeves. His college coach was Marvin Bass, with whom Dan developed a close rapport. When Dan became the head coach of the Denver Broncos, he gave his old coach a job. When the New York Giants hired Dan, the former South Carolina quarterback again offered a job to Bass, who was unable to join him in New York, owing to a stroke suffered by Bass' wife. At Dan's final NFL stop with the Atlanta Falcons, Coach Bass again became a member of the Reeves' staff.

From high school to college to the NFL, where he took four of his teams to the Super Bowl, Dan Reeves has always enjoyed a solid reputation as a coach and a gentleman — a determined competitor on the field, but a genuine nice guy away from the competition.

Dan Reeves' Pineapple Pie

Former South Carolina quarterback, and former head coach for the Dallas Cowboys, Denver Broncos, New York Giants & Atlanta Falcons

When Dan Reeves was playing for the Dallas Cowboys, he prepared desert on road trips for himself and his roommate, Walt Garrison. "Dan Reeves' Pineapple Pie" was a big hit. "It is easy to make and takes care of my sweet tooth," Dan says.

INGREDIENTS:

1 14-ounce can of sweetened condensed milk
1 20-ounce can crushed pineapple
1 16-ounce can sliced peaches
1/2 cup lemon juice
1/2 cup flaked coconut
1 12-ounce container of Cool Whip
2 Graham Cracker piecrusts

DIRECTIONS:

• Combine milk and lemon juice, and mix well. Drain pineapple and peaches well. Cut peach slices into thirds. Add peaches, pineapple, coconut and nuts to milk mixture and mix well. Fold in thawed Cool Whip and pour mixture into prepare piecrusts. Chill at least 4 hours. Serves 12 pieces. You can substitute any fruit for the pineapples and peaches.

it comes to interior decorating, Bob Davis says, "the sky's the limit." If you just have to have a Cockaboose — that is, if you can first find somebody who is willing to sell one — you will like have to pay $300,000 or more.

The networks, ESPN and CBS in particular, have featured the Cockabooses several times, and *Southern Living* magazine, among other publications, has featured the Cockaboose Railroad in its pages.

The Cockaboose Railroad gets my vote as one of the classiest and most unique tailgating ideas in college football tailgating. "I'll drink to that," says Bob Davis.

PAT HADEN ON TAILGATING

Few stories in college football feel better than the Pat Haden story.

Born in New York, Haden played high school football in La Puente, California, before enrolling at the University of Southern California, where he played in three Rose Bowl games and led the Trojans to two national championships. He would go on to play six years in the NFL with the Los Angeles Rams, but he was truly a scholar-athlete and was awarded a Rhodes Scholarship. Few players have excelled to greater acclaim athletically and academically than did Haden. High sports honors include induction into the National High School Hall of Fame, the Rose Bowl Hall of Fame and the GTE Academic All-American Hall of Fame.

Following his NFL career in which he frequently led the Rams to the playoffs, he began a broadcast career with CBS, which segued into becoming the NBC analyst for Notre Dame games. Next he joined a private equity firm in Los Angeles. Successful as a player, broadcaster and businessman, Haden listened when "mama called," becoming the USC athletic director in 2010. That was a good day for the Trojans.

While his multiple responsibilities keep him from tailgating on game day, he nonetheless is an impassioned advocate of the importance of tailgating in college football.

"Tailgating is part of the fabric of a college football Saturday at USC and across the country" says Haden. "I do not think it is much different at USC than it is other places, other than we probably serve a lot more Mexican food. Our tailgates are very much outdoors and family friendly.

"What strikes me about USC football games and tailgating in particular is that the audience is generational. What I mean is that you will see grandparents, their children and their grandchildren all at one tailgate. Then all will sit together in the stands. Some have been doing this for 10, 20 or 30 years. It makes it much different than professional football in my estimation.

"Every athletic director in America is concerned about enhancing the fan experience so fans do not stay home and watch the games on TV, which is admittedly much easier to do," Haden continued. "Thus, I am very interested in how much our fans both tailgate and enjoy the experience. We try to clear as many impediments as possible for them to be able to enjoy the game festivities."

Mexican Dip

**From Heather Dunn
Executive assistant to USC
Athletic Director Pat Haden**

INGREDIENTS:

Cream cheese, softened

Refried beans

Avocado, diced

Pace Picante Sauce

Cheddar or jack cheese, shredded

Tortilla chips

DIRECTIONS:

• This is a good appetizer I love to fix for parties. It is a Mexican dip that is layered in a baking dish. You start with a layer of softened cream cheese, then add a layer of refried beans, a layer of diced avocado, a layer of Pace Picante Sauce and a layer of shredded cheddar/jack cheese. Heat it at 350 degrees until the cheese is melted, about 15 to 20 minutes, and serve with warm tortilla chips. It is delicious!

THEY "BOULEVARD" AT SMU

"At SMU, fans don't tailgate — they 'Boulevard,'" says Skyler Johnson of Southern Methodist. "Instead of setting up in vast dull parking lots surrounding a stadium, alumni, students and fans at SMU set up on beautiful tree-lined Bishop Boulevard before every home football game. The Boulevard goes straight through the center of one of the most stunning campuses in the country.

"Underneath the canopy of the dozens of live oak trees, you will find fans grilling everything from burgers to frog legs (especially when we host crosstown rival Texas Christian)," Skyler continued. "If fans don't feel like grilling out, no worries, because they can get food catered from some of the local Dallas hotspots like Mi Cocina or Sonny Bryan's.

"If you are going to take part in Boulevarding, make sure to get on campus early and check out some of the great traditions that go along with game day at SMU. Greet the SMU football team during Mustang Walk, which takes place when the team walks through a portion of Bishop Boulevard on the way to the stadium. Then right before the game, follow Peruna, SMU's Shetland pony mascot, the SMU Mustang Band and SMU Spirit Squads to the stadium as they march down The Boulevard to the stadium for kickoff.

"Students and fans all dress up for Boulevarding, which helped SMU to be named in *Southern Living* magazine as a 'style setter' in its list of Best Tailgates in the South in 2013.

"No matter what opponent the Mustangs are facing, you can count on The Boulevard being packed with SMU fans and people from the community wanting to be a part of the party."

Ramen Cabbage Salad

From Ron and Cheryl Ridlehuber
Former SMU player, friends of head coach June Jones

INGREDIENTS:

1/2 large head cabbage, coarsely chopped (or one bag shredded cabbage)

1 3-ounce package ramen noodles, crushed

1/2 cup sunflower seeds or almonds

Dressing:

1/2 cup vegetable oil

3 tablespoons white sugar (We substitute Splenda)

3 tablespoons white vinegar

DIRECTIONS:

• Toss together the cabbage, noodles and sunflower seeds (or almonds). Whisk together the ramen flavor packet, oil, sugar and vinegar. Pour over cabbage mixture and toss evenly to coat. When tailgating we pack everything separately and put together right before serving.

Pulled Pork Sliders

From Ron and Cheryl Ridlehuber
Former SMU player, friends of head coach June Jones

INGREDIENTS:

1 or 2 pork tenderloins

1 bottle of your favorite barbecue sauce (We like Sweet Baby Ray's)

1 or 2 packages of slider rolls

DIRECTIONS:

• The day before tailgating, I put my pork tenderloin in a slow cooker, smother it with a bottle of barbecue sauce, cover it and cook it for 6 hours. When done, do not pour off the liquid. Using two forks, shred the pork and mix in the liquid. The day of the game, either heat your pork before going and wrap your container in newspaper to keep it warm, or heat it on a grill. Serve on slider rolls with your favorite condiments and side dishes.

STANFORD IS A UNIQUE PLACE

"**U**nder the eucalyptus trees in Chuck Taylor Grove is the only place in the world where undergraduate students rub shoulders with Silicon Valley venture capitalists and billionaires," says Mary Ann Guzy, a longtime Stanford tailgater. "Trucks painted Cardinal red cover the grounds. The open tailgates contain a delicious surprise of overflowing beer kegs, fine Napa Valley wine and culinary delights. Regulars include Heisman Trophy winner Jim Plunkett, Condoleezza Rice, Chuck Evans and other Stanford greats. Even a local Native American chief comes in his full traditional attire in commemoration of the days of the Stanford Indians.

"At this extremely casual event, there is no need to pretend to be anyone, because everyone is someone," Mary Ann continued. "This is the only place on Earth where academics, athletics and tech fortune collide; there is no need for formality. This is the birthplace of Google, Intel, Facebook — this is Stanford. Even amongst the elite crowd, there is anticipation for more. Fulfillment only comes as the Stanford football team makes the traditional march to the stadium through the swarm of fans. Led by the infamous five beautiful Dollies and the Stanford Tree, they dance on the grassy ground and the tailgate is easily mistakable for a wild house party as everyone is joined by the irreverent Leland Stanford Junior Marching Band.

"Though while this is a rambunctious party, don't be mistaken, because this has been a family event for over a century. Several generations gather together on The Farm as Stanford football creates a reunion of classmates and family alike. Fall in Palo Alto is cherished as a time the community comes together. The fondest memories of anyone lucky enough to be touched by Stanford happen here on warm Saturday afternoons.

"A faint rhythm from afar gets closer and louder, and people start to dance as a giant tree comes spinning into the party. The one, the only, the truly incomparable Leland Stanford Junior Marching Band has no time for formation as they swarm the Cardinal family and the rhythm turns into boisterous singing. Surrounded by the smartest yet wildest people the NCAA has to offer, with a cold beer in one hand and a 'Beat Cal' pin over your heart, you're left with the immortal lyrics, 'It's All Right Now.'"

Sourdough Crab Dip

From Jim and Sara Harbaugh
Former Stanford head coach,
head coach of the San Francisco 49ers

INGREDIENTS:

1 loaf of sourdough, French or Italian bread (hollow out the middle)

1 can white lump crabmeat, drained

1 package cream cheese

1 bag sharp cheddar cheese

1 bunch green onions, sliced

1 bottle Black Label Real Bacon Bits

DIRECTIONS:

- Mix all together and then stuff inside the loaf of bread. Wrap in foil and bake for one hour at 350 degrees. We use bruschetta toasts for dipping.

THE VOL NAVY

"The Vol Navy is an over-50-year-old tradition allegedly started by a UT broadcaster," says Sammy Jones, a Vol Navy "tailgating" captain. "It has evolved into a weekly event that swells to several hundred boats on early season big-game weekends.

"What the average person likely does not know is that the Knoxville area is a boating paradise," Sammy continued. "We enjoy a huge amount of navigable waterways, including access to the Gulf of Mexico, albeit a 900-mile trip. Thus, the boating community here is enormous for an area of its population.

"The Vol Navy is an extension of this boating community. Boats large and small make the journey upstream in a caravan of orange. This starts as far as a week ahead for some games, especially for those who have a special place they like to tie up. The caravan continues to grow as game day approaches, reaching a peak on the morning of the game when the boats that make it a day trip begin arriving in droves.

"Our navy community is a very friendly bunch. There are a few dozen boats that are mainstays and can usually be found at the same spots every week. Impromptu meals and gatherings on the docks are the norm. Fans of the opposing team are always a part of the Vol Navy and are welcomed. Many of us make it a point to invite folks from the opposing team down to the boat for a drink or snack and to welcome them to Knoxville.

"The game-day atmosphere at the navy is a wide variety of reveling and fun," says Sammy. "The tailgating ranges from couples lounging on a ski boat to groups of 50 or more on a houseboat complete with a band, playing 'Rocky Top' of course. Satellite televisions and big-screen TVs make it possible to watch games from across the nation. Most every boat also has a group of tailgaters that show up to join in the fun, so the navy swells to several thousand as the game approaches. Adding to the atmosphere are the walkways and traffic of Neyland Drive adjacent to the docks, the major thoroughfare to the stadium. Thousands of fans walk along the docks on their way to the game and join in the fun, and impromptu singing of 'Rocky Top' is a very common occurrence. Of course, the reveling continues after the games well into the night, win or lose.

Hundreds of Tennessee fans navigate their boats to within walking distance of Neyland Stadium for home games. Photo by Wade Rackley.

REFLECTING BACK ON JOHN MAJORS

John Majors became a legend at Tennessee, where he was an All-America tailback in the single-wing offense that worked to near perfection by Gen. Robert Neyland and maintained by his successors Harvey Robinson and Bowden Wyatt. The oldest of four brothers who played college football, John Majors also played for a legendary coach at Huntland, Tennessee — his father, Shirley Majors.

In 1956, with Wyatt as his coach, Majors made All-America as a triple-threat tailback in the Tennessee single-wing formation. He led the Volunteers to an undefeated season and a berth in the Sugar Bowl, finishing the season as the No. 2 team in the country. Tennessee fans thought that Majors should have won the Heisman Trophy, but Notre Dame's Paul Hornung won the award, even though the Irish posted a 2-8 record.

Tommy McDonald of No. 1 Oklahoma and Syracuse's Jim Brown were also candidates for the Heisman, but finished third and fifth, respectively, behind Hornung and Majors, the runner-up.

Several years later, in the late 1970s when Hornung was doing television for Notre Dame, the Irish played Tennessee in Knoxville. Hornung asked Majors to be a guest on his TV show, and then needled Johnny about being jealous of him (Hornung) winning the Heisman Trophy.

Majors flummoxed Hornung so badly with his response that Hornung became speechless when Johnny replied, "No Paul, I thought Jim Brown should have won the Heisman that year."

Waldorf Salad

From Johnny and Mary Lynn Majors
Tennessee alum, former head coach at
UT, Pitt & Iowa State

INGREDIENTS:

5 Honeycrisp apples cut into bite-sized pieces (Only Honeycrisp will do!)

8 stalks medium-sized celery cut into smaller pieces

1/2 cup Craisins (combination raisins and cranberries)

1/2 cup pecans

Dressing:

2 tablespoons mayonnaise

6 tablespoons Chardonnay wine

DIRECTIONS:

- Mix and serve!

Lavender Cookies

From Johnny and Mary Lynn Majors

INGREDIENTS:

1 cup lightly salted butter, softened

2/3 cup minus 1 tablespoon superfine sugar

1 1/4 cups minus 1 tablespoon self-rising flour

1 tablespoon fresh lavender flowers

DIRECTIONS:

- Preheat oven to 350 degrees. Cream butter and sugar. Stir in flour and flowers. Drop by teaspoons well spread apart. Bake 12 to 15 minutes until just golden. Makes 3 1/2 cookie sheets. Double recipe for 7 cookie sheets.

Gridiron Chili

From Phillip and Vicky Fulmer
All-SEC guard at Tennessee and former
Vols head coach

INGREDIENTS:

1/2 pound dried pinto beans

2 16-ounce cans tomatoes, chopped

1 pound green peppers, coarsely chopped

1 1/2 pounds onions, coarsely chopped

1 1/2 tablespoons oil

2 cloves garlic, crushed

1/2 cup butter or margarine

2 1/2 pounds lean ground chuck beef

1 pound lean ground pork

1/3 cup chili powder

2 tablespoons salt

1 1/2 teaspoons ground pepper

1 1/2 teaspoons ground cumin

1/2 cup parsley, finely chopped

DIRECTIONS:

• Wash beans, cover with water in a pot and let stand overnight. Place beans and water in a saucepan. Bring to boil, lower heat and simmer just until tender. Add tomatoes and simmer 5 minutes. In a skillet, cook green peppers and onions in hot oil, just until tender, while stirring frequently. Add garlic and cook 3 minutes. In another skillet, melt butter. Add chuck beef and pork, and cook while stirring frequently, about 10 minutes. Add meat to onion mixture, stir in chili powder and cook 10 minutes. Add meat/onion mixture to cooked beans. Add salt, ground pepper, cumin and parsley. Cover and simmer 30 minutes. Remove cover and skim any excess fat from the top of chili. Heat 10 more minutes, and enjoy!

Vols Chicken Spaghetti

From Butch and Barb Jones
Head coach at Tennessee,
former head coach at Cincinnati and
Central Michigan

INGREDIENTS:

3 pounds chicken breasts

1 pound thin spaghetti

1 stick, or 1/2 cup, margarine

3 teaspoons chili powder (vary to taste)

1 can regular or mild Rotel tomatoes

1 cup celery, chopped

1 small onion, chopped

1 can cream of mushroom soup

1 can cream of chicken soup

1 pound Velvetta cheese

Salt

Pepper

DIRECTIONS:

• Cook chicken by simmering for 1 hour. Leave chicken broth in saucepan. Skin, debone and cut up chicken. Cook spaghetti in chicken broth. Drain, leaving a little broth with pasta. Sauté celery and onion in margarine. Add chili powder and stir. Add chicken, tomatoes, soups and cheese until melted. Add salt and pepper to taste. Pour into a 9-inch by 13-inch greased casserole dish. Bake uncovered at 350 degrees for 45 minutes, until bubbly. Casserole can be frozen; just thaw before baking. This is a perfect postgame meal while celebrating a victory with family and friends!

"One of my favorite stories took place a few years ago. We were tied up in our normal spot right next to the walkway to the stadium. I had given some of my guests my tickets to the game and was watching it on TV on the boat. I do this for most of the games. After 30 years, I have spent enough time in the stadium. With the docks in the shadow of the stadium, you also get the feel of the game with the crowd roars and the fireworks exploding over the water when our beloved Vols score.

"The game was with Florida, and it was sold out, with tickets commanding a premium on the street. It was a late game with kickoff around 7 p.m. Shortly after kick-off, a group of us were watching the game on the upper deck of the boat. The sidewalks and streets had gone from a mass of people to an occasional straggler or passing car. I noticed a middle-aged gentleman and a young boy walking from the direction of the stadium. As they passed, I noticed the young boy was hanging his head in disappointment. I yelled over to cheer up, it was a great Rocky Top day. The father then told me he had made a special trip with his son from North Carolina to see the Vols. They didn't have tickets and were not able to scalp any they could afford. I told them while we were not in the stadium, it was almost the same and to come on aboard the boat and watch it with us. We made that kid's day. He was a huge fan and seldom got to come to many games. He had never been on a Vol Navy boat. They stayed with us for the entire evening, and us losing the game made no difference.

"The greatest part was last year we were at the Vol Navy for one of the early games. It was blistering hot and everyone was doing anything they could do to stay cool. A group of us put on our swimsuits and were sitting under the waterfall that is part of the walkway area leading up to the stadium. A fellow walked up to me and showed me a picture of me with a young fan. It was the father I mentioned earlier. He had come looking for us to thank us and brought a large bag of tailgating food for us. He told us how his son always talked about his memories of the Vol Navy and how it was his favorite game ever."

You can enjoy a great view of Neyland Stadium when you tailgate with the Vol Navy. Photo by Sammy Jones.

THEY DO IT BIG IN TEXAS

Texas has a long and storied football history, with coaching legends like Dana X. Bible and Darrell Royal identifying new formations — Bible an early proponent of the T-formation and Royal the first college coach to use the wishbone — and winning championships. Both are members of the College Football Hall of Fame, and Mack Brown, who won the national championship in 2006, is likely to be tapped for membership as soon as he is eligible.

Texans are proud. They like it that their state has the reputation for being a top state in the country for producing college-worthy high school talent. High school football under the lights graphically defines the game across the state, which led to the movie "Friday Night Lights."

Tailgating at Texas has the same aura pregame that it has on the field for a big game in the presence of Bevo, the Longhorn mascot. Game day in Austin, one of the more popular music destinations in the country, centers around the traditional foods you might expect from its heritage. There is the Mexican influence. Barbecue is popular. Ribs. Burgers. Brisket. Anything that will sear over a fire. When you are served a tasty snack or main course, you get the thumbs-up in the form of the nationally recognized image of "Hook 'em Horns," one of the most identifiable images in college football. Fans greet one another by folding down the middle and fourth fingers of their right hand to create the image of the long horns of the famous Longhorn cattle, which can total up to 7 feet in length.

Kasey Johnson of the Texas Athletics Department staff identified her friend Patrick Flinn as one of UT's most passionate tailgaters. A retired bartender from Portland, Texas, Patrick has been a season ticket holder since 2004, making him something of a newcomer, but without peer when it comes to passion for Longhorn tailgating. He says he began by watching the team on television but then started attending games and became smitten at first. He didn't miss a home game and then he took on road games, taking his tailgate with him. Last fall, he traveled 12,200 miles to see the Longhorns play, tailgate in tow. "That is the best thing about our tailgate

Patrick Flinn gets his tailgating area set up early, before most fans arrive.

Chili master Conrad Arriola, left, scoops some of his special creation for Patrick Flinn.

crew," he says. "We take it everywhere!" The following is Patrick's testimony to tailgating, Texas Longhorn style.

"Enjoying a day of tailgating at the University of Texas is easy. Most everyone with a party going on is happy to have a few extra faces join their fun. On campus, the tailgaters tend to be in smaller groups of friends and family members while the really large company-sponsored parties are just off campus across MLK Boulevard. Our group has approximately 25 core members, and we generally have 50 to 60 people at our tailgates most game days.

"As with most tailgates in the South, barbecue is high on the list for many of the groups around Austin. Things start to smell good early when the pitmasters get their meat on. But not everyone goes that direction for tailgate meals, largely due to the diversity of culture in the state of Texas. If you were to take a stroll around the tailgate parties on and around campus, there is probably not any kind of food you couldn't find, even if you tried! We do our own traditional meals from week to week that include beef and chicken fajitas, chili and a shrimp boil — and because we are one of the only college football teams to play on Thanksgiving Day, we have the full spread, including turkeys, dressing, all the trimmings, and homemade pies and other desserts. As far as traditions go, the Thanksgiving Day tailgate is great! Most folks eat their turkey at home and then watch football on television — we get to do it on location and enjoy our game live and in person.

"One of our favorite tailgate activities is the game of 'washer pitching' — very similar to what they call 'cornhole' in the Midwest and Northeast (essentially a beanbag toss). We play it with 3-inch industrial-sized metal washers (custom-painted orange and white, of course). It's a Texas thing!

"Tailgating at UT is predominately a pregame activity. While we do play games occasionally at 11 a.m. or an afternoon game at 2:30 p.m., most of our important matchups are played prime time. So after a big win, the city of Austin beckons most tailgaters to put away their tents, chairs, games and equipment to celebrate in the Live Music Capital of the World! It's one of the truly great things about the University of Texas, being so immersed in — and in the middle of — the incredible variety of entertainment venues Austin has to offer on any given Saturday night!

"Our biggest and most important conference game is always the matchup against that team in crimson from north of the Red River. It takes place every year the first or second Saturday in October at the State Fair of Texas

Special K Bars

From Charlie and Vicki Strong
Head coach at the University of Texas,
former head coach at Louisville

INGREDIENTS:

1/2 cup sugar

1/2 cup Karo Syrup

3/4 cup peanut butter

1 cup chocolate chips

1 cup butterscotch chips

DIRECTIONS:

• Heat the sugar and syrup until hot, but not to a boil, in small saucepan. Add 3/4-cup peanut butter to saucepan mixture and mix until blended and creamy. Pour 4 cups of Special K cereal into a 13-inch by 9-inch buttered baking dish. Pour the peanut butter mixture over the cereal and press together. Melt 1 cup chocolate chips and 1 cup butterscotch chips and spread over top of cereal mixture. Refrigerate 30 minutes and then cut into squares. Store in an airtight container in refrigerator. Great for tailgate!

Dallas-Style Brisket Tacos

From Mack & Sally Brown
Former head coach at Texas,
North Carolina & Tulane

INGREDIENTS:

For the brisket:

3 pounds brisket, from the flat cut

Salt

Black pepper

1 tablespoon vegetable oil or bacon grease

1 large yellow onion, cut into quarters

8 cloves garlic

1/4 cup red wine vinegar

2 cups beef broth

1 teaspoon ground cumin

2 jalapeños, seeds and stems removed, cut in half lengthwise

2 leafy stems cilantro

1 bay leaf

For the tacos:

2 poblano chiles

1 teaspoon vegetable oil

1 large yellow onion, cut into slivers

1 cup shredded Monterey Jack cheese

Corn or flour tortillas

Salsa

DIRECTIONS:

• Preheat oven to 250 degrees. Sprinkle brisket with salt and black pepper to taste. In a large ovenproof pot, such as a Dutch oven, heat up oil on medium-low, and brown the brisket on both sides, about 5 minutes per side. Remove brisket from the pot and add onions. While occasionally stirring, cook until they begin to brown. Add the garlic cloves and cook for another 2 minutes. Turn off heat and pour the red wine vinegar into the pot, scraping along the bottom to loosen all of the pan drippings. Return to the pot the brisket, fat side up. Pour in the beef broth and add the cumin, jalapeños, cilantro and bay leaf. Cover the pot and place in the oven. Cook the brisket for 6 hours or until fork tender. When you take the brisket out of the oven, let it rest in the pot uncovered for 30 minutes.

• Meanwhile, to make the taco toppings, roast the poblano chiles under the broiler until blackened, about 5 minutes per side. Place chiles in a paper sack or plastic food-storage bag, close it tight and let the chiles steam for 20 minutes. Take the chiles out of the bag and rub off the skin. Remove stem and seeds and cut the chiles into strips. Heat up the vegetable oil in a skillet on medium low, and add the onion slivers. While occasionally stirring, cook until softened, about 10 minutes. Add the cut poblano strips and cook for 1 more minute.

• After the brisket has rested, remove it from the pot, cut off the fat cap and shred the meat with two forks until it is in long strands. To make the gravy, strain the cooled broth, throwing out the vegetables. Remove the fat from the broth with a gravy separator (or you can take a quart-sized plastic storage bag and pour some broth into it. Snip a bottom corner of the bag and drain the broth, stopping when you get to the fat layer that is on top). Add 2 tablespoons of the gravy to the shredded brisket, reserving the rest for serving. Taste the brisket and adjust seasonings.

• To make the tacos, place on one side of each tortilla some Monterey Jack and slide the tortillas under the broiler for 30 seconds or until the cheese is melted. Fill the tortillas with shredded brisket and top with some of the onions and poblano strips. Serve with the pot juices and salsa.

in Dallas. Due to the fact that it takes place at the Cotton Bowl, inside the Fair Grounds, there is very little tailgating. Everything you could need or want to drink or eat is available inside the Fair, and that's where most fans of both teams spend their time partying before the game. It is truly a unique environment, not to be missed if you're a true college football fan.

"Austin and the University of Texas are landmarks in their own right. The capital building and Lady Bird Lake are beautiful, and Darrell K. Royal Memorial Stadium and Bevo himself should certainly be on your 'must see' list! The one thing that I think most UT tailgaters would point to as the greatest Austin landmark would be the university's 307-foot clock tower when it changes from its typical lighting configuration to the 'Tower Orange' in celebration of a Longhorn victory! Hook 'em Horns!"

Only in Austin will you see an apple pie like this! Photo by Patrick Flinn.

The Johnsons' Bean Dip

From Kasey Johnson
University of Texas Athletics Department

The specialty dish we serve at our tailgate is an out-of-this-world bean dip that will change your life! It's an old family recipe out of Alpine, Texas, and we are willing to share it!

INGREDIENTS:

1 package of ground beef

4 cans of Rosarita's Refried Beans

2 packages of Mexican Velveeta

3 or 4 medium jalapenos, chopped

Fritos Scoops

DIRECTIONS:

• Brown ground beef and then stir in refried beans until mixture is warm. Stir in Mexican Velveeta and jalapenos. Simple! Just be sure to have plenty of Fritos Scoops on hand!

Mean TC's Pizza Dip

From Mac and Becky McWhorter
Former offensive line coach at Texas and many other schools

INGREDIENTS:

2 8-ounce packages cream cheese

1 jar pizza sauce

1 small onion, chopped

2 cups shredded mozzarella cheese

1 large package pepperoni, chopped

2 small cans chopped black olives

Family-size Fritos Scoops

DIRECTIONS:

• Preheat oven to 350 degrees. Use hand to press cream cheese into bottom of an ovenproof dish (souffle dish). Layer remaining ingredients, except for Scoops, in order listed above. Bake 45 minutes to 1 hour. Serve with Scoops. Transport to tailgate by wrapping with sections of newspaper and then in a beach towel, but it's good at outdoor temperatures as well.

THE AGGIES WILL KNOCK YOUR SOCKS OFF

You don't find abundant shade trees and plush lawns on the Texas A&M campus — the climate is simply too arid. You will, however, find school spirit and Aggie pride that will knock your socks off. There is never a drought of emotions and rah, rah, rah's for those Aggie aficionados clad in maroon.

You won't find an Aggie who is not hospitable, accommodating, welcoming — and thirsty. Seems that all Aggie fans have a tent, multiple coolers, grills and enough brisket to feed the entire base at Fort Hood, which is 100 miles west of campus. Visitors, even those wearing colors of the opposing team, receive the warmest of welcomes. If you are passing by and are just a bit inquisitive, you can sample your way to a full stomach long before kickoff. Guests, with a smile and the familiar Texas greeting, "Howdy," can do very well at College Station on game day. At kickoff, they want to bury you, but pregame, they might as well be holding hands with you and singing "Kumbaya."

As you might expect, you see cowboy boots, jeans and Stetsons. You also see shorts, bare feet (early in the season), fashionable blouses and the A&M logo tattooed on the cheeks of countless coeds.

There's a homecoming atmosphere every home game. There might be a special ceremony on the field at halftime when homecoming is officially celebrated, but when it comes to pregame, the Aggie social routine never changes. It is always over the top, just like Aggie school spirit.

Wherever you matriculated, you can't wait to return to campus for a big game, return to your old haunts where you developed enduring friendships and were given to yell like hell for alma mater at kickoff. But who shows up at midnight to practice a yell? Aggie students

Tim Higgins turns some beef for fajitas before an A&M game. Photo courtesy of Tim Higgins.

do. Who stands on their feet waving white towels for four quarters? The Aggie students. Who is imbued with affection for the military and where is there the greatest respect for ROTC programs? Texas A&M, and don't you forget it.

Also don't ever forget that it was an Aggie who led the Rangers up the cliffs on D-Day at Pointe du Hoc at the beaches of Normandy, France, in World War II. That would be Col. James Earl Rudder, who came back later in life to become president of A&M.

Other schools talk about winning the fourth quarter and have unique home-game traditions — some even have their own version of the "12th Man" — but the idea of school spirit giving its team an extra man on the field was born in College Station and lives happily ever after.

Reveille, a full-blooded collie and the official mascot, leads the team on the field for each kickoff. Out in the parking lots, a bearded Aggie fan plays taps when the fan of an opposing team walks by. Fans get to their seats at Kyle Field early just to watch the Cadet Corps march with the precision that would shame Prussian goose step-pers. There were a lot of Aggies, like Col. Rudder, who helped bring about the fall of the Third Reich, and the student body today is on call if America needs it. How many campuses would you find such a bent and respect for the military?

The seniors in the Corps always wear high-top boots made in town by Hollicks, which has been making them since 1891 — just another Aggie tradition to be remembered, revered and appreciated for generations.

Aggie pride is expressed enthusiastically whenever you visit a game in College Station. Alumni and fans, as soon as they recognize you are a visitor, are eager to engage in conversation about what takes place on the A&M campus.

"We are in love with the SEC," says Jacob Hannusch, who hails from Smithville, which is only 50 miles away from A&M. "We are now more relevant than Texas and OU (Oklahoma)."

Jacob then explained the importance of the ring dunk at Texas A&M. Everybody appreciates having a ring. "You come here," Jacob said, "and you want to graduate. You want to buy a ring when you are a senior and you wear it with pride. When you get your ring, you dunk your ring on your finger in a pitcher of beer and then drink the beer as fast as you can. It took me 24 seconds. Some coeds can drink up the pitcher of beer in 30 seconds. It is popular to do the ring dunk at a home-game tailgate

Slow-Cooker Beef Sliders

From Kevin and Char Sumlin Head coach at Texas A&M, former linebacker at Purdue

INGREDIENTS:

1/2 cup onion, finely chopped

3 pound beef roast

Salt

Pepper

2 teaspoons garlic powder

12 ounces beer

1/2 cup barbecue sauce

12 to 16 mini slider rolls or potato rolls

Optional: serve with extra barbecue sauce, cheese, pickles, hot peppers and/or crispy onions

DIRECTIONS:

• Place the chopped onion in the bottom of the slow cooker. Season the roast with the salt, pepper and garlic powder. Place the roast in the slow cooker. In a small bowl, mix together the beer and barbecue sauce, and then pour over the roast. Cook on low for 8 to 10 hours. Using two forks, shred the beef. Serve on rolls with any optional items you desire. Season with extra salt and pepper if necessary.

party, but a lot of coeds prefer to do the ring dunk at a house party."

Bob Starnes, class of '72, says, "I've been tailgating, Aggie style, since I graduated. *Sports Illustrated* published a story about the class of '72, and the members of Tom Potthoff's tailgate club wear T-shirts with the photo of the *SI* cover for all in his group to wear on game day. If you are a visitor who happens by and you are nice enough, you might be the recipient of a T-shirt and become an honorary member of the class of '72."

"Gov. Rick Perry," Tom Potthoff explained, "is a member of the class of '72."

Throughout the tailgating enclaves at College Station are bands that play everything from country music (the

Green Enchiladas

From R.C. and Nel Slocum
Former head coach at Texas A&M

INGREDIENTS:

1 dozen corn tortillas

1/2 cup cooking oil

8 ounces Monterey Jack cheese, grated

1 small onion, chopped (optional)

For broth:

1/4 cup butter or margarine

1/4 cup flour (plus 1 tablespoon)

2 cups chicken broth

2 or 3 mild jalapeno peppers, seeded and chopped

1 cup sour cream

DIRECTIONS:

• Make the broth first. Put margarine and part of chicken broth in a saucepan and heat until margarine is melted and broth is hot. Stir some chicken broth (not hot) into the flour to make a thin paste, or shake in a jar. Add to hot broth and melted margarine, and it should thicken immediately. Cook and stir on low heat until bubbly. Stir in chopped jalapenos and sour cream. Blend well, but do not boil because it will curdle. Keep warm or reheat later.

• In a skillet, cook one or two tortillas at a time in hot oil until soft. It only takes a few seconds for each tortilla, so do not overcook because they will get crisp. Put about 2 tablespoons of cheese and 1 tablespoon of onion on each tortilla, and then roll it up. Put in a Pyrex-type casserole dish, pour broth over enchiladas, and sprinkle with remaining cheese and onion. Bake at 375 degrees for about 20 minutes, or microwave on high for 3 or 4 minutes.

Note: Recipe can easily be doubled or tripled in size.

favorite) to rock 'n' roll to golden oldies to current titles preferred by the students.

Tim Higgins, who is from Kingwood, a suburb of Houston, suspects his routine is fairly typical for many Aggie tailgating groups. He cooks brisket for his group, giving it the TLC to make it special. At 7:30 a.m. on Friday, he puts the brisket on a grill at his home and watches over it until 4 a.m. Saturday. That is when game day begins for him. He loads up his truck and packs his multiple coolers and begins the 90-mile drive to Aggieland, parking his vehicle and setting up for the day. He cooks for 100 guests. Some Saturdays everybody brings chili for a chili cookoff.

An observer easily concludes that Texas A&M has always been in the University of Texas' shadow, something of an underdog, but the school spirit and the 12th Man reputation, along with membership in the Southeastern Conference, could propel the Aggies into prominence. There's academic diversity in College Station, everything from veterinary medicine to engineering to business to law. Aggie alumni are well heeled and they enjoy giving back to their alma mater. The $450 million expansion of Kyle Field makes it — at a capacity of 102,500 — the biggest stadium in the SEC. Anteing up for A&M these days is like preparing for a tailgate party: "Let's make it bigger and better."

Higgins is as dedicated as the football team when it comes to cooking for his tailgate. Now for the rest of his story:

"I smoke the brisket for 18 hours. When I put it on and when it comes off depends on game time. I have figured out how to control my smoker without having to tend it constantly, so typically I will only check on it a couple of times during the evening, adding smoking chips to the fire box and water to the water pan if needed, and making sure the temperature is staying between 180 and 200 degrees. The different families in our tailgating group will take turns cooking, and sometimes several of us will cook for the same game. We are called the Conchos Crew.

"We try to get a head count the week of the game to have a general idea. For Alabama last year, we cooked for about 120 people and fed at least that many. On some of the lower-key games, we will cook for about 50 to 75 folks.

"Typically once a season we will have an inner-tailgate chili cookoff (bragging rights only) where each family will bring their own chili recipe and we will have taste test and try to convince everyone ours is best. We also will have Cajun-themed tailgates where we will cook gumbo, jambalaya and such. Fajitas are another favorite, and if it is an early game, we will cook breakfast tacos. Of course we also have all the extras that go with the main course: beans, salads, desserts, etc.

"Cooking low and slow on the brisket makes it tender and doesn't dry it out too much. I use a dry rub on the brisket consisting of granulated garlic, black pepper, kosher salt and seasoning salt. I will usually start with mesquite, and then also add hickory and apple later in the process to build a more complex smoke flavor.

"For smoking the brisket I use a commercially available gas-fired box smoker. I have two different ones but they are basically the same, one is just a little bigger. Three of us guys also have custom-made propane cookers for doing fajitas and cooking pots of gumbo or whatever.

"The tailgate actually starts at noon on Friday before the game on Saturday. At this time you are allowed to go 'reserve' your spot. One of our group lives in Bryan/College Station so he generally does this for us. We are pretty lucky to always get about the same spot. Aggies are an honorable sort, so the fact that they have seen this group at the same spot for the last decade or so, they honor it as our spot. This is pretty common throughout Spence Park, where you typically see the same groups in the same area game after game and year after year.

"About 7 a.m., three or four of the more hardcore of the group begin arriving, setting up the canopies, washer boards, chairs and tables, and making sure the beverages are cold. We also set up a TV and satellite as there are always quite a few folks that couldn't/didn't get tickets, so they watch the game from our tailgate area. The next few hours are spent pitching washers, socializing, drinking beer or whatever your choice is, and generally just having a good time. We try to eat about two hours before the game starts. If it is an early game (say 11 a.m. or so) we will sometimes eat after the game instead.

"A good portion of our group were really good friends while at A&M. Some of the wives even went to high school and grade school together in the Dallas area. Others were roommates or just hung out together all the time. It makes for a lot of fun as our group has families in Austin, the Houston area, the Dallas area and the College Station area. It gives us a good chance to stay in touch with each other while enjoying something we all love: A&M. It is also really neat now that most if not all of the families still have kids at A&M or very recent graduates."

TEXAS A&M'S CLASS OF '72 TAILGATE

"**W**e first started 'tailgating' when I was a freshman in the Corps in 1968," says Tom Potthoff, Texas A&M class of '72. "Back then, we did not call it tailgating. Instead it was called 'We can't afford to eat out' on a retired navy chief's pension. The attendees were my family and my 'fish,' or freshman buddies in my outfit.

"After graduation, although I still had season tickets, my wife and I mainly had football game picnics, and it was not until 2001 when our daughter was an athlete (golf) that it became a much bigger production," Tom continued. "I had Pitt's and Spitt's make me a custom single-axle barbecue trailer, which my daughters' teammates nicknamed 'The Beast.' It had a meat smoker, fish smoker, twin fryers and a griddle for cooking eggs. Of course, it had multiple tables and places for storage.

"From 2001 to 2006 we tailgated at the south end of Kyle Field until the new indoor practice facilities were built and we had to move to another area. For the next four years we were located right next to the stadium until the construction of the new workout facilities were built, forcing us to move again. A fellow classmate asked us to join his tailgate group on the east side of Kyle

The class of '72 still knows how to have a great time at A&M games. Photo courtesy of Tom Potthoff.

Tom Potthoff carves a whole hog for his tailgating friends. Photo courtesy of Tom Potthoff.

Field in Spence Park. Claiming our tailgate spot is similar to the lining up of the famous Oklahoma Land Rush in the 19th century. The university does not allow any setting up in Spence Park until Friday at noon, and at noon, an alarm is sounded and several classmates lay claim to our site at that time.

"The most popular thing we cook is our smoked whole hog," says Tom. "We usually do one every other year. We usually prepare food for around 25 to 35 persons, but for the Mississippi State game last year, we smoked a whole pig and probably had close to 75 people show up at various times.

"We have fried turkeys, smoked brisket, ham, sausages, beer-butt chickens and even cook breakfast for early games. For libations, it is strictly bring-your-own-booze. We usually have a couple of TVs at the tailgate, and although most people prefer to stand, we set up around 25 chairs for viewing since not everyone who attends the tailgate has tickets to the game."

And what is Tom's proudest tailgating memory?

"In the fall of 1968, there was an article published in *Sports Illustrated* about Texas A&M titled 'The Proudest Squares.' In this issue, there was a crowd shot taken of our 'fish' class' first home game and I guess you could say we were the 'centerfold' for that issue. Sadly, not everyone in the picture stayed and finished their degree at

Bum's Favorite Dessert

From Debbie Phillips,
wife of the late Bum Phillips
Former assistant coach at Texas A&M,
former head coach for the Houston Oilers
and New Orleans Saints

INGREDIENTS:

2 1/2 sleeves Ritz crackers

1/2 cup pecans, chopped

1 large tub Cool Whip

1 stick butter, melted

2 small packages Instant French Vanilla Pudding

1/2 gallon Blue Bell Homemade Vanilla Ice Cream

1 1/2 cups milk

DIRECTIONS:

For the crust:

• Crush the crackers. Pour butter over cracker crumbs and pecans. Mix. Save 1 cup of this mix for the topping. Press remainder of mix into the bottom of a 13-inch by 9-inch glass casserole dish.

For the filling:

• Soften the ice cream in the carton at room temperature and then put in a mixer bowl. Add milk and pudding on top, and mix at a slow speed. Pour into the crust and allow it to cool in the refrigerator. Top with a large tub of Cool Whip. Sprinkle reserve crumbs on top. Chill overnight.

A&M but they have managed to stay in touch and some have even attended our tailgate. For our 40th reunion in 2012, I had the picture printed on one of our pop-up tents.

"Some notable members of the class of 1972 include Gov. Rick Perry, Texas A&M Chancellor John Sharp, Con-gressman Joe Barton, Houston businessman and phi-lanthropist Jerry Cox, U.S. Army Gen. Henry Osterman, Marine Corps Gen. Joe Weber and USAF Colonel Wayne Edwards, and I am sure I have left some others out. Since 2001, we have estimated we have had around 150 mem-bers of our class drift in and out of our tailgate."

AN AGGIE
AT ST. ANDREWS

Jack Willoughby, a Texas A&M Aggie, first came to Scotland in the early days of the North Sea Oil Indus-try around 1977 and worked in Aberdeen for several years. It was quiet common for Americans to follow their paychecks throughout the world while working in the oil industry. Jack is one of those.

Whenever he travels, wherever he lights, he shows off his Texas A&M colors. He and his wife, Sheena, pur-chased the Dunvegan Hotel, about .01 of a mile from the 18th green at the Old Course at St. Andrews. Texas A&M banners fly prominently and Aggie logos abound among the traditional photos and artifacts that reflect the rich tradition of the game of golf along with the history of St. Andrews.

"Following a stint in Lagos, Nigeria, and then Hous-ton, I returned to Aberdeen in the late 1980s for a third assignment in Aberdeen," says Jack. "Sheena and I began a relationship and I frequently visited St. An-drews on weekends (a 1 1/2-hour drive) to play golf and enjoy the charms of St. Andrews.

"The Dunvegan was pretty run down and nothing more than a 'drinking man's bar.' We had a vision about making it a true golfing destination, or 19th hole. After much soul searching, we decided to pull the plug and purchase it. We got married at about the same time.

"Other than family and friends, without question the thing I miss most about living in the USA is miss-ing out on college football and following the Aggies — during the season, signing day and spring camp.

"I graduated from Texas A&M in 1972 and was a football manager for four years under coach Gene Stall-ings (we still keep in contact somewhat and I attended an appreciation night for him hosted by the Alabama TV and radio folks in College Station in 2013). I get to see one to three games a year, mainly toward the end of the season when we can get away, along with the bowl game most years.

"Many Aggies have learned of us via word of mouth and the Internet," Jack continued. "We have hosted Coach Fran (Dennis Franchione) when he was A&M's coach, Coach (R.C.) Slocum, the Aggie men's and wom-en's golf teams, Gary Blair, the women's basketball coach, and many other Aggies, mostly from on golf trips. If Coach (Kevin) Sumlin showed up, I would prob-ably buy his first drink. We do expect him at some point, as Jacob Green (a former All-American at A&M who works for A&M as a fundraiser) is a regular customer and has promised to bring him over soon.

"With the Internet, it is fairly easy to follow A&M football, usually via an ESPN game package. The big games are carried via Sky TV. I can also follow news ar-ticles and recruiting on a daily basis via a pay site. It has not always been this easy. I can remember not long ago trying to dial in Armed Forces Radio to catch an Aggie game, listening to it fade in and out, which was very soul destroying. One time in Aberdeen we phoned a friend in Houston and listened to an A&M-Texas game on the phone. On odd occasions, I have journeyed home just to watch a big game.

"As I have lived overseas most of my adult life, I have not been able to participate in many tailgating activi-ties. I do join my friends when we are at a game and we have sponsored an Aggie letterman's tailgate.

"I am absolutely delighted we are in the SEC despite how difficult the league is. What I really like is that a large part of the country can get a feel of who Texas A&M is and what we are all about. It appears in the early stages the feedback, from those SEC folks who have visited us, is very, very positive. I like the 'family' feel the SEC brings to the table. That is the way it is with Aggies — a family tradition.

"Remember, if you want to enjoy the best tailgate opportunity in Scotland, come visit us at the Dunvegan Hotel in St. Andrews."

"AN UNFORGETTABLE HAPPENING"

John Simpson, a Lubbock attorney, finished high school in Houston and enrolled at Texas Tech, hanging around after undergrad days to earn a law degree. It was that simple. When he finished law school, he hung out his shingle in Lubbock. That was a simple exercise, too. He was too smitten and infatuated to consider living anywhere else.

"Once I came to school here, I fell in love with the town and campus, and have never wanted to leave," Simpson says. The offices of his firm Splawn Simpson Pitts are decorated with an emphasis on the Texas Tech heritage and colors. John lives for game day. "Always have," he says. "When I was a student, I enjoyed tailgating, and as an alumnus, a big game here is an unforgettable happening. When you do anything around here Tech style, you are doing it the best way possible."

Texas Tech has an interesting routine for homecoming in the fall. They have a celebrity grand marshal who tours the campus and picks the best tailgate. When that role is filled by Tech's popular former head coach Spike Dykes, it is like Eisenhower coming home following V-E Day in World War II. Texas Tech is where the western theme is forever dominant. Cowboy boots, Stetsons, jeans and flannel shirts — a rawhide environment if there ever was one on a college campus. If you want to enjoy a down-home atmosphere, you want to tailgate in Lubbock in the fall.

Tim Carmichael, left, and Jim Harmon prepare scrambled eggs and bacon for John Simpson's tailgating group. Photo courtesy of John Simpson.

West Texas Chili

From Spike and Sharon Dykes
Former head coach at Texas Tech

INGREDIENTS:

2 pounds coarse ground meat with fat

1 to 3 chopped onions, to taste

1 can beef broth

1 can Rotel tomatoes & peppers

2 tablespoons ground garlic

2 tablespoons paprika

Salt, a dash

3 to 4 tablespoons chili powder

1 tablespoon cumin

Cayenne pepper to taste

DIRECTIONS:

• Brown meat and onions in cast-iron skillet. Add broth and Rotel. Simmer for 15 to 20 minutes and then stir in all other ingredients. Cover and cook slowly for 2 to 3 hours.

Mad Ralph Madrid's Margaritas

From Ralph Madrid, Texas Tech Superfan

INGREDIENTS:

2 parts tequila

3 parts triple sec\orange liqueur

Fresh lime wedge, squeezed

Fresh orange wedge, squeezed

Salt on rim of glass (optional)

DIRECTIONS:

• A sweet margarita results from an increase of triple sec/orange liqueur, and a sour margarita results from an increase of tequila or lime juice. The quality of the tequila does not change the margarita that much. Anejo, Reposado or Silver tequila do change the taste, as does the triple sec or orange liqueur used. Other little things make a difference. Play with these ingredients until you come up with a margarita that meets your fancy. Practice makes perfect! Good luck!

John Simpson offered this perspective:

"Arriving two-and-one-half hours before game time and seeing the parking lot full of flags, smokers and fans warms this old boy's heart. Seeing good friends every Saturday as they stop by to have a bite to eat and visit is a recurring experience that brings about anticipatory feelings that make you feel blessed.

"Tailgating becomes a great business opportunity, as many businesses have their own tailgates and invite customers and prospects to come by and share the game-day excitement. Great networking! On high-profile conference games, the students camp out in tents for three to five days before the game to secure a place in line for entrance to the game. The university, businesses and individuals support their efforts by sending food for the campers (the students furnish their own beverages).

It is a fun party at Raiderville! The students even elect their own mayor.

"The university sponsors a tailgate called 'Raider Alley' that has live bands, food vendors, cheerleaders, a pompom squad, a masked rider — Raider Red — and cold beverages. It's open to all fans! I realize that other schools have great tailgates, but you haven't experienced the best in tailgating until you taste the burritos, brisket, fajitas and chicken bits prepared by Bill Tarro, who we think is the best tailgate cook in Texas. You don't want to get into a tailgate cookoff with Bill. If you want to enjoy a margarita that will tan your hide, come by our tailgate and try one of Ralph Madrid's margaritas. Just don't strike a match while he is pouring one.

"Buses and motor homes can move into the parking lot on the day before the game at 5:30 p.m. for night games. Most fans who come in cars or pickups arrive two or three hours before kickoff. When you arrive, it's party time. At Tech, the party begins when you switch off your engine. It lasts until kickoff and begins again after the clock shows double zero. Some of the best tailgating is done after the game, especially if we have a victory. For better or worse, as I suppose it is at every campus, alcoholic intake increases proportionally with the success of the team and the result of the game.

"No trip to Lubbock, game or no game, should occur without seeing the Buddy Holly Center and the Buddy Holly Museum, the Silent Wings Museum (a tribute to the American Military Glider Program during World War II; pilots trained in this area) and Will Rogers' statue."

If Will Rogers never met a man he didn't like, then Texas Tech fans will tell you they never met a tailgate they didn't like.

Texas Tech officials proclaim that their masked rider, dressed in black with a red cape, is the oldest established rider in college football, dating back to the 1954 Gator Bowl when a horse and masked rider led the team on to the field. Florida State, with the stallion Renegade, began its tradition in 1978. USC and Traveler officially appeared on the Coliseum sideline in 1961. Oklahoma State's Bullet became official in 1984.

There are statues honoring the mascot-horses on each campus, but Texas Tech has another important equestrian tribute: the statue of Will Rogers and his horse Soapsuds. The inscription at the base reads, "Lovable Old Will Rogers on his favorite horse, Soapsuds, riding into a Western sunset."

All this makes for interesting photo ops, and that would include, at Texas Tech, one with Bill Tarro and his tongs and Ralph Madrid with a tongue-lashing margarita.

Whether it's beef, pork or chicken, Tech fans excel at tailgate cooking. Photo courtesy of John Simpson.

Hickory-Smoked Beer Can Chicken

From Donny Anderson
Two-time All-American at Texas Tech

SERVES: 4

PREP TIME: 15 minutes

DRY BRINING TIME: 2 hours

GRILLING TIME: 1 1/4 to 1 1/2 hours

SPECIAL EQUIPMENT: 4 large handfuls of hickory or oak wood chips, soaked in water for at least 30 minutes; church key-style can opener; instant-read thermometer

INGREDIENTS:

For the rub:

2 teaspoons granulated onion

2 teaspoons paprika

1 teaspoon packed light brown sugar

1/2 teaspoon freshly ground black pepper

For the bird:

2 tablespoons kosher salt

1 whole chicken, 4 to 5 pounds; remove neck, giblets, wing tips and any excess fat

1 tablespoon extra-virgin olive oil

1 12-ounce can of beer, at room temperature

DIRECTIONS:

• Mix the rub ingredients and set aside. Sprinkle the salt evenly over the meaty parts of the chicken and inside the cavity (but not on the back). The chicken will be coated with a visible layer of salt. Cover with plastic wrap and refrigerate for 2 hours. Prepare the grill for indirect cooking over medium heat (350 to 450 degrees). Keep the temperature as close to 400 degrees as possible throughout the cooking time. Rinse the chicken with cold water, inside and outside, to remove the salt, and then pat dry with paper towels. Brush the chicken with the oil, and season all over, including inside the cavity, with the rub. Open the can of beer and pour out about two-thirds. Using a church key-style can opener, make two more holes in the top of the can. Place the can on a solid surface and then lower the chicken cavity over the can. Drain and add two handfuls of wood chips to the charcoal or to the smoker box of a gas grill, following manufacturer's instructions, and close the lid. When smoke appears, transfer the chicken-on-a-can to the grill, balancing it on its two legs and the can like a tripod. Cook the chicken over indirect medium heat, with the lid closed, until the juices run clear and an instant-read thermometer inserted into the thickest part of the thigh (not touching the bone) registers 160 to 165 degrees, or about 1 1/4 to 1 1/2 hours. After the first 15 minutes of cooking time, drain and add the remaining wood chips to the charcoal or to the smoker box. If using a charcoal grill, replenish the charcoal as needed to maintain a steady temperature, adding 6 to 10 unlit briquettes after 45 minutes. Leave the lid off the grill for about 5 minutes to help the new briquettes light. Remove the chicken-on-a-can from the grill (do not spill the contents of the beer can, which will be very hot). Let the chicken rest for 10 to 15 minutes (the internal temperature will rise 5 to 10 degrees during this time) before lifting it from the can and carving it into serving pieces. Serve warm.

2 PERSPECTIVES
FROM CHARLOTTESVILLE

Virginia's storied history would attract anybody to Charlottesville. You wouldn't even have to tailgate to enjoy this beautiful place, but where better could you enjoy an autumn afternoon in the setting that was influenced so profoundly by the third President of the United States, Thomas Jefferson?

Located in the Blue Ridge Mountains, the University of Virginia is one of the oldest seats of learning in the country. Founded in 1819, it was "conceived and designed" by Mr. Jefferson, who considered it one of his greatest achievements. Virginia was the first non-sectarian university in the United States and the first to use the elective course system.

When I asked Dr. Charlie Caravati, class of 1959, if he ever thinks about Jefferson's shadow when he tailgates at Virginia games, he responded enthusiastically, "It is impossible to take respite at Virginia and not think about its history. If you are a graduate of UVA, you appreciate how we came about and who started it all."

Charlie, a one-time member of the Board of Visitors, takes reminiscing tours to the campus today and never tires of visiting the Rotunda, which Jefferson planned on the order of the Pantheon at Rome.

"We have not had that many good days with our football team lately," Charlie says, "but we still can't wait to go tailgating, and we have been setting up in the same spot every home game for 45 years."

The atmosphere is what keeps bringing Charlie back. He and his wife Betty enjoy good food, fellowship and Cavalier traditions. Just like the architecture, the food seldom changes. "Fried chicken, deviled eggs, pimento cheese — traditional tailgate fare — and, of course, your favorite libation," says Charlie. "We enjoy ourselves whether the team is distinguishing itself or not. We enjoy setting up our grills and enjoying ourselves. We would prefer that we have a winning afternoon to celebrate, but if not, we still appreciate where we are, who we are and why we continue our tailgating tradition.

"Visitors are always welcome at our tailgate, and they all will tell you they have never seen a more beautiful setting than ours," continued Charlie. "We take great pride in that. We like to think that if you have never tailgated at Virginia, you have missed something special about the college football scene."

* * *

"My first reaction to tailgating at UVA during my first year of college was one of amazement," says Tee Noland, class of '99. "Coming from St. Louis, which is really more of a professional sports town, I was not used to all the fanfare that surrounded the college game. People spent days getting ready stocking up supplies, talking about the matchup, and planning the pregame and postgame festivities. It was really more of a culture and way of life than just a football game.

"Certainly with UVA, tradition is part of the entire experience, and football was no different," Tee continued. "Many alums and students would wear coat and tie to signify the importance of the event from their perspective. While that tradition has turned more casual recently, just walking through UVA's grounds on your way to Scott Stadium really took you back a time many years ago.

"Tailgating at UVA was really a social experience. It was about connecting with friends, relatives and alums to enjoy a fall day without having to worry about any responsibilities."

Texas Salsa

From Derek and Allison Dooley
Former Virginia wide receiver
and former head coach at Tennessee

INGREDIENTS:

1/4 onion

2 jalepeno peppers

2 cloves garlic

Handful of fresh cilantro

1 28-ounce can whole tomatoes

DIRECTIONS:

• Boil jalapenos for 5 minutes and then remove seeds. Combine onion, garlic and jalapeno in a food processor, and pulse until chopped. Then add cilantro and tomatoes, and blend. Add salt to taste. Serve with tortilla chips.

THEY'VE GOT IT GOING ON IN BLACKSBURG

"**V**irginia Tech tailgating is a sort of institution for our group of friends," says Rob Guidry of St. Petersburg, Virginia. "We are a close-knit bunch with some diehard tailgate traditions that will, no doubt, be passed along to future generations.

"Thursday night games at Virginia Tech in Blacksburg are the most elaborate tailgates," Rob continued. "Setup begins no later than 7:30 a.m. Lot 5, 'Chicken Hill' as we lovingly call it, outside the south end zone, begins its transformation into our miniature city, the Hokie Party Zone. Everyone arrives bright and early and begins the team effort: pop-up tents for food tables, table cloths, tailgate trailer setup, custom kitchen setup, kitchen preparation, food preparation, beverage coolers, bar setup, heat stations, chairs, televisions and cornhole — all to the sounds of D.J. Lee spinning the tunes. By the time breakfast is ready, Chicken Hill is an official tailgate and breakfast can be served. Mimosas and Bloody Marys begin to flow. The event is officially in action.

"Our tailgate is a large adventure. Everyone has a job and plays a role in the setup. While the miniature city is being erected, the aromas of bacon, sausage, biscuits, scrambled eggs and hash brown potatoes begin to fill the air from the custom-built kitchen and grill. Tailgating for us is more about the fun, the food and the friends — then the game — then more fun, more food and more friends.

"Our tailgate trailer is a customized, one-of-a-kind creation with a full factory-installed Bose sound system, a full DJ booth and mixing boards, six independent satellite televisions, a full bar, refrigerator, ice cooler, bathroom and even video gaming station for the kids. The trailer has a custom wrap featuring lockers with jerseys for each of the tailgaters, and graphics of the stadium. It also features a memorial honoring those who once tailgated with us. The tailgate trailer has even been signed by the members of the Virginia Tech coaching staff.

"The tunes continue to spin, beverages flow, guests continue to visit, games of cornhole commence, and pregame and rival games are on the satellite televisions throughout the day. Mid-day, the legendary wings hit

Coca-Cola Cake

From Frank and Cheryl Beamer
Head coach at Virginia Tech

INGREDIENTS:

1 cup Coca-Cola

2 tablespoons cocoa

2 sticks margarine

Add to the above in a large bowl:

2 cups flour

2 cups sugar

1 cup buttermilk

2 eggs

1 cup small marshmallows

1 teaspoon baking soda

1 teaspoon vanilla

Frosting:

1 cup Coca-Cola

3 tablespoons cocoa

1 stick margarine

1 box powdered sugar

DIRECTIONS:

• In a large bowl, first mix the Coca-Cola, cocoa and margarine. Then add remaining ingredients and mix well. Pour into a 13-inch by 9-inch pan and bake at 350 degrees for 45 minutes.

Frosting:

• Boil the Coca-Cola and margarine, add sugar and cocoa, and mix together. Pour over hot cake.

the grill, as do the sausages and grapes. These items are complimented by a variety of hors d'oeuvres. When the grill is cleared of the wings, the prime rib goes on — slow cooked — until the lights from the stadium start to show their soft glow at about 5 p.m. Then the baked potatoes go on the grill, and the salad and vegetables are prepared. Dinner is served at 6 p.m., and then blankets,

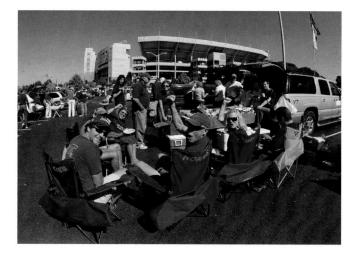

radios and Hokie garb is gathered for the 100-yard walk into the stadium.

"About 20 of us make the quick trip into Lane Stadium together. We have to get there 10 minutes early to hear 'Enter Sandman,' a Hokie tradition you don't want to miss! For the adults, we bring our radios and listen to the radio network calls. We love the game of football, and we love that we can root for Virginia Tech!

"After the game, and the Hokie win, we all head back to the tailgate and the trailer for more music, fun, pizza and beer to celebrate.

"While visiting Virginia Tech, it is a must to visit Burruss Hall, the signature building on the Virginia Tech campus. Many visit here annually to pay respect to those who lost their lives in the tragic massacre that took place on the campus on April 16, 2007.

"Another item of note is the beautiful facades on the newer Blacksburg campus structures. These buildings are covered in Hokie stone. The material, grey dolomite, is quarried exclusively for Virginia Tech projects."

The penetrating love of tailgating at Virginia Tech, shall we say, is written in stone!

Shutterstock

EVERYTHING IS FESTIVE IN MADISON!

Mark Nelson is a passionate Wisconsin tailgater. Born and raised in Madison, Mark lives in Beaver Dam about a half hour northeast of his hometown and the home of the Badgers.

"What is so special about Wisconsin tailgating," Mark says, "is that within a few miles of Camp Randall Stadium, tailgates are everywhere — in parking lots, in front and backyards, on business properties, on side streets and alleys — everywhere a grill, table and bag-toss game can fit. Although no two settings are the same, the Badger flags, tents, tables and fans combine to create a sea of red around the stadium.

"Each tailgate takes on its own personality with a variety of food, beverages and fun," Mark continued. "While settings vary, count on everyone being upbeat, nice and easy to get along with — even the opposing team's guests are heartily welcomed. While beer, brats and bag-toss are staples of most tailgates, variety makes Wisconsin tailgates special.

"Brad Oltrogge, a tailgating companion for years, and I use home-game tailgates to build up an extended trip we call 'Badger Invasion.' The Badger Invasion is a weekend trip of 50 or more Wisconsin fans on a bus charter to an away game. Home-game tailgates really serve as a gathering spot during the season for fans who participate in the Badger Invasion. Before this, we caravanned to road games. The Badger Invasion leaves Friday morning and returns on Sunday. Many activities and traditions are games, talent shows, movies with theme songs and a game of our own creation, 'Lug Nut Roulette.' There's also a night out on the town, the game-day tailgate and a 'Badger March' into the stadium.

Mark Nelson and his friends take their tailgating on the road when the Badgers play out of town. Photo courtesy of Mark Nelson.

"Something that takes place at Wisconsin, something that fascinates opposing fans and visitors, is our routine of 'Jump Around' between the third and fourth quarters, and the 'Fifth Quarter' — both are bucket-list experiences at Camp Randall Stadium. Jump Around sets the stage for team's fourth-quarter performance on the field. Fans are energized by the song and 80,000 fans jumping together — and the stadium literally rocks. The Fifth Quarter immediately follows each game, when the band takes the field to play fan favorites. The 'Bud Song' tops the list ('when you say Wisconsin, you've said it all'), with the 'Chicken Dance,' 'Badger Space Odyssey,' 'Tequila,' 'Varsity' and many more adding to the fun. Singing along after tailgating all day is inspirational. It gives you the best high! The Wisconsin band also 'let's go' with celebration and fun; instead of just marching, they do things like playing instruments while on their backs, rolling over other band members, making group pyramids and dancing, which all add to a crazy time. Thousands of fans stay for the Fifth Quarter fun.

"There is no one big tailgating location. Arrangements can be made for the day or for the same spot for the year. The Badger Invasion reserves its spot for the year before the season starts. We have had the same location for many years, so everyone knows where we are and can easily find us, even if they do not attend every game. While we tailgate, many people come and go — some may stay for hours while others stay for short time and hop to another tailgate. There are thousands of small to medium-sized tailgate parties. Each has its own character.

"Brats and burgers are a big hit for Badger tailgaters, and when it gets colder, chili is very popular. Oh, and don't forget the beer. Lots of beer. At our tailgate we typically have a theme for the day. Sometimes on early games we will do breakfast. We get a big pot of boiling water, and then people make their personal omelet by placing eggs and other items in a plastic bag. Plop it into the boiling water and three minutes later you have a perfect personal omelet made to your liking. That's a big hit. Other themes include barbecue day with ribs, chili wapatuli — with everyone bringing their version of chili and then mixing it all together — and, of course, there is the ceremonial christening of the wapatuli with a sacrificial beer added. Everyone cheers, the chili turns out great, thus warming a cold day in Wisconsin."

And then there are the Badger Invasion road trips.

"Badger Invasions started in the 1980s with a dozen Badger fans driving to another Big Ten school for a

White Chocolate Mix

From Barry & Cindy Alvarez
Athletic director and former head coach
at Wisconsin

INGREDIENTS:

1 1/4 cups Captain Crunch cereal

1 1/4 cups Cheerios

1 1/4 cups cashews

1 1/4 cups thin pretzels broken in small pieces

1 pound white chocolate

DIRECTIONS:

• Preheat oven to 200 degrees and then lower to 150. Melt white chocolate for 10 minutes, then check every 2 minutes. Mix all dry ingredients, then pour in chocolate and mix. Spread out on wax paper on cookie tray. Cool a little, then put in refrigerator for 2 to 5 minutes. Peel off the wax paper and break mix into pieces.

Jana White shares a cold one with a cardboard version of Bucky, the Wisconsin mascot. Photo courtesy of Jana White.

weekend of fun and tailgating but usually seeing another Badger football loss — yet, we still had fun!" says Mark. "Ten years passed before the Badger Invasion group, now 20 to 30 Badger fans, saw its first win. The game was in the Minneapolis dome and ended with Melvin Tucker tearing the football away from a Minnesota Gopher in the end zone. The Badgers snatched victory from the jaws of defeat! And the Badger Invasion had just witnessed its first-ever road win! We celebrated — boy, did we celebrate!

"Times kept getting better. Two years later, in 1993, we again caravanned to Minneapolis with a 6-0 record and going for 7-0. A win would put the Badgers on a track to an inconceivable trip to a major bowl. The Badgers got down early, 21-0, but rallied to take the lead 24-21. The scores kept piling up for both teams, but the game ended with another loss for Wisconsin and the Badger Invasion. For the year, the Gophers did not win any other Big Ten game, but the Badgers got a key win the very next week against Michigan. At the time, little did we know that the season would end with the Badgers playing in the Rose Bowl — the first time in 30 years — and with a first-ever UW Rose Bowl victory. Many of us made the trip. We celebrated — boy, did we celebrate!

"Planning for the first few Badger Invasions starts in the spring. A core group (really three or four of us) decide on the game to attend. This was a particularly difficult planning decision, since we could only speculate where our group may want to go. However, the process was not all bad; the planning sessions provided a solid reason to get out of the house. Of course, they took place in a local sports bar over a few beers. After a few meetings and much deliberation, we decide. The next few days required us to do a scramble and reserve a bus and hotel rooms, and order tickets. If everything worked out, we could create a flyer and send it to past participants and other friends. We estimated the costs and hoped enough people would sign up to use the tickets we ordered and to cover costs. Some years were better than other years. We learned from our experiences — some would say slowly — but we made changes.

"With tickets purchased, hotel and bus arrangements made, planning focuses on the fun aspects of the trip. Over the years, some activities have become traditions, and we do them every year. Additionally, we create a unique theme and activities to add interest and freshness to each trip. In general, we divide the trip into segments and plan each segment. Segments include the trip from Madison to the away school, Friday night on the town, the Saturday tailgate, Saturday night at a sports pub and the return trip.

"Each segment of the trip needs a plan. The first segment, the bus trip from Madison to the game-day destination, is perhaps the most important. Everyone on board is excited and ready to party. If it is a short trip, perhaps three or four hours, a fast-paced and efficient use of time is important. A long trip needs a consistent but a paced set of activities. Ohio State is a 10-hour trip, but it only takes three hours to bus to Northwestern."

On Wisconsin!

BEER, BRATS & A WINNING PROGRAM

Wisconsin has the distinction of winning the first Big Ten championship in 1896, when it was still called the Western Conference. Early on, there was success, but there have also been some lean years. When Barry Alvarez came on the scene as head coach in 1990 after three losing seasons, there wasn't anything to get excited about — especially when his first team went 1-10.

Good news was forthcoming, however, and it wouldn't be long until Alvarez was the toast of the Dairy State as he took Wisconsin to the Rose Bowl for the first time in over 30 years, causing Badger fans to literally lift their spirits — if you know what I mean. That is a statement that can be taken literally. UW fans are fond of imbibing, which makes tailgating at Camp Randall Stadium unparalleled when the team is victorious. Every toast is followed by a toast. Nobody at a Wisconsin game suffers from cenosillicaphobia — fear of an empty glass.

Today, Wisconsin is an annual factor in Big Ten title race and has been since Alvarez took over. He stepped down from coaching in 2005 but remains as the athletic director.

One of those Wisconsin alumni whose affection for Alvarez's leadership and what it has meant to the Badgers is Jana White, class of 2007. Jana grew up in Madison and experienced the glory days of the Barry Alvarez era. She remembers, as a kid, being able to walk into Camp Randall Stadium and "sit almost anywhere you like," to those splendorous years when tickets were being scalped for ridiculous amounts of money, especially if Michigan or Ohio State were in town, or if Iowa came to Madison to play for the Heartland Trophy.

It was natural that Jana would enroll at Wisconsin — "Never thought about going anywhere else," she says. She chose communications for her major and became a student assistant in the Sports Information office, which meant that she didn't get to tailgate until she became a graduate. But she knew about what went on pregame since her days as a high school student.

"Camp Randall is in the heart of campus surrounded by neighborhoods with a few street bars nearby as well," says Jana. "Therefore, you have everything from house parties to beer gardens (bar parking lots transformed to outdoor drinking spaces). The house parties feature beer bongs, flip cup and beer pong.

"No matter the weather, the fans show up," she continued. "Bad weather in Wisconsin is a given, but even unexpected things like rain and sleet won't keep fans from enjoying food and adult beverages outside. Badger fans are tough!

"There are two main staples at every tailgate — bratwurst and cheese curds. The best brats are ones that are boiled in beer and then put on the grill. Also very popular are 'breakfast brats' for those days that the tailgating starts very early. As for cheese curds, Wisconsin isn't called the Dairy State for nothing! The UW-Madison campus has one of the best dairies around, so it is only natural that cheese plays a large role in every tailgate. Squeaky cheese curds are the best because they are the freshest.

"It's no secret that Wisconsinites like to eat and drink, so when we have a Bloody Mary, we cram as many food items in them as possible. Sausage sticks, cheese curds, pickles and olives are the minimum. A Bloody Mary in Wisconsin is truly remarkable and unparalleled.

"If the game starts at 11 a.m., we might stop tailgating at 11:15 to head in. Wisconsin fans are notoriously late arriving, mainly because they don't want to stop tailgating. It is no secret to Wisconsin fans that Barry Alvarez influenced the party atmosphere for tailgating at Camp Randall Stadium. He made winning a tradition at Madison. You tailgate harder and more enthusiastically when you believe the team will bring about a winning season.

"One of the things Wisconsin is known for is the Fifth Quarter when the band comes down on the field after the game and plays for about an hour. Win or lose, rain, sleet or snow — even if it is a night game and midnight hour is approaching. They play Wisconsin fight songs, songs like 'Beer Barrel Polka,' which is everybody's favorite, and of course, 'On Wisconsin.'"

Brats, beer and winning football games. That says it all in Wisconsin!

You will always find brats on grills in Wisconsin, and Badger fans also wrap chicken drumsticks in bacon.

WALTER CAMP WOULD BE AMUSED

Walter Camp would likely be amused with what goes on outside the Yale Bowl today. It is nothing like it was in his day when he developed a reputation that led to many referring to him as "The Father of American Football."

Camp was a rules expert and had a lasting influence on the game. He also developed Yale into one of the most respected and successful football programs in college football.

When there were a plethora of deaths in college football, which got the attention of the White House and President Theodore Roosevelt, Camp suggested that the field be widened, but Harvard Stadium's width could not be altered without structural changes. That is why football fields are 53 1/2 yards wide today.

Yale, like all schools, has doting alumni who are anchored conveniently in the East — those who can find their way to the Yale Bowl every Saturday in the fall. Then there are the many alumni who can only make it to one or two games a year, which is why the game that brings them back to campus, more often than not, is the annual skirmish with Harvard.

When he was a student at Yale, Greg Wolf, class of '92, and his friends bought a grill and cooked burgers and hot dogs for their friends. That tradition continues.

Today, much of the tailgating is done by catering companies complete with call brands at the bar, upscale hors d'oeuvres and waiters at your beck and call. "When I go back," Greg says, "I can't wait to order pizza at two places that claim to have the best pizza in the world. You won't find many who will argue about that. Pepe's and Sally's are both in the Wooster Square neighborhood."

Many fans order pizza for pregame parties, including students who are famous for setting up hot tubs at their tailgates. Male alumni often wear, late in the season, long fur coats, which were a tradition in the 1940s.

And if you can get a table at Mory's, one of the most famous addresses in the world, at some point during the weekend, then you have achieved the ultimate social experience, which, if topped off by victory at the Yale Bowl, is an experience worthy of bronzing.

Crunchy Yale Bites

From John & Sally McHale
Parents of former Yale player Will McHale,
and CIO for Major League Baseball

INGREDIENTS:

10 slices French or Italian bread

2 cups smooth peanut butter

1/2 cup butter

2 cups graham cracker crumbs

1 cup crushed peanuts

DIRECTIONS:

• Trim crusts from bread slices. Cut each slice into strips. Bake on sheet at 350 degrees for 20 minutes. Mix peanut butter and butter in saucepan. Heat over low until smooth. Mix graham cracker crumbs and crushed peanuts. Dip each bread strip into warm peanut butter mix. Roll in crumb mixture. Refrigerate for 30 minutes.

A MOMENT WITH KEITH JACKSON

College football never had a better friend than Keith Jackson, who grew up in Carroll County, Georgia. The settlement where he lived was Roopville.

Keith rode a mule named Pearl to school and listened to sports on WSB radio. He was fond of the Georgia Bulldog teams of the 1940s, and had a great appreciation for the play of Charley Trippi.

Keith, the longtime football face and voice of ABC-TV, was big time, but functioning without a trace of ego or arrogance. He would be the first to say, even with all the problems out there today, college football remains the greatest of games.

When he was working a game at Georgia's Sanford Stadium a few years ago, we did a pregame radio show on the grounds on the east side of Field Street. I asked Keith to be a guest on the show before he moved into the stadium for his afternoon's work on ABC. As the interview began, he leaned in and said, "I've always been anxious to do this," and then he said, "Welcome South Brother," which is the phrase from which WSB gets its call letters.

Here is a salivating recipe from Keith and his wife, Turi:

"We never had time to do much tailgating since I went to the stadiums of the world early for work. Very seldom did we eat in the press box. Almost always, we ordered in our own food. There is a certain satisfaction to that and I guess you have to be in the media business to understand it.

"The following so-called menu for outdoor dining is basically designed for the back of the boat on fishing days, and sometimes for surviving ferry traffic.

"Start the day with a fried egg sandwich, on whole wheat bread, one or two eggs flat fried. One or two pieces of bacon or thinly sliced ham. Mayo or whatever fits your taste. If you want to give it a little pop, add a slice of jalapeno jack cheese.

"Back it up with sliced cantaloupe sealed in a Ziploc bag. Cantaloupe keeps better than watermelon...but you can do either or both in separate bags.

"Pepper cheese — Boursin is what we use with rice crackers — and Norwegian goat cheese on flat bread are great tasting and filling for snacks.

"And if there is a real demand for gusto, then another sandwich of any kind can be added. We like cold, thinly sliced strip sirloin, with horseradish and mustard on small slices of sourdough baguette.

"Top it with some real plain water. Skipper can't drink wine on our boat, and it makes him cranky if anybody else does."

Whoa, Nellie!

Sausage & Peppers Football Party

From Brad and Nancy Nessler
TV sportscaster and Minnesota State alum

INGREDIENTS:

Sausage Footballs:

1 package Hillshire Farm Beef Smoked Sausage

2 eggs, whisked

1 cup Italian bread crumbs

Glazed Peppers:

2 bell peppers, cut in quarters

1/4 cup mini pepperonis

2 tablespoons Parmesan cheese

1/4 cup Italian bread crumbs

DIRECTIONS:

• Cut sausage into 4 sections. Dip each section into eggs and then into bread crumbs, covering all the sausages. Bake at 350 degrees, turning sausages until all sides are dark brown and crispy. Cut into bite-sized slices (think mini footballs!). Then make a game of it by throwing pieces into each other's mouths for points. The winning team gets to chug a beer! No fumbles allowed!

Glazed Peppers:

• Preheat oven to 400 degrees. Remove seeds and stems from peppers. Heat peppers in microwave for one minute. Mix bread crumbs, pepperoni and cheese in small bowl. Spread olive oil on peppers and then cover them with the mixture. Bake 10 to 12 minutes or until mixture is crunchy. Enjoy!

VERNE
THE STORYTELLER

Verne Lundquist, who became the popular and familiar face and voice of Southeastern Conference football, which CBS turned into a national Saturday afternoon telecast, is a wonderful conversationalist and raconteur — which makes him a popular after-dinner speaker.

Egg Casserole

From Mike Tirico
ESPN and ABC-TV,
and Syracuse University alum

INGREDIENTS:

1 pound sage-flavored breakfast sausage
4 cups shredded potatoes, frozen
1/4 cup butter, melted
12 ounces sharp cheddar cheese, shredded
1/2 cup onion, chopped
1 bell pepper, chopped
1 8-ounce container sour cream
8 jumbo eggs
Salt
Pepper

DIRECTIONS:

• Preheat oven to 375 degrees. Lightly grease a 9-inch by 13-inch baking dish. Place sausage in a large, deep skillet. Cook over medium-high heat until evenly brown. Drain, crumble and set aside. In the prepared baking dish, stir together the shredded potatoes and butter. Line the bottom and sides of the baking dish with the mixture. In a bowl, mix the sausage, cheddar cheese, onion, bell pepper, sour cream and eggs. Salt and pepper to taste, but more pepper than salt. Pour over the potato mixture. Bake 1 hour in the preheated oven, or until a toothpick inserted into center of the casserole comes out clean. Let cool for 5 minutes before serving.

• NOTE: This tastes even better if made the night before and cooked in the morning. If you do so, add a few extra eggs.

Montana Bison Burgers

From Brent and Arlene Musburger
Longtime television sportscaster
and Northwestern University alum

INGREDIENTS:

1 1/2 pounds ground bison meat
1 packet dried Lipton Condensed Onion Soup Mix

DIRECTIONS:

• Mix together meat and soup mix, and form into four patties. Spray burgers with cooking spray and place on hot grill. Grill burgers 4 minutes per side. Serve with sliced Vidalia onion, Florida tomatoes and pepper jack cheese. Condiments should include Tabasco hot sauce, Heinz Ketchup and French's Classic Yellow Mustard. Serve on your favorite bun. This goes really well with a Lewis and Clark Beer from Montana! This recipe serves four people; just double it for eight, and so on. Enjoy!

Pepperoni Pizza

From Verne and Nancy Lundquist
CBS Sports and Texas Lutheran alum

INGREDIENTS:

1 12-inch pizza crust (ready to bake)
1 16-ounce package of shredded mozzarella cheese
1 cup pizza sauce
1 8-ounce package of pepperoni sausage
1 package of Italian seasonings

DIRECTIONS:

• Put pizza crust on a baking sheet that has been sprayed with non-stick oil. Spread pizza sauce over crust and add first layer of mozzarella cheese, followed by a layer of pepperoni. Sprinkle with Italian seasonings. Repeat this process and cover with mozzarella cheese. Bake in a 400-degree oven for 10 minutes or until golden brown.

His stories are classic and so well presented. He has a reservoir of countless humorous incidents — some real, some embellished, but all without rancor or contempt.

One of his favorites is the story about the legendary Bill Stern announcing an Army game in the days of the Cadets' Doc Blanchard and Glenn Davis, both of whom won the Heisman Trophy in consecutive years. As Verne remembers it, Stern had Blanchard running for a big touchdown when he realized that it was actually Davis who was carrying the ball. He quickly said on the air that Blanchard suddenly lateraled the ball to Davis for the score. Later in a conversation with prominent horse racing announcer Clem McCarthy, Stern chided McCarthy for having called the wrong horse winning a race. McCarthy's response to Stern: "Bill, you can't lateral a horse."

Verne takes up time with people wherever he goes. He enjoys tailgating after the game with friends, watching late televised games on fall Saturdays. He and his charming wife, Nancy, make every hostess feel special.

"One of my regrets," Verne says "is that I can't tailgate pregame. One of these days, I'll get to that."

Bonnie Bernstein's Ultimate (Healthy!) Tailgate Burgers

CampusInsiders.com,
former ESPN and CBS Sports reporter,
and University of Maryland alum

INGREDIENTS:

1 pound ground bison

1 package hot turkey sausage (six links)

1 packet Lipton's Onion Mushroom dry soup mix

Worcestershire sauce

Low-fat crumbled feta cheese

Salt

Pepper

Whole wheat or multi-grain buns or pita pockets

DIRECTIONS:

• Preheat grill to medium heat and lightly oil the grate. Combine evenly split bison and turkey sausage in mixing bowl. Knead together meat and Lipton's soup mix, Worcestershire sauce, salt and pepper to taste. Divide meat into 16 equal-sized balls, then flatten them into patties. Top eight of the patties with crumbled feta cheese. Place the other eight patties on top of those with cheese, and then press edges together so cheese is sealed inside. Grill 'em up to desired temperature, usually between 5 to 8 minutes per side. Top with desired garnishes (I love sliced tomato and avocado) and serve in buns or pitas. Bon appétit!

Carrot Souffle

From Phyllis George
Former CBS sportscaster and
Miss America

INGREDIENTS:

1 pound cooked fresh carrots

3 eggs

1/3 cup sugar

3 tablespoons flour

1 teaspoon vanilla (I usually use a tablespoon)

1 stick butter, melted

Dash of nutmeg

Topping:

1/4 to 1/2 cup of crushed corn flakes or walnuts

3 tablespoons brown sugar

2 teaspoons butter, softened

DIRECTIONS:

• Put cooked carrots and eggs in a blender (not a food processor). Add rest of ingredients and mix well. Pour ingredients into a 1½ quart pan or soufflé dish. Bake at 350 degrees for 40 minutes.

Topping:

• Mix together and spread on top of baked soufflé. Bake for an additional 5 to 10 minutes. Serves six.

White Chicken Chili

From David and Lindsey Pollack
ESPN "GameDay" crew,
All-American linebacker at Georgia

INGREDIENTS:

1 32-ounce box organic chicken stock

3 cans white beans, undrained (you can use different types to add variety)

5 cups cooked chicken, shredded (rotisserie or boiled)

1 16-ounce container salsa (use fresh salsa, as this is the key)

1 8-ounce block pepper jack cheese, grated

2 teaspoons ground cumin

2 cloves garlic, minced

Black or white pepper to taste

1/2 cup finely crushed corn chips (optional, if you like your chili thicker)

Sour cream, for garnish

DIRECTIONS:

• Place all ingredients except the corn chips in a slow-cooker. Cook on high until the cheese is melted (the chili can also be cooked on the stovetop over medium-high heat until cheese is melted). When the chili is ready, add the crushed corn chips, if desired, and simmer for 10 minutes to thicken. Garnish with more chips, cheese and/or sour cream, and serve. This will serve about six people.

Fusilli With Sausage, Artichokes & Sun-Dried Tomatoes

From Tracy Wolfson, CBS Sports and University of Michigan alum

INGREDIENTS:

3/4 cup drained oil-packed sun-dried tomatoes, sliced (2 tablespoons of oil reserved)

1 pound Italian hot sausages, casings removed

2 8-ounce packages frozen artichoke hearts

2 large cloves garlic, chopped

1 3/4 cups chicken broth

1/2 cup dry white wine

16 ounces fusilli pasta

1/2 cup shredded Parmesan cheese, plus additional for garnish

1/3 cup chopped fresh basil leaves

1/4 cup chopped fresh Italian parsley leaves

8 ounces water-packed fresh mozzarella, drained and cubed (optional)

Salt

Freshly ground pepper

DIRECTIONS:

• Heat the oil reserved from the tomatoes in a heavy, large frying pan over medium-high heat. Add the sausages and cook until brown, breaking up the meat into bite-sized pieces with a fork, about 8 minutes. Transfer the sausage to a bowl. Add the artichokes and garlic to the same skillet, and saute over medium heat until the garlic is tender, about 2 minutes. Add the broth, wine and sun-dried tomatoes. Boil over medium-high heat until the sauce reduces slightly, stirring occasionally, about 8 minutes.

• Meanwhile, bring a large pot of salted water to a boil. Cook the fusilli in boiling water until tender but still firm to the bite, stirring often, about 8 minutes. Drain the pasta (do not rinse). Add the pasta, sausage, 1/2 cup Parmesan, basil and parsley to the artichoke mixture. Toss until the sauce is almost absorbed by the pasta. Stir in the mozzarella. Season to taste with salt and pepper. Serve, passing the additional Parmesan cheese alongside.

Utah Texas Cake

From Holly Rowe
ESPN and University of Utah alum

Growing up as a Mormon in Utah, this is our "go-to" dessert, and we take this cake to everything from baby showers to funerals, reunions and football games. It's moister than a brownie, and more delicious than just cake — and it transports easily!

INGREDIENTS:

Cake:
1 cup butter
1 cup water
1/3 cup cocoa powder
2 cups sugar
2 cups all-purpose flour
Dash of salt
2 eggs
1 teaspoon baking soda
1/2 cup sour cream
1 teaspoon vanilla

Frosting:
1/2 cup butter
1/3 cup cocoa powder
1/3 cup milk
1 teaspoon vanilla
1 box confectioner's sugar, 4 1/2 cups sifted

DIRECTIONS:

• Preheat oven to 350 degrees. Grease a 15x10x1 jellyroll pan and set aside. Sift together flour, baking soda and salt. In a medium saucepan, combine butter, water and cocoa, and heat until butter is melted, then stir and remove from heat. Add in sugar, eggs, sour cream and vanilla, blending well. Carefully whisk in flour a little at a time, making sure there aren't any lumps. Pour batter in to jellyroll pan and spread evenly. Bake 20 minutes or until toothpick comes out clean. Remove from oven, and frost immediately.

Frosting:
• Mix well using hand mixer. Spread over hot cake.

Easy Cheese Potato Casserole

From Jill Arrington
Fox Sports and University of Miami alum

INGREDIENTS:

1 bag frozen hash brown potatoes (2 pounds chopped)
1 can cream of chicken soup
2 cups sour cream
2 cups sharp cheddar cheese, grated
1 stick butter, melted
1 tablespoon salt

DIRECTIONS:

• Preheat oven to 375 degrees. Grease 9-inch by 13-inch pan. Mix all ingredients in a bowl except the butter. Pour mixture into pan. Pour melted butter over the top of the casserole. Bake for 1 hour.

Chocolate Peanut Butter Balls

From Tony and Maria Barnhart
CBS Sports and University of Georgia alum

INGREDIENTS:

For the balls:
12 ounces peanut butter
1 teaspoon vanilla
1 stick butter or margarine
1 16-ounce box confectioner's sugar
For the chocolate:
6 ounces semi-sweet chocolate bits
2 teaspoons shortening

DIRECTIONS:

• Combine the ingredients for the peanut butter balls and refrigerate for at least 30 minutes before dipping into the chocolate sauce. To make the chocolate sauce, melt the shortening and chocolate together in a small pot over low heat. Then use a toothpick to dip each peanut butter ball three-fourths of the way into the chocolate. Place the chocolate-covered balls on wax paper on top of a cookie sheet. Store in the refrigerator for several hours or overnight before serving. You can also add chopped pecans or walnuts to the peanut butter mixture.

ABOUT THE AUTHOR

In his collegiate years at the University of Georgia, Loran Smith captained the track team, was sports editor of the campus newspaper, *The Red and Black*, and was also sports editor of the *Athens Banner Herald*. He has spent a great portion of his life as an author and journalist.

Following six months of active duty with the Coast Guard in 1962, he joined the Georgia staff as assistant sports information director, and has held the positions of business manager and executive director of the Bulldog Club. Smith was Georgia's first football sideline announcer. He originated the "Tailgate Show" and also originated the coaches locker room show. He was the executive producer of the "Vince Dooley Show" for over 15 years. He is a freelance columnist and author, having authored or co-authored 15 books, including the *University of Georgia Football Vault®: The Story Of The Georgia Bulldogs, 1892-2007* and the *Florida-Georgia Rivalry Football Vault®* for Whitman Books.

Smith was elected to the State of Georgia Sports Hall of Fame in 1997. He has covered countless sporting events, including the Super Bowl, World Series, Kentucky Derby, Indianapolis 500, Wimbledon, the French Open, Tour de France, Henley Regatta, the four major golf championships and the Palio de Siena, which is called the most dangerous horse race in the world.

He and his wife, Myrna, have two children, Camille and Kent, both UGA graduates, and four grandchildren, Alex, Zoe, Sophie and Penny.

ACKNOWLEDGMENTS

The team effort to produce this book began at home where my beautiful wife, Myrna, managed the manuscript through the computer and chased down information and facts, with our daughter, Camille Martin, providing research and editing.

My thanks, too, to the athletic staff at the University of Georgia for compatibility with this project: Greg McGarity, athletic director; Claude Felton, director of Sports Communications; and Mark Slonaker, director of Development. A special thanks to Karen Huff and Jana White for general assistance; Ben Beaty, for much needed IT direction; and Anne Noland, Ann Drinkard, Kate Burkholder Copp, Brittany Adams, Caitlin Connell and Laurel Hosmer — for tasks which aided and abetted the end result. Also special thanks to Grant Teaff, Executive Director of the American Football Coaches Association, and his wife, Donnell, of the AFCA Wives Association, for permission to use several recipes from *Married to the Game*. And thank you to Shay Griese for providing several recipes from her cookbook, *Griese Spoon*.

My thanks to Whitman Publishing for the opportunity to showcase the pregame hospitality and fervor that enraptures this nation on fall Saturdays.

And to Alex, Zoe, Sophie and Penny. It is for them that I can summon the energy, commitment and enthusiasm for fun projects like *Spread Formation* with the hopes that they will someday join the ranks of college football's most passionate tailgating fans.

And to all those seasoned fans, with a deep and abiding love of alma mater, valued contributors to this project, the most generous of "high fives." Many are strangers except that the Internet has brought them into my circle of friends. I am grateful. They have confirmed that in the fabric of the college football scene, tailgating has become just as important as the games themselves.

SEND US YOUR TAILGATING RECIPES, PHOTOS & STORIES!

Do you and your friends tailgate before college football games?

If yes, then send us a few photos from your tailgate parties along with your favorite recipe and a short 200- to 400-word description of how your tailgate got started and in what year, what you cook before a game, how many people show up and any entertaining anecdotes you may have.

Your submissions may be used in a future Whitman Books publication on fans tailgating before college football games.

Please send your photos, recipes and stories to: fanstailgate@whitman.com. Make sure to include the names of fans in your photos, which should also have food pictured.

This is your chance to be part of the college football tailgating craze!